D1461404

Pullingthe**trigger**®

There is recovery and a place beyond. We promise.

Adam Shaw, a mental illness survivor and mental health advocate, and Lauren Callaghan, an industry-leading clinical psychologist, are the founders of the global mental health publishing enterprise, Pullingthe**trigger**®. With their TV appearances and global education programmes, Adam, Lauren and their amazing team are helping more people around the world understand, recover from, and talk about their mental health issues.

The Pullingthe**trigger**® range – user-friendly self-help books with an innovative approach to supporting people recovering from mental health issues.

The**inspirational**series™ – remarkable, real-life stories of men and women who have overcome mental illness to lead fulfilling lives.

Why have we called our books Pullingthe**trigger**®?

Many things can 'trigger' mental health issues. So what do you do if something makes you feel bad? You stay away from it, right?

I bet you've been avoiding your triggers all your life. But now we know that avoiding them only makes things worse. So here's the game changer: you need to learn how to pull those triggers instead of running away from them – and our Pullingthe**trigger**® series shows you how. Your recovery is within reach, we promise.

This is more than recovery, it's a way of life.

Adam Shaw & Lauren Callaghan.

First published in Great Britain 2017 by Trigger Press

Trigger Press is a trading style of Shaw Callaghan Ltd & Shaw Callaghan 23 USA, INC.

The Foundation Centre
Navigation House, 48 Millgate, Newark
Nottinghamshire NG24 4TS UK

www.trigger-press.com

British Library Cataloguing in Publication Data

A CIP catalogue record for this book is available upon request
from the British Library

ISBN: 978-1-911246-19-0

This book is also available in the following e-Book formats:

MOBI: 978-1-911246-22-0
EPUB: 978-1-911246-20-6
PDF: 978-1-911246-21-3

Cover design and typeset by Fusion Graphic Design Ltd

Project Management by Out of House Publishing

Printed and bound in Great Britain by TJ International, Padstow

Paper from responsible sources

Comhairle Contae
Átha Cliath Theas
South Dublin County Council

The**inspirational**series™
Overcoming adversity and thriving

Life After Care
From Lost Cause to MBE

By Mark Edwards

We are proud to introduce The**inspirational**series™. Part of the **Pulling**the**trigger**® family of innovative self-help mental health books, The**inspirational**series™ tells the stories of the people who have battled and beaten mental health issues. For more information visit: www.pulling-the-trigger.com

THE AUTHOR

Mark Edwards spent the majority of his childhood in foster care and then in a children's home. Following this, he was sectioned under the Mental Health Act and admitted to the local mental institution.

Mark is now a vicar in Newcastle upon Tyne and is a volunteer Ambulance First Responder. He is police chaplain to Northumbria Police and has also previously served as a lifeboat crew member. In 2010 he received an MBE for his services to the public.

Mark is now happily married with four children and one grandchild.

Thank you for purchasing this book.
You are making an incredible difference.

All of The**inspirational**series™ products have substantial enterprising and philanthropic value and generate proceeds that contribute towards our global mental health charity,
The Shaw Mind Foundation

MISSION STATEMENT

'We aim to bring to an end the suffering and despair caused by mental health issues. Our goal is to make help and support available for every single person in society, from all walks of life. We will never stop offering hope. These are our promises.'

Pulling the Trigger and The Shaw Mind Foundation

the *Shaw* **mind**
FOUNDATION

Supporting children, adults and families
for better mental health. **#lets**do**stuff**

The Shaw Mind Foundation (www.shawmindfoundation.org) offers unconditional support for all who are affected by mental health issues. We are a global foundation that is not for profit. Our core ethos is to help those with mental health issues and their families at the point of need. We also continue to run and invest in mental health treatment approaches in local communities around the globe, which support those from the most vulnerable and socially deprived areas of society. Please join us and help us make an incredible difference to those who are suffering with mental health issues. **#lets**do**stuff**.

In Memory of my Father-in-Law, Mr Elfed John, 1935–2017.

Trigger Warning: This book contains details of self-harm and attempted suicide.

Disclaimer: Some names and identifying details have been changed to protect the privacy of individuals.

Comhairle Contae
Átha Cliath Theas
South Dublin County Council

INTRODUCTION

A MOMENTOUS ACHIEVEMENT

As I took in my magnificent surroundings, I felt exhilarated and nervous at the same time. It had taken many years and a whole lot of hardship and pain to get to where I was right now.

I walked through the palace state rooms with my fellow men and women, and staff directed me through to where the investiture was to take place. I couldn't help but stop in my tracks every so often as I stared, open-mouthed and in absolute wonderment, at the beautiful and lavish furnishings around me.

I still couldn't believe where I was. A sumptuous sight awaited me at every turn: white walls with ornate golden gilding, incredibly high ceilings, breathtaking chandeliers, magnificent centuries-old paintings, golden antique clocks, and columns with black marble busts.

Along with a number of other guests, I took my place in a queue at the side entrance to the Buckingham Palace ballroom. They were all dressed in their finest clothes, waiting with anticipation on plush red chairs with golden trim. I could see my sister sitting in the audience.

Before too long it was my turn to enter the room. My heart rate shot up and butterflies fluttered in my stomach.

The Lord in Waiting Viscount Hood called out my name – 'The Reverend Mark Edwards, for services to the voluntary sector in the North East.'

At the sound of my name, I walked forward towards the dais. Right in front of me, looking splendid in his Royal Navy uniform, stood Charles, the Prince of Wales. The Yeomen of the Guard, the oldest royal bodyguard in the world, stood behind him in their red, gold and black uniforms, their top hats adorned with flowers in the colours of the British flag.

In my slight nervousness, I ended up standing a bit further away from the dais than I'd been instructed to, and dear old Charles had to lean forward to pin the medal insignia onto my jacket. He smiled at me warmly.

'It's nice to see a police chaplain looking so smart,' he remarked.

I was thrilled that he knew I was a police chaplain, though I guessed there was someone behind him prompting him a little bit before each conversation. 'Thank you very much, Your Royal Highness,' I replied, grinning from ear to ear.

'You've had quite a chequered past, haven't you?'

'Yes, sir. I was in and out of care, and then in a mental institution as a teenager, before becoming ordained and joining the ambulance service.'

If I had been thrilled before, I was ecstatic when the prince replied, 'You have done very well to overcome all the obstacles placed in front of you, and to be here today. I am sure your story will inspire others.'

As a warm feeling of gratitude swelled in my chest, Prince Charles shook my hand, signifying the end of our brief but wonderful conversation. What a charming man. I later learnt that he gave so much time to each individual that day that he ran over his timetable by half an hour. He helped us all to relax, at the same time as allowing us to revel in the specialness of the moment.

And what a special moment it was. I bowed my head slightly, still in complete awe, and turned away from the Prince. I walked towards the ballroom exit, all eyes upon me, my MBE hanging proudly on my chest.

CHAPTER 1

DRAGGED AWAY FROM HOME

My earliest memory is of when I was three-years-old. Not only can I remember it, but I can see it clearly in my mind. Visualising things comes easily to me, for some reason.

I can see social workers walking into the room. I'm clinging to my mum as they try to pull me away from her. My brother Paul is only a year old, and another social worker is holding onto him. There is pandemonium. Mum doesn't want to let me go and she is holding onto me tightly. I am holding on to her too, tears pouring down my face at the trauma of being dragged away from my family. My brother is crying because he hasn't a clue what's going on. Dad isn't on the scene, and so Mum is powerless to stop anything. It is not a pleasant first memory to have.

After that harrowing scene, my brother and I were taken into care by Lincolnshire Social Services.

Our home life had never really been stable. Mum had been mentally ill for a while at this point. Dad was in the army, and so Mum had had to raise my three older sisters and me mainly on her own in Boston, Lincolnshire. She then suffered postnatal depression after giving birth to Paul, and had to spend some time in psychiatric care in a mental hospital. She had alcohol issues too, and this is one of the main reasons why we were always in and out of care. I remember one social worker telling me that Mum had a 'sickness in her head'. Of course, I was far too young to understand what this meant at the time, except that it was something scary.

Whenever Dad returned home on leave, there was always conflict. I have a lot of memories of them rowing – screaming and shouting at each other. Living under such stressful conditions, the air thick and heavy with tension, inevitably took its toll on all of us. There's no wonder, really, that eventually my parents divorced.

We had always been pretty much left to our own devices even as toddlers, although our sisters did their best to bring us up when we were at home with them, because they were older than us. Shene and Jenny, the twins, were seven years older than me, and Maxine was just five years older. But with all the coming and going into foster care, we barely saw our big sisters. It was sad really; it was yet another thing that meant I never really knew what it was like to be part of a proper family. When your sisters are strangers, your mum is too ill to look after you and your dad can't cope with parenthood, how could I have possibly understood what a real family was?

After the divorce, things became very erratic. My brother and I lived with several different foster parents, but even foster care wasn't consistent. Sometimes we were allowed to stay with Mum in between her hospital stays, or Dad in between his various jobs, but for the most part we were fostered.

I didn't go lightly whenever I was taken into foster care. I would often scream and shout and kick out at the people taking me, but eventually I learnt that that wasn't going to do anybody any good. I soon learnt that I was achieving nothing except frightening Paul, and so I began to internalise and bottle up my fear and anger from a pretty early age.

There's something truly heartbreaking about a young child feeling completely helpless, out of control, and unsure of what's going to happen next. Those first few years of my life I lived in four, five, six – I've actually lost count – foster homes. The fact is, when you're moved from home to home, you're just taken. You're just snatched and whisked away to the next home. You have no control. You internalise all your pain, your frustration, your sense of rejection, your anger. You internalise all that as children, because expressing it gets you nowhere. People say that children are very resilient, but they're not. Not always.

No one explains to you what is happening when it's happening. Instead, there's a whole lot of confusion and panic, with no real outlet for it. When I was old enough to ask what was happening, I'd be told, 'Come along, don't be silly.' And so the panic attacks started very early on. What was doubly unhelpful was that, when I was having a panic attack, it looked like I was having a tantrum. So the adults around me just thought I was being petulant. I didn't stand a chance of turning out undamaged, really!

I constantly bottled up my frustration, whether I was with my real family or foster parents. I would start to hyperventilate if things became too distressing, and Paul would too. Every day sheer dread wrapped itself around my body like a coat that was too tight. Far too many times I was told by an adult – who I didn't know very well – to trust them. That everything was going to be okay, and that we would be back with our mum and dad and family again soon.

'Just trust me. Everything's going to be okay.'

Those words came out a lot. Even today, they still cause me to bristle. Nowadays, if someone tells me to trust them, my immediate knee-jerk reaction is to think, *You must be joking!* (I've often joked that if the bishop told me it was a Wednesday, I'd check the calendar! Nothing against the bishop, of course!) To this day, though I trust people generally, I struggle to trust them to see the real me – the Mark whose childhood was one long string of broken promises.

Up until around the age of eight I can remember being back with my dad in short bursts in a council house, and then later in lodgings, in between foster placements. What you have to understand here is that my dad had, in a way, become institutionalised himself. He had spent time in the services and so he struggled to cope with the responsibility of looking after me and my little brother when Mum wasn't around. He eventually formed a relationship with his landlady, Maggie, and he became very hands-off. In a way, he left it to her to bring us up.

Dad argued with her a lot, just like he had with my mum, but I think what caused a lot of the conflict is that we weren't Maggie's kids and yet she was being left to look after us as though we were. And I can understand that, looking back. We both regularly wet our beds up until we were around ten years old. Who would want to deal with that when, as Maggie put it, it was our dad that she'd taken on, not us? Ironically enough it was the pain of abandonment and fear of rejection, of constantly being dragged into care against our will, which caused the bed wetting in the first place. No child wants to be taken away from their family, and the consequences manifested themselves physically as well as mentally. Maggie was frustrated with our dad for not putting in enough effort, and resentful of the fact that she had children that weren't hers to contend with.

Perhaps it was inevitable, then, that in the summer of 1970, our lives became even more turbulent. I remember the night we left our dad permanently – or perhaps I should say the night that he gave us away more or less for good. I was eight and Paul was six. This is yet another memory that is still very vividly lodged in my brain.

After a particularly heated row with Maggie late one night, Dad came upstairs into our room.

'Boys, get dressed please,' he said, admittedly sounding rather upset. 'I'm taking you to your Aunt Violet's house.'

Fear and dread snaked their way up my back. This scenario felt all too similar.

We didn't ask him any questions though. There was no point. Paul and I got dressed and Dad gathered some of our things into our suitcases. We'd had to use those far too many times before. Without a word to Maggie and more or less in silence, we left and walked to

Aunt Violet and Uncle Jack's house in another part of town. It was quite a long walk and a fairly cold night; I was already feeling weary and upset. I was distressed and tearful, but I managed to hide it fairly well in the darkness.

Dad asked us if we were alright before knocking on the front door. Aunt Violet answered, looking distinctly unimpressed at being woken so late. When she saw us, she was very surprised but not unkind. She hugged us tightly and then turned to Dad, berating him for uprooting us yet again.

'There's nothing else I can do,' he said, defending himself. 'Their mother's back in hospital and Maggie's not having any of it. This is the best thing for them.'

Shaking her head, Aunt Violet ushered us inside. I was just glad at this point to be in a warm house. I was too tired to stay too worked up about what was going on.

Aunt Violet looked after us well that night. She gave us hot milk and comfortable beds to sleep in, showering us with affection and generally being very motherly towards us. The house smelt of her perfume and whatever she'd been cooking earlier that night, it smelt of love and care and family. I had forgotten what those things felt like, but it was very comforting being in Aunt Violet's home.

As I curled up in bed beside Paul a little while later, my eyes stinging with tiredness and my head hurting from holding back tears, I appreciated for the first time how quiet and calm things were – so different from how things were at home. I started to think that maybe this was a blessing in disguise.

Mark aged 5.

CHAPTER 2

LIFE IN A FOSTER HOME

But of course, if it really was a blessing in disguise, you wouldn't be reading this book today. Life is rarely so simple.

The next day began with our father waking us up very early in the morning. But if I had any hopes that he was taking us back home, they were quickly dashed when he took us out of the house and walked us towards the social services building.

I felt that familiar feeling of panic squeeze at my chest as I did my best not to hyperventilate. Paul looked nervous but he was keeping himself together.

'Can't we stay with Aunt Violet?' he asked Dad in a small voice.

'Yes, I wish we could just stay there,' I agreed, nodding and looking up at my dad hopefully. I desperately wanted to stay with Aunt Violet. She made me feel safe and protected, and I craved that kind of affection. Lord knows there was a lack of it in our household when Mum was away! Perhaps if he knew we liked it with Aunt Violet, he would change his mind?

But no such luck. 'I wish you could, too,' Dad replied. 'But she hasn't got enough room for you both. Won't you prefer it somewhere where there's plenty of room for the both of you? It's not going to be for long, I promise you.'

I'd heard that one before. I wonder why I wasn't too convinced this time?

With my heart sinking right down into my boots, I followed my dad and Paul into the social services building. At this point I broke into tears. I couldn't help myself. Dad was abandoning us yet again and I was helpless. As Miss Vernon (my social worker since I was three years old) ushered us into a separate room so that she could talk to Dad in private, I hugged my brother. He sobbed into my shoulder and all I could do was sit there, afraid. I was the big brother but that didn't mean anything.

After a few minutes Miss Vernon came to collect us. 'Come on, boys,' she said kindly. 'Let's get your stuff into the car. I'm taking you to your new home. It won't take us long, come on now.'

Unable to say a word, Paul and I dragged our suitcases out into the car park and Miss Vernon loaded the boot of her small red car. As I climbed into the back seat, I deliberately didn't look in my dad's direction. My heart hurt too much to deal with it. Paul climbed in after me, looking as distressed as I felt, but he'd stopped crying. He clearly felt as resigned as I did.

At the last second, though, I couldn't stop myself and I turned to look out of the back window. That memory of Dad standing there in tears, waving us goodbye, as we drove away is another memory that is etched firmly into my brain. It was to haunt me for years. And despite his many promises, we saw very little of him or Mum after that.

'You're going to be okay,' Miss Vernon reassured us, after a short time. 'Mr and Mrs Tait are lovely people. They'll take good care of you.'

At that moment, I didn't feel reassured by anything. I'd been in foster care before. It was never permanent. And at times it had definitely not been lovely. I'd suffered at the hands of foster parents before. There had been times when I was locked in a cupboard, screaming and crying to be let out, banging on the doors and nobody coming to help me. The fear and anxiety and claustrophobia had been overwhelming, and still I had to comfort my little brother through the worst of it. There'd been a lot of verbal abuse too. I learnt from a very early age how to block traumatic things from my mind, but when I was distressed I found it very difficult. No wonder I felt so nervous going somewhere new.

As it turns out, I needn't have worried. Mr and Mrs Tait were lovely. They lived in a smart semi-detached house the next town over, and were kind and caring souls. Mrs Tait was a plump ageing woman with greying hair. Her husband was more reserved but friendly. They had two children called Laura and David, and I could tell that they were a settled family – the complete opposite of mine. Walking through their house made me feel calmer. It was tidy, homely, and colourful, with squishy couches and an open fire. As Miss Vernon worked through the necessary paperwork, Mrs Tait got started on making us a hot meal, holding our hands and fussing over us while the chips cooked in the oven.

And so it was that we came to live with our new foster family for the next two years. Life was happy, secure, safe. There were a few hiccups now and then. Paul and I continued to wet our beds, a side effect of all the trauma and instability we'd experienced in our young lives. The first time it happened, I braced myself for a beating or telling off. But Mrs Tait was so kind. She just pulled the sheets off our beds, and with a breezy 'Don't worry, boys, we can clean this right up,' the problem was solved swiftly and peacefully. It made such a wonderful change from being constantly on edge.

We missed our real mum and dad and our big sisters, who we rarely saw. On the odd occasion that Mum visited, she was always drunk. It just put our new life in stark contrast with our old home, and I found myself feeling more comfortable in our new environment. The Taits were strict and they smacked us if we were naughty, but it wasn't abuse. At that point I sadly knew the difference. Paul and I just saw the smacking for what it was: discipline. And we'd been sorely lacking discipline for years. All the smacking was to me was a sign that for once, a parent figure cared enough to pay attention to what we were doing. They were giving us structure and doing what real parents should do. It might sound strange, but I came to love how strict the Taits were. It meant they loved me. I'd clearly needed this all along.

The following summer brought another positive change for us. Paul and I were returning from playing outside in the nearby field one bright, breezy day when we saw Miss Vernon's car pull up at the Taits' house. Immediately I felt sick. Were they taking us away again? Had something happened to Mum and Dad?

'Lovely to see you, boys!' Miss Vernon greeted us with a beaming smile as we entered the house. That was a good sign. Perhaps nothing bad had happened after all.

'Hi, Miss Vernon,' I said to her. 'What are you doing here?' She hadn't visited us very often in the past year or so.

'Well,' she said to us, sitting down on the couch next to us, 'I've come to ask you and Paul how you feel about staying with Mr and Mrs Tait permanently?'

I looked at Paul and he looked back at me, unsure what to say.

'Does this mean we won't see our real family again?' I asked, scared to know the answer.

'No, of course not,' Miss Vernon reassured me. 'But your father still lives with Maggie and your mother and her new husband only live in a tiny house. They can come and visit you here, where there's more room for you.'

I mulled this over. Things had never been good at home. As much as I wanted to go back and live with Mum and Dad and my sisters, I knew it could never really happen again. They were both with different people now, and so home was no longer home. It had never been enjoyable anyway. It had been loud and stressful and upsetting. Not like here, with the Taits. Here we had space to run around and play. Here we got to go out on trips, play at the seaside with Laura and David. Here we didn't have to worry about Maggie hitting us if we accidentally wet the bed. Here things were fun and peaceful. Stable.

Quietly I nodded my head. I looked at Paul and smiled reassuringly. He looked unsure, but I knew even at such a young age that this was the best thing for me and my brother. A real home at last.

Over the next year, it became obvious that Paul and I had made the right decision. The paperwork still needed to be processed to keep us there permanently, but neither of us worried. We loved living with the Taits. For the first time since I could remember, Christmas was a happy, exciting affair full of great food and presents. We went to church regularly, though I didn't think much of God. A father that loved you and never left you? Oh yeah, a likely story!

The seasons passed and soon the spring of 1971 had hit us in full bloom. One morning at school, Paul and I were excited because there was an important village football match coming up that night, and our minds were on nothing else but what a big deal it was. We spent the day giggling and bantering with our friends about it, and were in good spirits that afternoon in art class. But it wasn't to last.

As I worked away on my project, I spotted two cars drive into the car park next to the playground. I didn't think anything of it until I realised that one of the cars was Miss Vernon's red Mini. When she climbed out of the front seat and started walking towards the school entrance, I could hear my blood rushing in my ears. What was she doing here?

The occupant of the other car climbed out and I recognised her as Mrs Robins, the educational psychologist that we'd seen the previous week. She'd given us a bunch of tests to do, square pegs and drawing and the like. I couldn't fathom why she was here, either. But I was about to find out.

Miss Vernon and Mrs Robins walked into our classroom, accompanied by our headteacher. After exchanging some inaudible words with our teacher, the headmaster called my name and asked me to follow them outside. Nervously I did as I was told, feeling increasingly anxious. Had something awful happened to Mum? Dad? My sisters?

I was led to the headmaster's office where Miss Vernon and Mrs Robins smiled at me awkwardly. We waited for the headmaster to bring my brother in before anybody spoke. There was a lump of fear in my throat and I could feel my heart pounding.

'What's going on?' Paul asked, looking as worried as I felt.

'Boys, sorry to have to pull you away from class,' said the headmaster. 'But something's come up.'

'Yes,' Miss Vernon agreed. 'Mark, Paul, if you could gather your things and follow me, we're going on a little trip.' She and Mrs Robins stood up and they each took hold of one of our hands.

But I wasn't falling for that one. 'What do you mean? Where are we going?' I demanded, through my rising panic. Holding onto us tightly, they ushered us along as we were led out of the headmaster's office.

'Where are we going?!' Paul yelled, twisting his arm out of Mrs Robins' grip.

'Calm down!' Miss Vernon yelled back. 'We have to go quickly. Just trust me.'

Trust her? Was she having a laugh? Here we were again, being pulled away against our will by another untrustworthy adult, with no explanation. And she was telling us to trust her? When had we ever been able to trust an adult?

'I want to know what's happening!' I shouted, anger pushing aside my fear. The two adults continued to shuffle us along and lead us out to their cars.

Here Miss Vernon knelt to eye level with us and whispered quietly, 'Try not to make a fuss, Mark. We're taking you to a children's home. Just until we can find you another foster placement.'

A sob choked my throat, and hot tears spilled down my cheeks. *Not again*.

Paul began screaming 'No!' over and over again as the two women wrestled us into the car, carefully avoiding our kicking and ignoring our cries. Against our wishes, we were wrenched once again from yet another family home.

CHAPTER 3

ENTERING THE CHILDREN'S HOME

There's a stark contrast between life in a foster home – where you are given at least some passable form of personal love and attention – and life in a children's home, where you are given your own number to distinguish your property from others'. I was given the number 14 on my first day there. Hardly personal, is it?

Ivy Cottage Children's Home in Lincolnshire wasn't as pretty as you would perhaps imagine it to be. It was big, red, and a bit characterless. I guess it was difficult to make a care home too homely, though. It was, essentially, a building for children who were either unwanted or unmanageable for whatever reason. Paul and I lived in the care home with fifteen other children. Thankfully, we were kept together though. We shared a comfortable, but slightly out-of-date, bedroom with two other boys called Richard and Brian. We shared wardrobes, drawers, mirrors, and a few worn-out toys. It wasn't a luxury but I guess it provided for us well enough.

The home was run by Uncle and Aunty Andrews and a bunch of other house parents. All of the women in the home were called Aunties. Perhaps that was their way of making things feel more family-like, but it was hardly a substitute for the real thing. They treated us fairly, though, and at that point it was the most I could ask for.

It took a little bit of time for Paul and me to adjust to life in a children's home. Even with all the to-ing and fro-ing we'd done in our young lives, it was new and strange territory for us. During our first few nights there, Paul threw a few tantrums and cried a lot. I can't say I blamed him. The only reason I didn't do the same was because I was so scared of getting into trouble. But I felt as angry and hurt and let down as he did. Why had we been taken away from the Taits? Didn't they want us any more? Had we done something wrong? Why didn't anybody *want* to tell us?

Life in the home was strict and regimented. We each had our own chores to do, such as setting the table, washing dishes, and peeling potatoes. We were paid 50 pence each week for pocket money. There was one quite humiliating aspect of life in care that I found particularly hard to adjust to, and that was the bathing and toilet arrangements. Looking back, I do question them now, although at the time we just did as we were told. It was all such an embarrassing affair. Whenever we had a bath, Aunts would 'supervise' us. Basically, they would watch us closely to make sure we bathed correctly. This even happened with the older boys; there were no exceptions. Some Aunties kept a discreet distance, but others didn't. Don't get me wrong, no harm was done and we weren't abused in any way, but looking back on it now it is very strange to think about.

What was even worse was we were asked to go straight to the toilet after our meals and stay there until a member of staff came up to join us. They would then check to see if our bowels had moved! Talk about a draconian system!

Despite these strange rules, however, the children's home was safe and we were well looked after, fed, and treated with respect. I felt secure within the boundaries of the institutions I was in, but I felt insecure in terms of my abandonment issues. My emotions were never simple.

Before long, Aunty Freda told me and Paul that we'd be attending the nearby primary school. That put me on edge a little bit because it meant we'd be there for the foreseeable future. But in a strange sort of way, a part of me felt like maybe the children's home was for the best. If I didn't grow to love anybody, then it wouldn't hurt so much again the next time I was rejected. Perhaps the easiest way to live was knowing that while no one really loved me, no one could turn my life upside down again. A song that Maggie often used to play back at my dad's lodgings often floated into my mind when I thought about this: *I'm nobody's child. Nobody loves me, nobody cares*.

I was tired of being scared all the time. And I had a duty to repress whatever I was feeling in order to look after my little brother. It wouldn't have been any good for both of us to fall apart. Soon I became very good at swallowing my feelings. Expressing them never got me anywhere.

But trauma and abandonment issues can never be repressed forever, and someday I was going to learn that the hard way.

During my first day at school, I was thrilled to find out that the kid sitting next to me in class also lived in the children's home. His name was Gary and we hit it off straight away.

'Me and my brother Robin have been at the home for two years,' he told me. 'You get used to the strictness after a while. It's the bullies you need to watch out for really. Keep your head down and you'll be okay.'

'Bullies?' I asked him, voice wobbling.

'Yeah, there's a handful of them about. But Uncle normally gives them a good hiding. Just try to stay out of their way.'

As was just my luck, I didn't always manage to stay out of their way. The first few months in care were difficult precisely because I was bullied. Add that to my growing resentment, abandonment issues, lack of self-confidence, fear and distrustfulness, and things felt pretty miserable for a while. Until slowly but surely, things started to improve...

As time passed, the other children in the home started to feel like my brothers and sisters. My best friends were Richard, Brian, and especially Lee. And other than the odd bit of bullying which Uncle managed to tamp down most of the time, Paul and I got on well with all the other kids. We had annual holidays in the summer in Mablethorpe, with donkey rides and penny arcades and ice cream kiosks. We played games together, ate together, and did our chores together. It was fun and while it wasn't loving or affectionate, it started to feel okay.

My mind was often a dark and difficult place to inhabit during my years in the children's home, though. Mostly I kept my anxiety and deepening depression to myself, but if I ever did try to speak up about how low I was feeling, no one ever truly listened. I was just a kid! There was still that idea of 'children should be seen and not heard' in those days (that phrase makes me feel old!) and I was one of those children. It made me feel so undervalued, and I'd had more than my fair share of that over the years.

It's hard to imagine now, because there are so many resources out there for young people to use. But when I was in care, there was no one who was interested in what I had to say. There was no Childline at that time. And this was before the days of Esther Rantzen!

So who on Earth did a young person turn to? Miss Vernon visited but only occasionally, and though I still looked forward to her coming over, I no longer hugged her or greeted her quite so warmly. After all, she'd proven that I couldn't really trust her. She always seemed to break her promises. She was always the bearer of bad news too. After all, it was her who told us that our sisters had been taken into different foster homes themselves. Our family truly was broken up and fragmented.

She always reassured us that she was trying to find us a foster home, though, and one autumn when I was eleven and Paul was nine she called in to see us.

'Mark, Paul, I have some news for you,' she said with a bright smile on her face. I was starting to get a sense of déjà vu, and not the good kind.

'What now?' I asked warily.

'It's nothing to worry about. In fact, it's great news! Mr and Mrs Bradshaw have expressed interest in becoming your foster parents. What do you think of that?' She asked both of us the question but looked straight at me, waiting for an answer.

Once again I looked at Paul for some kind of signal of what he wanted me to say. But he just stared at me with those big wide eyes and I knew it was down to me to say the right thing again. Only, I didn't know what the right thing was any more. Even the adults didn't seem to have a clue. What chance did I have of getting it right?

I weighed up the pros and cons in my head. We'd settled in Ivy Cottage and we'd made some friends. It was safe, but it never truly felt like a home. It felt like I was always at school or something. And the rules and routines only made that feeling stronger. Perhaps … perhaps the Bradshaws could give us something different? Maybe things could work out this time. In a real home with a proper family. Surely they wouldn't throw us out like the Taits?

'Okay,' I said. 'We'll meet them.'

Over the next few weeks, Mr and Mrs Bradshaw took us back to their home to meet their family. They were both tall, slim, and, though they looked quite formal, were friendly and jokey. Their kids were nice and they made us feel welcome. Their home was tidy but comfortable and inviting. They didn't seem the type to be overly strict. Eventually they won us over, with the added bonus of some great toys and gifts thrown into the mix. We made it clear that we were keen to move in with them and eagerly awaited the day they came to bring us home for good. It gave us something to look forward to.

Paul and I decided to invite the Bradshaws over as our guests for a Bonfire Night party at Ivy Cottage. It was brilliant. We had hot dogs, a bonfire, sparklers, fireworks, and roast chestnuts. Everybody was laughing and having a wonderful time. The night air was cold and fresh and made our cheeks go bright red. We were in good spirits and things got even better when the Bradshaws arrived bearing gifts for me and my brother.

Together, already seemingly as a family, we watched the fireworks and Catherine wheels and laughed in delight at people's jokes. We spent the night chatting with the other children and staff; it seemed like a perfect night, one like I'd never really had before. It was for this reason that I followed Aunty Andrews willingly when she called me into her and Uncle Andrews' office. I went to find Paul who was mingling somewhere in the crowd. As we entered the office, though, a pang of anxiety hit me. I had just heard a car driving out of the car park outside, and I had a horrible feeling that it was something to do with us.

'Boys,' said Uncle Andrews, looking grim. 'I'm sorry to tell you that we have some bad news.'

No. Please, please, no ... not again.

I could feel my breathing becoming shallower and faster. I shook my head, trying to drown out their words.

'Why?' Paul asked, tears running down his face. 'Why?'

'We did something wrong. What did we do wrong?' I said.

'Nothing. You didn't do anything wrong at all. Don't blame yourself,' Uncle said.

'Then why? *Why* don't they want us?' I pleaded.

Suffice to say, they gave me no explanation. Both Paul and I started yelling in anger and frustration. The scene became completely chaotic as we tried to push our way out of the office and were held back by Aunty and Uncle Andrews. But I just wanted to get out. Rage boiled over inside me and I lashed out, telling them that I hated them. I hated both of them. I hated Miss Vernon, who always lied. And I hated God for continually ruining our lives.

Sobbing, I wrenched my arm free of Uncle and headed out of the door. 'I don't *ever* want to be fostered again!' I yelled.

CHAPTER 4

LIFE IN CARE

For once, it seemed like the house parents had decided to listen to me. They never tried to get another foster home for us after that. Ivy Cottage was to be my home for the next few years. And for the most part, I felt safe and secure there.

Church played a part in everyday life. From very early on, Paul and I were frogmarched down to the Methodist church. Whenever I tell this story it always causes a little bit of amusement, because four of us got so disruptive in the group, even with the Uncle that came with us, that the minister had a quiet word with him and said, 'Look, we need to split these kids up. It's disruptive. We need to move them elsewhere. Mark and his brother Paul, and the other two.'

As a result, me and my brother ended up being sent to the local Baptist church, and our friends were sent to another. The Baptist church took me under their wing. We went to Sunday school and Boys' Brigade there too. I mostly enjoyed it, although I never really felt particularly 'religious'. It was just part of the routine of life. I had a Bible but I never read it. It just sat on my bedside table like an ornament. I always scoffed at the idea of a father who loved me unconditionally. What a joke that was!

I remember horrifying the church staff when they asked me what my hobby was and I said, 'I like burning things!' I didn't set any buildings on fire, but I did like to take a match to park bins and things like that. We still had chores to do in the home and one of them was burning rubbish. I was always the one to volunteer for that job. Health and safety personnel would throw a fit at that nowadays!

Ivy Cottage was good in that it instilled good morals into us. We knew where the line was. We knew that if we stepped over the boundaries that we'd be punished, and rightly so. I still maintain that a form of strong discipline is a good thing. I had structure and routine for the first time in my life, and it gave me a sense of security. I'd been craving that kind of consistency since I could walk!

Gary, Richard, Brian, Lee, and the other boys kept me happy and entertained. I felt like I was surrounded by friends. There was so much laughter and joy around the holidays, and a little bit of mischief too! Yes, the house parents were strict, but generally we were allowed to just be like normal young boys, as long as we didn't cause anybody any harm.

There was one boy that put me a little bit on edge. His name was Barry, and he was bigger and older than me. He was moody, with long greasy black hair and an acne problem. He rarely spoke to the younger kids, but for some reason I couldn't fathom at the time, he always seemed to have time for me. He hugged me a lot, and bought me sweets.

In the beginning, I thought nothing of it. Why would I? I was an innocent little kid. But as time went along, I noticed how much attention he was paying to me. I didn't necessarily think it was dangerous, but it confused me. I wasn't used to anyone paying me quite so much attention.

One night I came out of the steamy bathroom just before bedtime. I was trying to fasten up my pyjamas and wasn't really concentrating on where I was going. I started to walk down the corridor and there I ran into Barry, who smiled down at me. He stood quite close in front of me, and I couldn't get past him to go to my bedroom. 'Let me help you with that,' he said, fastening the last few buttons on my pyjama top. I had no choice but to let him.

'Thanks,' I said, trying to inch my way around him. But he was too big and there was no room.

'You settling in okay?' he asked me. 'Can't be easy, being taken away from your family to come here?'

'It's going okay,' I responded. Why did he care? We were all in the same boat here.

'Maybe a cuddle will make you feel better,' he said, pushing me lightly back into the bathroom.

No, it wouldn't, I thought, but no words came out. I didn't know what was happening, only that it was starting to make me feel uncomfortable. But he needed no encouragement anyway. He started to run his hands up and down my arms. My throat tightened in fear and I felt frozen to the spot. It was hot and steamy in the bathroom, and the mixture of the soap scent, and Barry's sweat and aftershave made me feel sick. He whispered something in my ear, something I didn't catch. I pulled myself away from him, but there was only a tiled wall behind me now and he pushed his full body weight against me. His hands began to roam all over my body, touching me in places that I knew were utterly wrong. Seized by panic I took a deep breath in, ready to yell – but he put his hand over my mouth and growled, 'Be quiet!'

Unable to make any noise, I started wriggling and squirming out of his grip. He held on even more tightly, but in my panic I had found some strength. Finally I managed to pull my mouth away from his hand and scream at the top of my voice.

'Shut up!' Barry shouted at me. 'Shut up!'

But I kept on screaming, repulsed at what was happening, terrified of what he was doing to me. Eventually, after what seemed like an age, I heard a loud banging on the bathroom door. Aunty Freda and

Uncle were on the other side. I continued to scream as Barry tussled with me. The last thing I remember about this incident was them entering the room and pulling Barry away from me.

Not long after that, Barry was sent away from the home and he never came back. Aunty Freda told me that he'd been sent away to another home for troubled children, and that I was safe again now. I was told to forget about the whole thing, and somehow I managed it. I'd become so good at repressing the awful memories of what had happened to me in the past that it was surprisingly easy to do it again.

As I grew older and became an adolescent, my mind became a far darker and more confused place to live in. School had always been a struggle because of my turbulent upbringing, and my grades continued to suffer. I felt useless in almost every subject and I was given a lot of negative feedback. Can you imagine what that did to me, when such negativity was fed into my psyche every day? No matter how hard I worked, I just couldn't keep up with everyone else. I felt worlds apart from them intellectually and this did nothing for my self-esteem.

It also became harder to hide my true emotions around people. Everything touched me deeply and affected me emotionally. The smallest things made my anger flare up. I was almost sixteen-years-old and puberty was hitting me hard, messing with my mind and my body. My past haunted me and I never felt good enough. Day after day I could feel myself sinking deeper into depression.

I became more cynical at anything anyone said, especially when it came to family or supposed 'loved ones'. Dad only visited once, my mum was hardly ever sober when she showed up, and Miss Vernon left for Scotland and I didn't see her again. My new social worker didn't seem that interested and he didn't last long either.

Eventually the home became a bit less strict with the décor of the place, and we were allowed to put up our own pictures and posters. I chose Lindsay Wagner, who played Jaime Sommers in *The Bionic*

Woman, and kept a large poster of her over my bed. Over time, Jaime Sommers became much more than a teenage crush to me; she became a kind of saviour.

She was stunningly beautiful and every teenage boy's fantasy, so there was that aspect to it. She was more than that for me though. She came to represent someone who I could pin all my negative emotions onto, while knowing that in my fantasy world she would remain loving, caring, strong, firm, and compassionate. I especially loved those episodes of The Bionic Woman where she had the responsibilities of looking after difficult and challenging young people. I related to her other films where again she was having to deal with young people and their challenging behaviour. I'm still convinced that it was my infatuation with her that kept me from giving into despair, depression, and suicide. Sometimes I even had imaginary conversations with her.

The poster seemed to remind me that I had a lot to live for. I would replay in my mind episodes of The Bionic Woman where Jaime Sommers' warmth, compassion, firmness, and love would make me feel that yes, life was worth living. Lindsay Wagner was beautiful and everything I was looking for in a woman. I wanted Lindsay Wagner to be my guardian, someone who would love me and set boundaries and who would encourage me to excel and give me hope beyond the reality of my difficult life. The problem was she was just a fantasy, a character in a television programme, an actress who lived on the other side of the world. I should have had real people around me who made me feel that way. But I didn't.

The only times I felt in any way valued as part of my biological family was when Shene, my oldest sister, and her husband Graham invited me to sleep over at their house on the occasional weekend. I would often see my other sisters, Maxine and Jenny. These were the only people I really, truly felt anything for, the only real people who I really loved and craved validation from.

At least, they were until Aunty Lindsay came onto the scene.

CHAPTER 5

AUNTY LINDSAY

I remember the moment I first set eyes on Lindsay. She was gorgeous and sexy as hell. She looked amazing in her tight blue jeans and her light brown hair framed a beautiful, smiling face.

Look, I was a teenage boy. Of course I noticed!

Aunty Freda introduced Lindsay as a new house parent when I got home from school one afternoon. I couldn't stop staring at her. She was only young, 23 or 24, and fresh out of university. She had shoulder-length light brown hair, lovely blue eyes, and a happy smile. She was slim and shapely, and my mind immediately compared her name and her looks to Lindsay Wagner. She didn't really look a lot like her, but her characteristics were the same, and that was enough for me. In my mind she became another Jaime Sommers, and instantly I was smitten. I could finally live out my fantasy, in the flesh!

'Hello, Mark,' she said to me with a sweet voice. 'It's lovely to meet you.'

I greeted her with as much cool as I could (which really wasn't a whole lot) and scurried off to my room. There on the wall hung the picture of Lindsay Wagner. I was astounded at what I'd just seen; my mind made it seem like Lindsay Wagner and Aunty Lindsay were identical. And they had the same name, too!

Turns out I wasn't the only boy in the home to recognise Aunty Lindsay's attractiveness. On her first night at Ivy Cottage, we were all sitting around in one of the dormitories wearing our dressing gowns, waiting to have our supervised bath.

'You go first!' one of the boys giggled at Richard.

'No, Mark can go first!' Richard said, throwing a cushion at me, which I dodged.

'Nah, one of you can go first,' I joked back. 'You've only got little ones – she won't be shocked at yours!' In our shyness we all laughed, feeling nervous at having Aunty Lindsay supervise us. But Lindsay was actually very discreet, not like some of the other Aunties. She made sure she stayed well away and gave us our privacy, which only made me admire her even more.

Lindsay was also kind and helpful. She would help me with my homework, have a laugh and a giggle with us, and generally spend more time socialising with us than the other Aunties. She was prettier, less strict, had a nicer figure, and was easier to talk to. She wore the most intoxicating perfume and didn't mind physical contact, in a completely platonic way, of course. She always had time to talk to us if things bothered us. She never really noticed that I was flirting with her, because of course she only saw me as a kid at work, but that never entered my head. I became smitten very quickly.

I might not have been very academically bright at the time, but that doesn't mean I wasn't clever. I started manipulating the situation in the home so that she'd have to spend more time with me than the other kids. If she did spend more time with any of the others, I got jealous. Aunty Lindsay was mine and I didn't want anyone else to have her. Well, no one ever said I was mature!

I was a 15-year-old, but mentally I was much younger. I was a depressed, underdeveloped little kid (Mrs Robins had been right after all!) and I wasn't prepared to share this beautiful new house parent. At every opportunity I would try to make her laugh, and whenever she had a giggle with me or showed me the slightest hint of attention, I would beam with happiness.

Things started to get quite boisterous in the home, especially as we were all growing bigger and the boys enjoyed play-fighting with one another. Occasionally things got out of hand, and play-fighting turned into real arguments and fall-outs. I argued a lot with Lee. We weren't always the best of friends any more anyway due to arguments we'd had in the past, and he'd obviously noticed that I'd become a bit silly over Lindsay. He'd caught me gawping at her one night and often took the mick out of me for it. Other kids played along too, playing Donny Osmond's *Puppy Love* on the stereo when we were both in the room in order to embarrass me. My temper being what it was, I would pretty much blow up at them, and things got often got physical. Aunty Lindsay hated that. 'What's all the racket about?' she would yell at me. 'Stop it right now!'

Often I would completely ignore her when she tried to tell me off, or I would answer back to her, and this would transform her from a laughing, smiling friend to a person of authority with deep anger in her voice. She had no patience for any kind of disrespect and wouldn't hold back from grabbing me roughly and yelling at me to behave. Over time I think she started recognising me for what I was: a bit of a headache. And I admit, I was always playing up. I didn't know how to handle my emotions. I was desperate for any kind of acknowledgement.

After a few weeks of swinging between getting along with Lindsay and being reprimanded by her, I realised something. Even though it wasn't great when Aunty Lindsay was unhappy with me, I actually kind of liked the conflict. Deep down, warped as it may be, I wanted her to prove that she loved me enough to discipline me. No one else, in my world view, cared enough to even really pay attention to what I did day-to-day, outside of making sure I did the chores and went to school.

And because I craved the kind of attention that Lindsay Wagner's character Jaime Sommers gave her charges on television, I started playing out a fantasy in my mind. Aunty Lindsay *became* Jaime Sommers, who had conflicts with her charges because she loved them. I wasn't seeing Aunty Lindsay; I was seeing Lindsay Wagner. I was losing touch with reality where Lindsay was concerned and was struggling to separate what was real from what wasn't. I preferred the fantasy, because the reality was too painful.

On Bonfire Night everyone was in high spirits. I enjoyed all of the time I got to spend with Aunty Lindsay, and I felt better than I had for a long time. Throughout the night Lindsay was happy and playful with me, and I felt like I could do anything. As a result I got far too carried away and, in an effort to make her laugh, I tried to trick her and did that joke move that makes you feel like you're having an egg cracked on your head. Unfortunately I did it way too hard and actually ended up badly hurting her neck. The problem was that I didn't realise I'd hurt her, and I laughed loudly right in her face. In her shock and pain, she reached around to try to sit me down but instead accidentally slapped me hard across the face. I was gobsmacked because I didn't expect it, and immediately she looked horrified at what she'd done. I don't think she'd meant to do it at all.

'Mark, I'm so sorry,' she said to me, her mouth open in horrified surprise. But I didn't want to hear any of it. My own fury bubbled up inside me, and I didn't let her finish.

'You act like you care about me, but you don't!' I yelled in her face. 'You're just like everyone else!' I then stormed off in a dramatic huff, and locked myself in my room, away from her and everyone else. I skipped dinner that night, determined to make her feel as bad as I felt myself. I wanted to play mind games, to kick back at authority, to make her worry about me.

But she wasn't just an authority figure to me any more. To me, it felt like she was different from everyone else. People kept telling me it was a childish schoolboy crush, but I knew it was becoming much more than that. I was falling in love with Aunty Lindsay and I was in no mental state to stop it. I didn't even really want to. It made the slap feel even more like a huge betrayal. Yet another betrayal by another person who loved me.

I was a messed-up kid, though, and my love for her didn't stop me from making her life a bit of a misery for a good few months. I avoided her to the best of my ability, punishing her and provoking whatever emotion from her that I could. I would throw dishes into the sink when she was nearby, splashing her with water. I would refuse to eat my dinner and throw the cutlery around. I would shout and scream at her, and start fights with the other children. I'd create tension and hostility, and I couldn't stop myself from doing it.

Why was I doing this? Every day I grew to love Aunty Lindsay more and more. I fantasised about her every night. I craved her love and attention but then threw it back in her face whenever she tried to engage with me. I told myself I hated her when I really felt the opposite. I was confusing myself, becoming less aware of why I was doing what I was doing. Was I protecting myself from being hurt by another loved one? Was I punishing her for everything I'd had done to me over the years, by the people who were supposed to love me the most? Was I projecting my hatred of my many past abusers onto her? I no longer knew. And I hated, *hated* that I didn't know what was going on with my own mind.

I loved Aunty Lindsay so much, and I wanted things to be good between us. So why was I constantly making things horrible?

For years I'd been living in an institution that had worked nicely for a long time. And then suddenly I reached puberty and fell in love with a house parent. The home had absolutely no idea how to handle that. The only thing they could think of was to tell me I had to suppress my feelings. And so it was that I ended up in Uncle's office one late afternoon, after I had caused yet another commotion.

Sitting myself in the chair in front of Uncle's desk, I kept my head and eyes down at the floor. I could feel a telling off coming my way.

'Mark, it's come to my attention that there's a problem between you and Aunty Lindsay,' Uncle Andrews said to me. I said nothing. 'Do you have anything to tell me?'

I shook my head. Uncle sighed deeply.

'We're trying to run a happy home, here, Mark,' he said. 'We can't have you causing tension, and making Aunty Lindsay feel bad. She's just doing her job. She's only young, she's only just started with us. You mustn't keep making her feel uncomfortable. We can't let this carry on.'

I said nothing, but inside I was seething. Lindsay had obviously told on me. She'd betrayed me. How else would Uncle know about all of this?

'If there's anything you need to talk to me about, you can do so right now. Would you like to tell me anything?' he asked, his tone softer.

I shook my head again. 'No.'

Uncle sighed again. 'Okay. Well, I trust that now we've had this chat, you will behave yourself far better than you have been doing, and you will stop giving Aunty Lindsay a hard time. No more attitude. Is that clear?'

'Yes, Uncle,' I said to him, my eyes still on the floor.

'Good,' he responded. 'You can go.' He opened the office door so that I could leave.

At that, I ran out into the garden where no one else could see me, parked myself under a tree, and sobbed. I stayed there for a long time, resenting the fact that no one inside the house seemed to care that I was nowhere to be seen.

'I hate her for betraying me,' I thought to myself. 'I thought she cared about me, but all she wanted to do was report me to Uncle.'

I sat there in the cold December night, letting the dampness of the grass seep into my trousers, ripping up the weeds from the ground in my anger. I was too wrapped up in my thoughts to hear Aunty Lindsay come outside to look for me, and I didn't realise she was there until she spoke.

'Mark, what are you doing out here?' she asked me, wrapping a coat around herself. 'What's wrong?'

I looked up at her with tears in my eyes. 'You reported me to Aunty and Uncle,' I accused her.

She looked surprised at this. 'No, I didn't,' she responded, quietly but firmly.

'I don't believe you,' I told her. 'You betrayed me.'

'Now, Mark,' she said to me, putting a hand on my shoulder. 'I did no such thing. Let's not be dramatic.'

I wrenched my shoulder away from her. 'You're lying to me! I don't want to speak to you! Stop pretending you give a damn!'

She sighed heavily, clearly worn out. I turned and ran back into the home, leaving her knelt down on the ground.

Christmas was rapidly approaching and my moods were erratic and unpredictable. I managed to avoid Lindsay quite successfully over the next couple of weeks, often treating her with contempt if our paths crossed. Further arguments occurred, most of them my fault. I continued to confuse myself. I loved Lindsay deeply, and yet I couldn't stop making her life difficult.

And she was the only one who seemed oblivious to my love. During one or two rare, calm moments when we were happy in each other's company, I found it impossible to hide my admiration from all of those around me. The staff became increasingly aware of my obsession; the kids carried on taking the mick. I was infatuated and couldn't help myself – I stared at her every chance I got, sought physical contact whenever I wasn't angry with her. But it was also humiliating to know that everyone else was watching all of this happen. I couldn't escape my own feelings. I lived in constant fear. I was simultaneously worried that someone would report me for being around Aunty Lindsay, and yet I felt powerless to keep away from her.

It later transpired that eventually Aunty Lindsay was reprimanded by Uncle and Aunty Andrews. She was taken aside and told not to encourage me or my crush. But she never had! I don't know whether anyone had the impression that I was being groomed or something, but nothing was further from the truth. She never encouraged me; I want to make this very clear. In fact if anyone was doing the grooming, it was me! I was the one manipulating her into spending her time and energies on me, by playing up or hogging her time. She was told that she had to take a firmer hand with me, but she'd always disciplined me well.

In the run-up to Christmas it was Aunty Lindsay's turn to supervise us while Uncle and Aunty Andrews went away for a short break. Aunty Freda went away too, and Aunty Gwen was ill, so we had Lindsay all to ourselves. Needless to say I was happy with this; it meant we had more freedom to mess about, and some closer time with Lindsay. Over the next few days Lindsay and I laughed and joked together, playing games with the other kids, finally enjoying each other's company. Whenever her arm or leg brushed against mine, I felt a jolt of excitement rush through me. She was so beautiful, and so kind and gentle when we weren't arguing. The smell of her perfume did something to me – I was drawn to the smell of it. When we chatted about everything and anything, she would smile and chuckle at me like I was the funniest person in the world. In my mind, she was so much like Lindsay Wagner that it almost felt as though Jaime Sommers was actually in the room with me, taking care of me, proving that I was important and that I was loved.

Lindsay encouraged me to join her at the Baptist church, and we would walk home together afterwards, discussing the sermons and chatting about God. She clearly loved him dearly. I didn't trust him as far as I could throw him! But it made me feel close to her and made me love her even more. During these times I wondered to myself why I sometimes felt the need to make things hostile and awkward between us.

And yet, because I was so messed up in my head, it never lasted. One day after school Fram, one of my close friends who was the local paperboy, asked me if I could help him out with his paper round. I was hesitant because I thought I'd get in trouble if I was late back, but I liked the idea of the extra money and I wanted to help him out. His mum had often invited me over to their house for huge meals, and I owed Fram a favour.

Even with two of us it took us quite a few hours, though, and I didn't come crawling back to Ivy Cottage until gone seven o'clock. I walked through the kitchen to find Lindsay sitting at the table, looking distraught. Instead of facing her, I did the cowardly thing and ran upstairs to my room. But she followed me anyway.

'Where on Earth have you been?' she shouted at me.

I kept quiet, staring at my fingernails. I wasn't going to tell her.

'We were worried sick about you! Why didn't you tell us where you were?'

Still I stayed silent.

'You need to grow up, Mark!' she said. 'You have got to stop treating me as though you hate me.'

I didn't hate her. I *loved* her. If only she knew.

'Fine, forget it,' she said, looking disgusted with me. 'If you're not going to talk to me, if you're going to mistreat me at every turn, then you're not worth my time! I have far too many other children to take care of without worrying about your issues!'

With that, she turned to walk away. Suddenly I became furious that she'd decided not to pay me any attention any more. That wasn't what I wanted! In a fit of rage and immaturity I picked up a hairbrush from the bedside table and hurled it towards her as she walked out of my bedroom door.

It missed her by centimetres. I held my breath, my heart pounding away in my chest. Why had I just done that?

She stopped in her tracks and slowly picked up the hairbrush. She was shaking – I could see it in her hands. I swallowed hard, unsure of what was going to happen next. For a split second I thought she was going to hit me with the hairbrush, and I found myself wanting her to do it. *Go on, discipline me, I thought. Show me you care!*

'Don't you ever do that again, you stupid child,' she shouted, brandishing the brush at me. 'Be thankful this didn't hit me! You can start bucking up your ideas, young man!' She left the room and went downstairs, leaving me lost and confused. Why did I keep doing this? Why was I pushing away the person I loved most in the world?

Lindsay was due to spend the holidays at home with her parents, and I just couldn't face Christmas knowing things were bad between us. I'd been feeling incredibly guilty about my behaviour towards her recently. So I decided to write her a letter:

Dear Aunty Lindsay,

I am writing this letter because I know I have caused you a lot of problems since you started working here, and I really want to say how sorry I am ... I wrote.

I went on to tell her about all of the adults who had pretended to care about me over the years, only to let me down when I had just started to trust them. I explained why this made me act out and become hostile towards the only people who ever showed me any love.

Please don't give up on me, I wrote. *I do feel bad about the way I've behaved. I hope we can be friends.*

Love, Mark

I then went and slipped the letter underneath her bedroom door and went back down to my own, anxious about how she would react to it. I prayed to a God I only half believed in that she would forgive me.

I needn't have worried. Lindsay always was, and still is, a wonderful and kind woman, and she left a letter on my bedside table before she set off for home the following day. Her response was kind and uplifting:

Mark,

I was absolutely delighted to receive your letter. I'm sorry if I've hurt you. I never meant to.

As far as I'm concerned it's all in the past and forgotten. I will never give up on you. I want us to be friends. Let's put all this behind us after Christmas.

I pressed the letter to my chest and smiled to myself. She really, truly, cared about me after all. I could now get through Christmas knowing someone out there had my back, and that I could finally trust someone after all. My heart soaring, I ran downstairs to join my friends and get ready for the Christmas celebrations.

Christmas was fantastic, but over the next few months certain aspects of my life started to decline rapidly. My schoolwork was suffering badly and I struggled in all of my CSE exams. More than one of my teachers expressed concern to Uncle and Aunty and I felt humiliated every time the topic was brought up. I also started having horrific nightmares, most of which I couldn't remember when I woke up. I would wake up covered in sweat, and my friends told me that I screamed out in my sleep numerous times. I had built up such a mental wall over the past few years that the only time the bad memories and thoughts had free rein in my mind was during sleep.

I also found myself unable to eat. Every bit of food made me feel sick. I was on edge and stressed all the time, and so my stomach hurt and my appetite disappeared. I didn't touch my meals at school, and that got reported back to the home too. Paul frequently asked me if I was okay, telling me I looked like garbage. House parents had to order me to choke down my food at mealtimes, not without aggressive protest from me. I started arguments and fights over and over again, in a constant vicious cycle of anger and defiance against authority. Why were they all being fake? None of them actually cared whether I ate or not. My teachers didn't give a monkeys whether I did well in school! No one had cared before and I wasn't about to fall for it now.

One day in science class, I was helping the teacher and some of the other kids put away the equipment in the supply cupboard. That day we had been dissecting animal organs and there were lots of knives and scalpels that I needed to collect and lock away. I was just placing a box of scalpels and blades wrapped in plastic on a shelf when something new and scary popped into my mind.

Why don't you take one?

I didn't even really take the time to question myself or my own motivations. The teacher called out my name, hurrying me along, and walked towards the back of the room where I was standing. Before she could get too close and before I could really think about what I was doing, I had snatched a scalpel and some blades and buried them deeply in my pocket. I closed the door just as I was being reprimanded for taking my sweet time in getting things packed away. I stepped away from the cupboard and carried on acting as normal.

Later that night, I had almost forgotten about what I'd done when another argument erupted over the dinner table. Lindsay had noticed that I wasn't eating my food again. The first time she mentioned it, she asked me simply to eat up. When I ignored her, she spoke more loudly.

'Mark, eat, please,' she warned me.

'No! I don't have to eat if I don't want to!'

'For heaven's sake,' she sighed heavily. 'Stop making everything so difficult. Eat your food.'

'Stop ordering me around!'

At this, I fled upstairs to my room. I didn't even really take much provoking any more. My mind was foggy with fury already. I felt sick and tired of conflict, sick and tired of myself for causing it, sick and tired of not understanding myself. My emotions were becoming more and more erratic and out of control. There never, ever seemed to be a way out.

Except … I *did* have the scalpel.

I stared up at the poster of Lindsay Wagner. *Why couldn't you be real?* I asked her. *You would have taken care of me. You wouldn't have got angry at me. You would have understood me*.

Slowly, I pulled the scalpel out of my pocket and attached the blade onto it. It was incredibly sharp and the metal felt cold against my skin. My heart was thumping at a thousand beats per minute and I asked myself if I could really do it.

But what was the alternative? Life was just too hard. I hurt all the time. Every day I tried to keep the wall between my past and my present, between my emotions and rationality, between reality and fantasy as high as I could. But it was slowly crumbling and there was nothing I could do about it. There was nobody on my side. It would be easier for it to just end.

I pressed the blade just a little bit harder against my skin. I didn't draw blood, but it was starting to hurt. *I can do it, I can …*

Suddenly the door crashed open with a loud bang, and Lindsay traipsed in. 'Listen here, Mark …' Her voice trailed off as she spotted the scalpel in my hand. She walked towards me slowly.

'Leave me alone,' I said to her, scalpel still against my skin.

'Let's just talk,' she said to me, her voice shaking. 'Put the scalpel down and talk to me. You're punishing no one but yourself.'

I shook my head, staring down at my wrist. I had dug the scalpel in a bit deeper and drawn out a bead of blood. But I hadn't gone any further than that. *I can do it.*

'Drop it, Mark,' Lindsay said in my ear, a lot closer than she'd been before. My head shot up in alarm, and I realised that she'd inched her way towards me while I wasn't paying attention. She wrapped a hand around my wrist, and instinctively I started to struggle. Panic gripped me as we wrestled; Lindsay desperately tried to knock the scalpel out of my hand, but I was strong for a teenager and so we fought on.

'No! Stop it!' I yelled, terrified I was accidentally going to stab her. I didn't want to hurt anyone but myself, especially the woman I loved. But she didn't let go. I twisted and turned, trying to pull my wrist from her grip. For a split second I thought I'd managed to fight her off but then I felt a hot, sharp, searing pain flash across my thumb. 'Arrrgh!'

'Oh my God!' Lindsay cried, staring down in horror at my hand, which was now covered in blood. I kept on wailing. She pulled out a handkerchief from her pocket and pressed it down on the gaping wound in my thumb. Then she led me into the bathroom, telling me to keep calm and that it wasn't as bad as I feared. 'FREDA!'

Freda ran into the room. As her eyes surveyed the scene the blood drained from her face. 'What did you do?' she said to me, panicked, helping me wrap my bleeding thumb in a towel. With orders to Lindsay to look after the other kids, she whisked me off to hospital in the car. Thankfully, I only needed six stitches and was back home within a few hours, but it was a traumatic experience. When I got back I expected a huge fallout, but after a lengthy lecture from Uncle and Aunty Andrews and several reassurances to Paul that I was okay, things returned to normal quite quickly. The house parents kept a close eye on me, and Lindsay made me promise I'd never do anything so silly again. I was given a stern warning from my teachers about stealing school equipment, and that was it. No one really asked me anything about my suicidal tendencies.

Of course nothing changed in my mind. Eating still made me feel sick. The nightmares kept on haunting me. Every day I struggled with my schoolwork, and I lashed out at my teachers and the house parents. I continued to follow Lindsay around like a lost puppy, and I also argued with her over and over again. I knew that my time in the children's home was coming to an end, as it was customary for kids to leave and find their own way in the world when they reached 16. I kept thinking about how I would cope without Lindsay and my brother. I worried about how I would get a job. I worried about everything. I became exhausted, Lindsay was at her wits' end, and Aunty and Uncle Andrews finally lost their patience with me.

One morning, as I was packing up my bags ready to visit my sister Shene for a couple of weeks, Aunty Andrews walked into my bedroom.

'Mark, can we chat?' she asked me, standing near the bedroom door.

I nodded, packing socks and underpants into the suitcase.

'We've had a staff meeting,' she said quietly. 'We've discussed your problems with Aunty Lindsay and your ongoing problems with your anger and emotions. The hostility and bad behaviour isn't going away, despite our numerous efforts to discipline you.'

I swallowed hard, feeling a bit nauseated. She continued.

'We just can't take any more of this teenage rebellion. We've done our best to calm things down, but it's not working. We're also aware that your feelings for Lindsay are intense, and they're not fading.'

She was right there. At least now she realised it wasn't just *puppy love*. It was real.

'But we do feel that they are inappropriate, and there's not a lot we can do here about that. For these reasons we feel that it's best if you stayed with your sister indefinitely and didn't come back to Ivy Cottage after your holiday.'

'Don't come back?' I asked, tears welling up in my eyes. Aunty Andrews nodded and held my hand.

'Look, it's not so bad,' she said to me kindly. 'You were going to be leaving in a few months' time, anyway, weren't you? I hear your older sister was kind enough to agree to take you in for a while until you landed on your feet. This way you're just going a bit earlier, right?'

I nodded, my head feeling foggy and my heart hurting. I didn't know why I was still so surprised every time this happened. Yet again I was being forced away from my home against my wishes. What was I going to do without Lindsay? Away from my home?

The next morning, after an utterly sleepless night, I packed the last of my things together and went downstairs to say goodbye to the other kids in the home one by one. I felt desperately sad saying goodbye to Gary, Richard and Brian, and even to Lee. I hugged my brother and knew I would miss him for the next few months. I hugged the house parents and said goodbye to the cook and cleaners.

But of course the most heart-wrenching experience was saying goodbye to Lindsay. She hugged me tightly and promised to write me letters.

'I will always be your friend, Mark. Remember that,' she whispered into my ear as tears ran down my cheeks. *But I love you*, I thought, my heart breaking.

She squeezed my hand and then let me go. I was driven off in Uncle's car towards the train station, feeling as though the floor had been ripped from underneath me once again.

The last photo of Mark in the children's home before he was forced to leave.
Lindsay, the house parent, is standing next to him on the left.

CHAPTER 6

A DRASTIC DECLINE

And so here I now was, living with my big sister Shene and her husband Graham back in Chester, sleeping in the little box room at the back of the house. I'd been snatched once again from a place I called home, pulled away from my brother, rejected by the woman I loved and misunderstood by everyone, including myself.

It seemed like I was destined to be subjected to an onslaught of misery, abuse and pain. The negative experiences just kept hitting me like falling bricks, over and over again, and I felt lost. No one ever taught me how to deal with all these awful emotions that were swirling around inside my brain day in, day out.

I missed my friends, I missed Paul, and I missed Aunty Lindsay. And for that reason I had no motivation whatsoever to go out and forge a new life for myself. I didn't want to hang around people my age; they all seemed so juvenile compared to Aunty Lindsay (a bit hypocritical of me, I know). My social life diminished to nothing. I spent my days sneaking alcohol into my room, laying on my bed and brooding over the unfairness of everything that had happened to me in the past. Why had our parents failed us so badly? Why hadn't Mum or Dad wanted us? Why were we so cruelly pulled away from the Taits? What kind of system allowed people who locked kids up in cupboards to be foster parents? And how had a sexual abuser been able to attack me in a children's home that was meant to be safe?

Why didn't the children's home want me any more?

To his credit, Graham tried to help me get back onto my feet. He was a lovely, cheerful bloke, with a full head of thick hair and an infectious laugh. He and Shene made things just about bearable for me, and deep down I appreciated him taking me in with him and my sister when he didn't have to. After a few weeks he helped me get a job in a local menswear shop. I told the manager about my dark past in the interview, and miraculously it didn't put him off. I functioned okay in the role, but outside work my life was a shambles. Beer and lager were my only friends, and I began to drink more and more. At first drinking was just something to do to quell the boredom, but after a while it became a coping mechanism. It was in this manner that I saw through my 17th and 18th birthdays: holed up in my own misery and going nowhere in life.

True to her promise before I left Ivy Cottage, Aunty Lindsay regularly sent me letters. I lived for them; I would spend hours upon hours reading and re-reading them, searching for any kind of indication that she might love me. She had left Ivy Cottage a few months after I had, and was now a teacher somewhere in Sussex. Knowing she was so far away hurt me, but her letters made me feel better when depression came knocking on my door. I desperately wanted to tell her again that I loved her, but I was terrified of pushing her further away. She was all I had now, and my heart ached with longing for her. What if she cut me off altogether?

Throughout all this I clung onto one little ray of hope: that when Paul left Ivy Cottage, we could move in together and start a new life. But I was to be handed yet another huge disappointment when he called me one day and told me he'd decided to join the navy. I spiralled into yet another pit of despair, lying around in my room for days with ABBA music on an endless loop. Clearly I wasn't destined to be happy.

But if I expected sympathy, I was to be disappointed because Shene had no patience for my wallowing or my self-pity. Looking back, I realise how awful things must have been for her. She tried her hardest to look after me, despite having my two little nephews to look after and a house to run. Technically I was still under the care of social services, but my sister just wasn't getting any help from anyone. Social services had washed their hands of me and she was left to sort things out herself. She tried to understand me, but even she had her limitations. She wasn't that much older than me, but some of her childhood experiences had been quite different to mine. She didn't know about a lot of the stuff that had happened to me, and so she genuinely believed that my drinking and moping was some kind of teenage rebellion.

'For heaven's sake, Mark!' she yelled at me in the kitchen one day, struggling with shopping bags and her two young sons who were acting up. 'Start helping me a little bit more around here, with less of the anger and attitude, and grow up! We all had bad childhoods, but that doesn't mean you have to become an alcoholic and shut out the rest of the world!'

I slammed my cup hard on the kitchen side, which only made her angrier. 'I'm not an alcoholic,' I snapped at her.

'You could have fooled me!' she said. 'All you do is sit around and mope!'

Once again I felt that familiar stab of anger. 'Leave me alone, Shene! All you do is nag at me!'

'Nag at you?' she yelled, wrestling with a bag of groceries as my nephew tugged at her trouser leg and started to whine. 'I'm trying to help you! You need to cheer up, learn not to give up all the time, and stop driving me crackers!'

'Cheer up? That easy, is it?' I snarled at her, standing at the kitchen sink and filling up a glass of water. 'And how do you suggest I do that, when every time I try to be happy, something comes along to mess it up?'

'Get some friends!' Shene yelled at me. My fists clenched up. 'Get a grip!' I closed my eyes tightly, trying to drown out her words. 'Go out and get a life!'

Shut up. Shut up …

'SHUT UP!' I screamed at her, white-hot rage coursing through me. The pressure built up in my head, in my whole body, and there was nowhere for my anger to go but outwards. Before I even knew what I was doing, I had grabbed something off the side. Something with a wooden handle.

Suddenly everything went quiet. I was breathing heavily, blood rushing in my ears, but I still had no real idea what had just happened. Why was Shene looking at me like that?

'Mark,' she said, quietly and slowly. She had a terribly frightened look on her face, and her arm was stretched out towards me. 'What are you doing? Put that down, Mark.'

Put what down? I looked down at my hand and flinched in shock. Subconsciously I had grabbed a big bread knife from the kitchen side and was holding it in front of me. I was threatening my sister with a knife.

The horrible realisation hit me with full force. I felt dizzy and my breathing was laboured. Suddenly I felt my legs giving way beneath me. Darkness closed in on me as I collapsed to the floor.

'Mark!' Shene screamed, and it was the last thing I heard before I lost consciousness.

'It was stress,' said the doctor, a short while later. I was lying on my bed, eyes still closed, feeling exhausted and deeply upset about what had happened. I could hear the doctor talking to my sister and Graham downstairs: he had a loud, booming voice. 'Stress caused him to have a fit, probably brought on by emotional distress. He needs to take things easier.'

'He's not exactly exerting himself,' Graham responded, sounding deeply unimpressed. 'I don't know what he has to be stressed about.' I winced at this. Graham had always listened to me. Surely he knew what my pain was about?

'I just wish he'd help himself,' Shene responded, sounding exhausted. 'I'm tired of asking him to get up and sort his life out.'

A pang of guilt hit me and I buried myself deeper into the bed covers. I couldn't face the shame of what I'd done; sleeping was the only way to escape it.

I fully expected things to become awkward after that horrible episode, but clearly Shene and Graham wanted to put it behind us as much as I did. I wasn't sure whether Shene was scared of me now. I was scared of me. What had I been playing at, wielding a knife around? The guilt of what I'd done hung heavy on my shoulders. I felt suffocated by all of the terrible emotions I carried around every day. Nothing I did could shake off my depression, and I was sinking further and further …

I went back to work after a couple of days despite the doctor's recommendations, just to get out from under their feet. Graham asked me how I felt about seeing a doctor or a psychiatrist to talk about my issues, and I didn't have the strength to say no. I didn't trust doctors or psychiatrists any more than I trusted any other adult who'd come and gone in my life, promising to make things better for me. But I was still mortified by what I had done, so I told Graham what he wanted to hear and agreed to it. I didn't expect him to bring it up again anyway.

Life continued in a haze of drunkenness and sadness, but what really kept me going were Aunty Lindsay's letters. After getting home from my shift one afternoon, I noticed that I'd received another letter from her. Joy swelled up in my chest and I grabbed a can of beer. Running up into my room, I tore open the letter, a smile plastered across my face. I loved getting new letters from Lindsay. It broke up the monotony of my new life.

Dear Mark, it read.

I hope you're okay and that you're enjoying living with your sister. It's good to hear about your job.

My own job is going well. I'm enjoying teaching and the move to Sussex has gone well ...

I read through each paragraph carefully; her joy and happiness about her job was heartwarming for me. But then one word caught my eye.

... married ...

Wait, what was that? I re-read the sentence, certain I'd got it wrong.

... his name is Geoff and last week we got engaged. We hope to get married sometime next spring ...

Married? My Lindsay was getting married? A wave of nausea hit me as the truth sunk in. How could she do this to me? How? After everything she'd promised me? She'd told me she'd never abandon me!

A deep wail escaped my lips. My heart hurt and my head felt cloudy. Another rejection. When was the rejection going to end? Was I so unlovable? Did I really not deserve to have anything constant in my life?

Another wave of dizziness hit me and I was terrified I was going to pass out again. I tried to breathe in deeply but it felt as though the pain was gripping tightly onto my lungs. I did my best to stop myself from hyperventilating and I got my breathing under control, but still the pain and the humiliation and the heartache kept on their war of attrition against my sanity.

The next few days disappeared into a black hole of numbness. I barely spoke or moved unless I had to; I was terrified of jolting myself out of the calming alternate reality my mind was creating for me. I listened to sad music and shut out the real world. My mind had retreated to somewhere else completely. I'd simply had enough.

Irritated and worried about me in equal measure, Shene and Graham left me to my own devices. I didn't tell them what had happened. I'd had enough talking; no one ever listened anyway, and that was nothing new. Instead, my mind kept taking me back to the incident with the scalpel a couple of years ago, and I wondered if I had the courage to try cutting my own wrists again. Was there any other solution?

Did I actually want to do this?

My question was answered for me one day when the house was empty. I stumbled, zombie-like, into the bathroom and grabbed hold of a razor blade out of the cabinet. *Oh God, am I strong enough to do this?*

Memories of what I'd done with the scalpel as a boy came flooding back to me. Could I get it right this time? With shaking hands and my eyes closed tightly, I slashed the razor blade across the vein in my wrist. I cried out, terrified but strangely spurred on by the searing pain. Blood splashed out onto my clothes, onto the bath, onto the carpet. Fear gripped me but this time my determination was stronger. I willed myself to do it again on my other hand.

As I dragged the blade down the vein on my other wrist, I felt the strength slowly start to ebb away from my body. I had done it now, but something in my mind didn't quite believe I had gone through with it. I started to panic: had I made a huge mistake? Now that the blood was rapidly pouring out of me, something deep inside me called out to the God I still wasn't sure I believed in. *If it's true you'll never leave me when everyone else has, please prove it to me,* I remember myself thinking. *If I am truly worth something, please don't let me die.*

CHAPTER 7

GETTING SECTIONED

Perhaps the Lord truly did listen to me, or maybe it just wasn't my time to die. In sheer panic, I'd dragged myself over to Graham's sister Jill's house, where I'd collapsed, semi-conscious, onto her floor. Jill called Shene and Graham, who rushed home as quickly as they could. Unsurprisingly, I don't remember much after that, except the sound of my sister wailing, the severe pain in my wrists, and the loud siren of the ambulance as it sped me towards the local hospital.

The next few days were a haze of pain, distress, and frustration as I was supervised by hospital staff no matter where I went or what I did. I guess I should have been used to this kind of control after Ivy Cottage, and I'm well aware that they were trying to stop me attempting suicide again.

And so it went for a full week while they treated my wounds and assessed my mental condition. It shouldn't have come as a surprise when Shene told me that I was being sectioned under the Mental Health Act. Poor Shene had to make the difficult decision and sign the papers to say she approved of the decision. She had no other choice and no clue what else to do, and so I was to be admitted to a local psychiatric hospital for treatment. I was absolutely horrified.

Even more upsetting was leaving the ambulance when we pulled up to the psychiatric hospital. I was a 10-year-old in an 18-year-old's body (I even looked about 12!) and I was scared and overwhelmed. I saw the big red building looming through the ambulance window, and it didn't look like a hospital. It looked like a prison. There were bars on the windows and big doors that were clearly securely locked. It was a Victorian structure, with big chimneys and thick brick walls.

It was daunting. The ambulance drivers literally had to pull me off the ambulance because I was so adamant that I wasn't going into the hospital. I didn't want to go in there.

The only reassuring indication to me that it was a hospital – and not a prison – was when the nurses came out in their blue and pink uniforms and hats. Those uniforms were reassuring to me, because it showed that there were staff who were going to look after me. The men's uniforms were grey suits, and they were not so reassuring. They didn't look very trustworthy, but thankfully I reassured myself that they mostly worked upstairs where the padded cells were.

Inside the hospital was a bit depressing. There were long corridors and dark colours, a complete contrast from the bright summer sun and colours outside. But I was put at ease when I met one of the nurses, who introduced herself as Nurse Alex. She was young and attractive with a sweet smile, and I liked her. She led me into a lounge from which led a dozen small bedrooms, and helped me put my suitcase on my bed. My bedroom was small and simply furnished, with bars on the window. I suddenly felt very tired.

Next, she introduced me to some of my ward mates. I met Annie, a large woman in her forties, who suffered badly with depression like me. I liked her, but I knew I would have to learn to read her properly, as I didn't want to get on her nerves if she was feeling low. Then there was Sandy, a tall skinny girl who couldn't have been any older than me. She had brown hair and big eyes, and she greeted me with a degree of hesitation. I later learnt that she had been sexually abused and so was uneasy around men. That was fair enough, I thought.

Then there was Jack and George. I liked George; I didn't like Jack. George was an overweight, 30-something lad, and he smiled at me warmly and shook my hand. He seemed affable enough. Jack didn't; he reminded me of a weasel. He seemed jumpy and there was just something about him that put me on edge. I found it hard to adjust to the hospital in the first few days. I was still obviously incredibly depressed and feeling suicidal, and I'd never been any good at adjusting to new situations, as many as I'd had over the years! I was prescribed medication and took it without question to begin with. Having lived in an institution for such a long time, there were some things I didn't really question.

I did start questioning things, however; in my first session with the psychiatrist, he actually asked me if I'd ever had any sexual fantasies about my mother or father. I was astounded! Was this what life in a mental hospital was going to be like? Me being humiliated with such ridiculous questions and accusations?

My first appointment with the doctor wasn't the easiest either. He was Indian and I struggled to understand his heavy accent. Eventually I just let him do most of the talking, which was okay. He was a nice guy. He understood the need for me to get out what I was feeling, but he also understood that I had real issues opening up to people because of my abandonment complex.

'Mark, have you ever considered writing a diary?' he asked me in the session, staring at me over the rim of his glasses.

'No, I haven't,' I answered truthfully. It had never occurred to me to do that.

'Well, it might be worth giving it a go. Maybe it will help you release some of the anger you're holding onto. If you don't feel you trust anyone enough to talk to them, perhaps writing things down would be a good substitute.'

It took me a few days to come around to the idea, but when Shene and Graham visited me and gifted me with a typewriter, I found it the perfect opportunity to write Aunty Lindsay a letter and give diary writing a try. And that's precisely what I did.

The following chapter consists of diary entries from my time in the home, and they paint a picture of what I went through far better than any rewriting could do.

West Cheshire Mental Asylum, where Mark was sectioned.

West Cheshire Mental Asylum's dark, Victorian corridors.

CHAPTER 8

DIARIES OF A TEENAGER
IN A MENTAL HOSPITAL

11th September 1980

Dear Aunty Lindsay,

Since I left the children's home I have loved keeping in touch with you. Your letters have always cheered me up when I have become depressed. I don't know how I would have coped without your friendship over the last two years. You have always encouraged me in everything I have done and I am grateful that you have let me keep in touch with you.

I often think back to my time at Ivy Cottage and remember when you first arrived. I don't know if you are aware of this, but you were the first house parent ever to wear jeans.

From the moment I saw you, I thought you were the most beautiful woman I had ever seen. You reminded me so much of the actress, Lindsay Wagner. You know how crazy I was about her in the science fiction programme The Bionic Woman. You always said you looked nothing like her and that it was all in my imagination. In all honesty that was true, but I didn't care. I lived in a fantasy world. It was my way of coping.

My social worker and other house parents told me that my feelings for you were not normal. They warned me that if I didn't get my feelings under control they would have to send me away. I couldn't cope because of the stress I was under.

That day I tried to cut my wrists with the scalpel blade, it wasn't so much because you had told me off, but because I had snapped. I couldn't take any more. I desperately wanted to tell you what they were doing to me, but my social worker told me not to.

After the scalpel incident they were more sympathetic towards me, but still made me feel like my feelings were wrong. Aunty Lindsay, forgive me, but I have been in love with you since the first time I met you. I fell for you in such a big way. I couldn't handle my feelings. I didn't know what to do. You were the first house parent to take a genuine interest in me.

I cannot forget those times I spent with you. I liked it so much when you were helping me with my homework. I remember the night you discovered me in the bathroom, working late with my books, and confiscated them. You looked so beautiful in your dressing gown, with your long tawny hair hanging loose.

When I left the children's home I was so depressed, bitter, and resentful. I hated everyone who sent me away from the children's home. I was in so much emotional pain, I felt like my heart was breaking. I am in love with you. Please forgive me. I can't help my feelings. These feelings for you won't go away. I wish they would, because I hurt so much.

A couple of weeks ago I tried to take my own life and now I am in a mental hospital, well that's what it's called around here. Aunty Lindsay, I need you to understand the depth of my feelings for you. By writing to you and sharing with you, I am taking a big risk. I hope you will understand and will forgive me for the trouble I am causing you. Aunty Lindsay, will you write back to me and tell me you understand, and that you want to help? If you turn your back on me now, then I don't think I will want to live. I am scared – scared that you will not want anything more to do with me.

I love you, Aunty Lindsay. I love you so much and I need you now more than ever. You are a Christian. Ask your God what you should do. I hope he guides you to write back to me. I feel so unhappy. I am so sad and depressed. I love you so much and I want to be able to let you go, but it's difficult for me to accept that you are only a fantasy.

My sister doesn't know what to do to help me. She has sectioned me in this mental hospital for trying to commit suicide, and they think I am an alcoholic because of my heavy drinking. I am sorry to put this on to you. I don't know what to do. I am so scared – this place is horrible! Please, if you can't write to me direct, please get in touch with my sister. Just tell me you understand and that you won't reject me. That's all I ask, please.

Love,

Mark xx

13th September 1980

I have posted my letter to Aunty Lindsay. I am worried. I don't know how she will react when she discovers that I have been in love with her for the last two years.

I have told the psychiatrist, the one with the double chin, that I am angry with everyone who I feel has rejected and misunderstood me, especially Lincolnshire Social Services. I also told him that I found it difficult to trust people. I think he listened to me (you can never be sure). He was writing a lot and stroking his many chins, which amused me. He didn't look up from his notes and avoided making eye contact with me. He has increased my sleeping tablets and anti-depressants. He says they will help calm me down. I hope so, because I feel so angry – like a volcano that could erupt.

14th September 1980

Nurse Alex was on duty this morning. I waited for an opportunity to catch her on her own but had to go to occupational therapy (OT). Later that afternoon she came over to me while I was sat on my bed staring out of the window. She placed her hand on my shoulder and asked me if I wanted to talk. I did want to talk and showed her the letter that I had written to Aunty Lindsay. I told Nurse Alex that it had been a difficult letter to write. As she read the letter, my mind drifted to the last few moments I had spent with Aunty Lindsay.

I would never forget our final embrace the morning I left the children's home. Aunty Lindsay had hugged me and whispered in my ear, and told me to have faith. She did her best in those final moments to reassure me that everything would be okay. I can't help wondering how she will react to my letter. Will she want anything more to do with me? My heart is breaking. I am facing an uncertain future and everything isn't okay! I want Aunty Lindsay! I need Aunty Lindsay! Why did they make me feel that my love for her was so wrong? I hate them! I hate them so much for causing me so much pain.

After reading the letter, Nurse Alex said that it read well and it must have taken courage to write it. I asked her what she would do if she received such a letter. She told me that she would reply. That gave me hope. I told Nurse Alex that if Aunty Lindsay rejected me now after receiving this letter, I would kill myself, and I meant it. I couldn't bear it if she rejected me. I loved her so much. My love for her had not lessened since I left the children's home – it had grown stronger.

How could I not love someone who had shown me such love and understanding when she came to work at the children's home? Like the song *Puppy Love* goes: 'No one knows how a young heart feels and why I love her so.' Alex hugged me then reminded me that occupational therapy would be starting in half an hour, and not to be late. As she walked away I felt comforted. She had hugged me and made me feel special, just like Aunty Lindsay had done. At 18 I needed to feel special, I needed to feel loved. Right now, I felt misunderstood and lonely. No one, not even my sister, understands my inner turmoil or depression, God, I am so depressed. Who wants to live like this? I feel like I am in a prison, not a hospital. A nurse has just told me that I am late for occupational therapy. I had better go otherwise I will be in trouble again.

15th September 1980

Nurse Alex is on duty. I am mad at her and I don't want to talk to her. I wanted to talk to her last night, but she was too busy. She had come across to me at the table and said she would speak to me before she went off duty. After waiting for an hour, I told her it would keep. I know I should have spoken to her earlier when I had the opportunity, but when I tried to, she was too busy. When she came back I had clammed up and refused to speak to her.

I should have gone to occupational therapy this morning but, instead, went to the hospital gym and managed to stay until 11 o'clock. I much prefer the gym to occupational therapy. Once they discovered I was at the gym they sent someone to get me. The head of OT wasn't happy with me and made her feelings known.

I am sat in the occupational therapy room writing while pretending to do some art. I am worried about the letter I have sent to Aunty Lindsay. I don't know how she will react when she reads it. I feel tense and anxious. There is so much I want to share with Nurse Alex but don't know how. My words become muddled every time I try to speak to her. It reminds me of the time that I couldn't speak to Aunty Lindsay back in the children's home. I had ignored her for so long that it became difficult for me to approach her and talk to her. She had been patient with me, only losing her temper occasionally.

I think I am trying to replace Aunty Lindsay with Nurse Alex, pushing the boundaries with her like I did with Aunty Lindsay, to see if she will give up on me. Aunty Lindsay never did. That is why I love her so much. No matter how much I pushed her away she still tried to understand me. I wish I could have said the same for social services. Where was my bloody social worker when I needed him?

Since coming to live with my sister in Chester two years ago I have become more and more withdrawn, depressed and suicidal. My sister feels guilty at having me committed to this hospital, sectioned on a mental health ward. She said that, after cutting my wrists, she didn't know what else to do to help me. So now I am stuck in this bloody mental hospital.

It's so bad here – I am surrounded by crazy people. I hope Aunty Lindsay will feel sorry for me when she reads my letter. I remember how kind and loving she had been after I had tried to cut my wrists in the children's home. I can still remember her kneeling down beside me in the quiet room, stroking my hair and making me promise that I wouldn't do anything silly like that again. I have broken that promise and I am still as depressed as I was back then.

I hate myself, and I hate my life. I have so much unresolved anger within me – hatred towards the people who caused me so much pain. I wish I could relive my time with Aunty Lindsay. Maybe if I had another chance I wouldn't be so difficult or challenging, I don't know. I am so confused, so bewildered and so frightened. I am only 18. My sister says I have all my life before me, but I cannot see beyond my pain or this prison they call a hospital.

So many people have let me down and betrayed me that I find it difficult to trust anyone. I have lost count of just how many times someone has said to me: 'Trust me'. After a while you stop trusting, you stop believing, you stop hoping. I trusted those foster parents who abused me. I cannot talk about it – it is too painful. I blame myself. I will never share my feelings of disgust with anyone.

I have just taken a piece of broken glass to my wrists, and have tried to cut them just above the other wounds that are healing. Who cares whether I live or die? I don't. Selfish, I know, but I don't bloody care. The wounds are superficial; I don't have the courage to cut deeper. Last time I cut my wrists I couldn't feel the pain because I was so drunk.

I asked Miriam, who was the head of occupational therapy, if I could change rooms. The workshop with all the machinery is too noisy. I can't stand it. The cow got angry with me and told me to stop being melodramatic and said I could not change rooms. She said that I am wasting the hospital's time, and treating this place like a holiday camp. She told me to pull my socks up and snap out of my depression, warning me that if I didn't stick to the programme, then there was no point in my being in the hospital.

How could anyone treat such a horrible place like this like a bloody holiday camp? There are crazy people here roaming around the corridors screaming and yelling. Some have been here years. They look like zombies and are scary. I shouted back at her, telling her that I was not treating the hospital like a bloody holiday camp. She ignored me and forcibly sat me down at the table to play scrabble with the other loonies. I told her that I couldn't spell, but the ugly cow made me play the stupid game!

16th September 1980

I slept badly last night. I couldn't get Aunty Lindsay out of my mind. I kept thinking about her, remembering how I felt when she first came to the children's home, recalling how special she made me feel and how gorgeous she was, the love-hate feelings I had towards her, before she broke down my barriers and reached into my heart. It had felt good to be in love. Although most people simply said it was a teenage crush, I didn't. Then it all went horribly wrong and I had to leave the children's home, the only real home I had known. I can't let go of her now. I love her so much. They call it puppy love but it is real enough to me.

I suppose I had better go and queue for my tablets before breakfast. I should refuse to take them because they make me feel so drowsy and not with it, but I have seen what they do to others who refuse to take their tablets. They hold them down and inject them, so I had better not refuse to take mine. I hate needles.

A tragic accident has occurred. Anna, a confused elderly woman on my ward, has died. She fell or jumped into Chester Canal. Some of us feel guilty about her death, because we knew she was planning on leaving the hospital, to make her own way home. I tried for twenty minutes to talk her out of it, but in the end I left her on her own. I feel guilty now, as I should have told a nurse. Sandy (she is the same age as me and not bad-looking) saw Anna leave the hospital and did nothing, so she feels upset.

I think Sandy likes to feel like that. She is one for the dramatics and likes to have everyone, including myself, fussing over her. The truth is, no one could have stopped Anna, as she was a large woman, confused and determined. It took several nurses to bring her back the last time she got out. Since Anna's death, we have to have a nurse escort if we want to go to the shop opposite the hospital. I even had a nurse go with me this afternoon, which annoyed me. I wanted to buy Nurse Alex some chocolates. I didn't get them. I didn't want anyone asking me who they were for.

I think Aunty Lindsay should have received my letter by now. I am still worried about what I wrote. I hope she doesn't think that I am mad. I hope she remembers the mixed-up kid she tried to help and is sympathetic. I know that I pushed her too far at times and pushed her away, but she had stuck with me. She loved me even when others thought I was a waste of time. I know I was just one of many children in the home, but she went the extra mile with me. She understood me when no one else did. I love her so much it hurts. It wasn't my fault I fell in love, it just happened. I didn't know how to handle my emotions at 16 – I still don't. Help me, please someone help me. Don't leave me to rot in this place

The psychiatrist keeps increasing my medication. I feel like a zombie most days, out of touch with reality. I create my own reality – a fantasy world – with Aunty Lindsay. I am so drugged up I don't know what is real or what is part of my imagination. I have not said anything to anyone, but I think I hear voices in my head telling me to end it. I am not going to tell the shrink that. Everyone in here hears voices; he will just think I am as crazy as they are. I must stop writing now – lights are out in ten minutes.

Dear God, if you're real, I pray that Aunty Lindsay will answer my letter. Amen.

I feel sleepy now the medication is having an effect. I cannot stop crying. Tears flow so easily in this place. I can hear people screaming.

I am in hell.

17th September 1980

I saw the shrink this morning. I told him how depressed I was. He just kept making a humming sound while writing away in his little book. I told him that I was anxious all the time. I tried to tell him about the letter I had written to Aunty Lindsay, but he didn't seem that interested. I sensed that he felt that it wasn't important. It was to me! My whole life is dependent on whether Aunty Lindsay rejects me. I will kill myself if she does.

The doc, as usual, made little eye contact with me. He just scribbled away with his stupid pen, making notes. He didn't ask me why I was so depressed. He didn't ask me why I felt suicidal. He just asked about my mother and if I had sexual fantasies about her? Sexual fantasies about my mother disgusted me!

Then he asked me if my dad had touched me anywhere? I told him, 'No.' I didn't tell him that an older boy had abused me in the children's home, or that one of my foster parents had abused me. I tried again to tell him about Aunty Lindsay, but he still didn't seem interested. He was too fixated on my mother's breasts. I don't like this doctor. The day I came to this ward he had made me strip naked in his office in front of Nurse Alex.

The shrink has noted my depression and mood swings without asking me why I feel depressed. He has warned me, though, that they might consider using the electric treatment on me if my depression and mood doesn't improve. That scared me. I have seen patients that have had that done to them. They look like zombies afterwards. He has told the nurse to increase my medication. He says the tablets should help me feel calmer and less depressed.

I went to occupational therapy, not because I wanted to, but because if I didn't, I would be in trouble with Miriam. She is a hard, stony-faced woman. I don't like her. She is always doing her dragon imitation, huffing and puffing and blasting flames all over anyone who crosses her, especially George and me.

18th September 1980

I have had an 'emotional breakdown.' That's what the shrink told my sister. He said that I will remain in hospital, sectioned under the Mental Health Act until they think I am no longer a danger to myself. My sister told him I threatened her with a knife before collapsing on her kitchen floor and having a fit, back in June. She also told him that I was drinking excessively before I tried to cut my wrists. They don't think I am an alcoholic, she told me, but my excessive drinking, my attachment to Aunty Lindsay, and that I still feel suicidal, does concern them. She also told me during her visit that they had mentioned the possibility of using the electric treatment on me. I begged her not to allow them to fry my brain and got upset about it.

I finally got out of the hospital grounds, unnoticed, to go to the shops without an escort and bought Nurse Alex some chocolates. When I gave her them she thanked me and said that it was thoughtful of me, but I shouldn't have bought them. I went to the occupational therapy room. I picked up some sandpaper and started to sand the wooden horse George had been working on. I was aware that an occupational nurse was watching me. It wasn't long before she came and stood by my workbench. She told me that I needed to go back to the ward immediately.

As I was walking back to the ward with my nurse escort, I kept thinking about Sandy. I hoped that she hadn't done anything silly. I need not have panicked; the shrink wanted to see Sandy and me with the ward sister. I knew then we were in trouble and I was right. Someone had heard us talking about suicide last night and reported us. In front of the shrink the ward sister gave us a stern talking to. He threatened us with electric treatment if we did anything silly. Sandy walked out of the office, slamming the door so hard the window shook. I just looked straight at sister and smiled. She was clearly angry and gave me one of her disapproving looks. She is not bad-looking, but I wouldn't want to get on the wrong side of her. She is just as fierce as Miriam if you push her too far.

I found Sandy mooching in the day room; she was looking 'down in the dumps.' I suggested a trip to the canteen just to get off the ward. At least we don't need an escort with the canteen being in the hospital grounds. I wish we hadn't gone – it was so depressing. The mentally ill hang out in the canteen. We sat watching them for ages. They staggered from one vacant chair to another, where they sat all hunched up, while others like them wandered the long dark corridors. Old and dishevelled, they looked like the walking dead. They reminded me of those pictures in the history books of the Jews in the concentration camps. You would think the hospital would dress them in decent clothes. I think their families have just forgotten them, out of sight out of mind. Bloody hell, it is so flipping depressing here. Sandy and I shouldn't be in a place like this! I've just been reminded that I have my weekly session with the doc. I had better go.

My session with the shrink was a waste of time. He does nothing to relieve my anxiety or depression. He has given me even more tablets – I can barely focus or think straight, I am on so many tablets. Sometimes I just feel like I am not here, that I am somewhere else in a dream. I hear voices in my head. My mind is playing tricks on me. They are voices from my past, haunting me.

The pervert of a doctor asked me more questions about sexual abuse. He wanted detail, but I didn't want to talk about it; it was too shameful. I became so agitated that I grabbed hold of his notebook and flung it off his desk. The nurse on duty in his office looked embarrassed and tried to calm me down, while he looked alarmed. He was about to press the alarm button for help, but the nurse stepped in and calmed me down and comforted me. The shrink told her to take me back to the ward and increase my medication at bedtime.

The nurse was lovely, but I wish it had been Nurse Alex comforting me. She is older than the other nurses, but still attractive, with her blonde hair. She looks sexy in her uniform.

The ward sister has just given me a telling off for my outburst in the shrink's office and said that I was lucky they had not sedated me and put me into the padded room. I hate that bloody head doctor!

I spent the evening talking to Nurse Alex, sat at the table in the dining area of the ward. She held my hand. It felt so good. I could not help but feel aroused. Alex stroked my forehead and moved my hair out of my eyes. She gave me a warm smile. I asked her if I could visit her once I left the hospital. She looked concerned but then said she would think about it. She didn't want me forming a dependency on her. I felt knocked back and sulked. She lifted my chin and told me firmly to snap out of it. Aunty Lindsay had done the same on many occasions. It made me feel secure and loved. She squeezed my chin and told me to be good or else! I smiled as she walked away and went into the staff room. I didn't see her for the rest of the evening. I think she went off duty. I just sat in the corner of the ward for the rest of the evening, rocking backwards and forwards, before we had to queue for our happy pills.

19th September 1980

It is eight o'clock, time to queue up for our morning pills before breakfast. There is the usual pushing, shoving, yelling, screaming, with patients refusing medication. This happens every bloody time we have to queue for our pills, day and night. If they don't take the pills they have to have a needle where it hurts – twits!

It's Friday again and we have the usual discussion groups on the ward. Lee, as usual, is drawing attention to herself. She must be about 40 but acts like an old woman. I asked her if she liked ABBA and she thought it was something to eat. Idiot! Some of her property is missing and she thinks someone has stolen it. She has said if it's not returned by two o'clock she will call the police. She was waving her arms all over the place accusing everyone including me, daft bat. No one has stolen anything! She is barmy!

After group discussion, we played musical chairs and pass the parcel. I felt so embarrassed. Sandy refused to take part and sat in the corner watching. Lee's new deadline is now eight o'clock this evening before she calls the police. She is still flipping nuts! Someone has told me that Nurse Alex might be leaving and moving to Scotland. The thought of losing someone else who has shown me love makes me feel so depressed. This always happens to me!

Flipping OT this afternoon – we had to play more stupid games just like we did this morning, passing a stupid balloon between our legs to each other then back, using our chins. I didn't want to take part. I felt silly and pulled a face when they told me what we were going to be doing today. I didn't have much choice. I had to do it as part of my treatment; so did Sandy this time. Some idiot kept bursting the balloon, which frightened one of the other patients. He kept screaming every time the balloon went near him. Lee kept being rude, George couldn't stop laughing, and Sandy walked off. The rest just wandered around, not sure what to do. The student nurse enjoyed it. I just enjoyed watching her passing that balloon between her legs. She looked very sexy.

I think I am in trouble with Nurse Alex. She is not happy with me. She had been escorting me back to the ward. I sat down under the big oak tree and I refused to go any further until she told me why. She tried to pull me to my feet, but her nurse's cloak kept getting tangled up around my arms. She told me to stop acting like a child and get up. When I still refused, she became so mad that I thought she was going to slap me. There are many similarities between how I behave with Nurse Alex and how I behaved with Aunty Lindsay in the children's home. I wanted Nurse Alex to discipline me just as I had wanted Aunty Lindsay to.

Alex confronted me in the day room this evening about my behaviour this afternoon. I told her that I had felt like a child when she had yelled at me. Her reply was that I had been acting like a child, although Nurse Alex did say that, because I was ill, she was trying to be sympathetic towards me. However, she said she would not tolerate such childish behaviour again. Even as she said it, I looked at her and fantasy and reality became distorted. Was she Nurse Alex or Aunty Lindsay?

After Nurse Alex had gone off duty the ward sister called me into her office and told me off. She said she would not tolerate me treating a nurse on her ward with such contempt. I am sat in the chair sulking, angry with Alex for reporting me. Looking around the ward, the bars on the window, the shabby appearance, patients wandering around, confused and looking into space, I am reminded that this place is hell.

20th September 1980

Jack had a row with George. Jack prodded George in the stomach with his finger and shouted at him. I asked him why he was getting at George. He told me to shut up and called me 'stupid.' Then he turned his back on me and shoved George. I knew I shouldn't have interfered, but the sight of poor old George being treated like that, and Jack ignoring me, made me mad. I told him that a kiddie fiddler shouldn't be on this ward but in prison. He didn't like that. He shoved me, and so I kicked him. Once I started I couldn't stop. I was so angry that I jumped on Jack's back and held on, with my arms around his neck. The whole ward erupted. He swung me around and I fell to the floor. It was mad – arms and feet flying in all directions.

Alarm bells were ringing. It was crazy! Nurses were running from all directions, ordering us back to our beds while they tried to separate Jack and George. I managed to stop fighting before the nurses arrived, otherwise I would have been in trouble again. Jack and George were put in padded rooms.

Jack is not talking to me. He blames me for the fight. I don't care – it doesn't bother me. I hate him. I have been abused and I feel sick at the thought of sharing a dormitory with him.

I have been thinking about Aunty Lindsay today, remembering when she first came to the children's home. She was young, attractive and sexy. No wonder I was smitten with her from the first day. It saddens me to think I gave her such a hard time, after she had slapped me for a silly prank of pretending to crack an egg on her head. I didn't mean to hurt her but I did. After she slapped me around the face I didn't speak to her, unless I had to, for seven weeks. She did her best to penetrate my wall of silence, firm but kind. I was just stubborn. Perhaps I needed another slap and who would have blamed her?

The superintendents told me that my behaviour towards Aunty Lindsay was unacceptable. Little did they know that I was in love with her! In the end, she succeeded in breaking through my wall of silence. I liked how she helped me with my homework, laughed at my jokes and, when I sulked, lifted my chin, forcing me to look into her eyes. In her naivety, she didn't know that I was in love with her and everything she did, even when she told me off, just reinforced how I felt.

I wish she would write back to me and let me know that she hasn't rejected me. I go to the nurse's office every day to see if there is a letter. Perhaps Nurse Alex is right. Aunty Lindsay will need time to respond. Enough writing, I have to go. It's visiting time and my sister, Shene, has arrived with my brother-in-law, Graham.

Sandy flipped this evening after her mum and dad had left, and went into a rage. They gave her an injection and put her to bed. I asked my sister to write to Aunty Lindsay, but she said, 'No.' She said the same as Alex – to give Aunty Lindsay more time to write back.

21st September 1980

I am so depressed today. A black mood has come over me. I still haven't heard from Aunty Lindsay. I am convinced that if I go on like this much longer I will lose the will to live. Why doesn't she write? Should I write again? I need to talk to Nurse Alex about this.

I am worried about Sandy. She has been more depressed than usual since her parents visited. I am wary of trying to talk to her in case she flips like she did yesterday. I know how she feels. Most of the time I just want to be on my own too, but I find people just don't take the hint. Nurse Alex is off duty today. I miss her not being around. I like talking to her. She listens, just like Aunty Lindsay used to. The pain I feel is so intense that I would do anything to make it stop. Every time I think about Aunty Lindsay I am hurting.

Since I left the children's home two years ago I have found it difficult to move on with my life. I don't know how to. My favourite pop group, ABBA, sings: 'I have a dream to help me cope with reality'. I have many dreams – my reality is too horrific, too painful. I can't go on feeling like this. I flow between reality and fantasy. Some days I can't tell the difference and that is worrying.

I wish Nurse Alex was on duty. She understands me better than some of the other nurses. I think that's because on the day I arrived in the hospital she comforted me, reassured me, then stayed with me until I felt settled on the ward. She reminds me so much of Aunty Lindsay. At times, I play the same games with her as I did with Aunty Lindsay, pushing her to see how she will react. I know I am doing it, but I cannot help myself. I get a thrill out of seeing if she will discipline me. It makes me feel secure. I think I must be weird!

22nd September 1980

My sister brought me an old typewriter. I am going to use it to type my diary. Perhaps one day I can put it into a book to help others. Bad start – the damn typewriter is not working – the ribbon has gone.

Sandy is still quiet. I don't know what to do to help. I am struggling with my own pain. She can be difficult with her tantrums. Sometimes they have to give her an injection in her bottom, like the other night. It's the only way they can calm her. Jack continues to snub me. I swear I will swing for him. I am feeling hostile towards him because of my own abuse.

I have to go to relaxation classes. I am told they will help me. I was watching all those old dears trying to relax last week. The occupational health nurse couldn't get them to stay still long enough to relax. As soon as the music started, they got off the bed and started dancing – so funny. It's 3.15pm and relaxation classes still haven't started. I have sat here outside the flipping ward where they take place for ages. If they don't start soon I am off, and I don't care what the ward sister says.

I got sick of waiting so I went back to my ward, got my gym gear and went to the hospital gym. Gordon, the gymnast, suggested that I work with Doug, a new guy who was attending the hospital as a day patient. Doug is a big guy and reminds me of that Indian guy in *One Flew Over the Cuckoo's Nest*. He seems like a good bloke, rough maybe, but a good old boy nonetheless. From what he has told me he might have to go to prison for thumping someone. Gordon's an ex-army sergeant major. He can handle Doug, but OT can't. I suppose I could ask Doug to duff Miriam up if she keeps getting at me! On second thoughts, best not, as Doug would go to prison if he did.

Earlier today I went to the dormitory, closed the door behind me and confronted Jack. He ignored me. I walked towards him as he tried to leave. I tried to stop him and he punched me in the face. I said to him, 'So help me God, if I had a knife I would knife you now!' He stood laughing and told me to do it if I dared. I pulled out my pen and held it to his stomach and pushed. My second mistake – he punched me again, then he opened the dormitory door and went back onto the ward.

After I got over the shock, I went and told George what had happened. He told me to report it, but I wouldn't. Another patient butted in and said that I had provoked Jack. I told him to shut his bloody mouth, otherwise I would get a knife from the kitchen and stab him for real. That shut him up. Nutter!

I am feeling suicidal, all this aggro between Jack and me, and no letter from Aunty Lindsay. I keep planning in my mind how I will commit suicide. I favour jumping in front of a train. It will be quick and painless. I think about killing myself all the time. I feel so depressed, I just want to go to sleep and never wake up.

At least when I dream, I am back in the children's home with Aunty Lindsay, feeling secure and loved. I hate my life! I have been so depressed since leaving care. My sister has tried to make a home for me, I feel guilty I have not settled. I miss my brother too. It's the first time we have been apart. I wish I was still with him in the children's home. At least Aunty Lindsay's not there any more. She is teaching at a girls' boarding school in Scotland. I miss her so much.

I meet with the shrink every week. The sessions don't last more than ten minutes. He keeps going on about me having the electric treatment, while reminding me just how important it is to keep going to occupational therapy. I don't know why he keeps increasing my medication though. I am drugged up enough!

23rd September 1980

I am more depressed than usual, if that was possible! I feel so drugged up my head spins and everything appears hazy. It's a drunken feeling. I am hurting, but at least it confirms that I am still alive. Sometimes I stagger around the ward dragging my feet.

Still no letter from Aunty Lindsay. Why doesn't she write? Does she hate me? Does she care?

I've seen Nurse Alex around this morning. I have ignored her. I don't want to speak to her. Why should I, after the way she spoke to me earlier today? She was angry with me and said I was selfish and childish, and I should stop wallowing in self-pity. I heard what she said but, to be honest, I could barely focus, my head hurt so much. Alex told me that she would no longer tolerate my stubborn behaviour, even if I was ill. All I had done was to refuse to sit down at breakfast when she had told me to. I ignored her and walked away. She grabbed my arm and told me to sit down and eat my breakfast. I told her that she couldn't make me. That made her mad. She forced me to sit down and yelled at me, then walked away.

I had similar battles with Aunty Lindsay at the children's home, with her yelling at me. I will only talk to Nurse Alex if she approaches me first. I need to talk to her, but cannot bring myself to make the first move. I see so much of Aunty Lindsay in Nurse Alex. She makes me feel good, even when she is firm.

George and I sneaked out of the hospital and went to the local shops without an escort. We bought Sandy some flowers and chocolates to make her feel better. When we gave them to her, she said that we did care and gave us both a kiss on the cheek. I have asked the ward sister twice today if any letters have arrived for me. She just said, 'No' and that I shouldn't keep asking. She knows that Aunty Lindsay's letter is important to me. She is just like everyone else; she treats me like a child. Nurse Alex said to me that if I act like a child they will treat me like a child. I don't care! I do what I want!

It's teatime and I have still not approached Nurse Alex. I have tried, but chickened out twice. She knows I am sulking. I think she wants me to say sorry for what happened at breakfast. I am not going to. Why should I? She hurt me when she grabbed my arm and forced me to sit at the table. A nurse has told me to put my notebook away. Better do as I am told – I don't want them thinking I am childish.

24th September 1980

A female nurse took me into town on a bus so I could go to the library. Why do they have to wear their bloody uniforms? It just draws attention to the fact I am a patient from the mental hospital. Some people on the bus were giving us funny looks. I pulled faces, stuck out my tongue, rolled my eyes, and acted like I was a mental case. She slapped my thigh, said I was embarrassing her, and told me to stop it!

I am fed up, depressed, and anxious. I am kept on drugs to keep me calm. Without them I would be more aggressive. My sister is refusing to let them try electric treatment on me. I am relieved! The thought of them frying my brain scares the hell out of me. The psychiatrist has told my sister that I am not responding to treatment, so they are going to increase my medication.

Aunty Lindsay is on my mind. Everywhere I look I see her face. Two years ago, social services sent me away from the only real home I have known, all because I fell in love with a house parent. I just wanted to feel loved and to love in return. Was that so wrong?

If only I hadn't tried to cut my wrists or gone on hunger strike, maybe social services would have let me stay for longer. I don't know. No one cares what happens to you after you leave care. I hate social services. Bastards! At 18 I have no life, I have no future, and I have no hope. The stigma of being in a mental hospital will follow me around forever. I used to joke about this place at work. Now I am a patient and the joke is no longer funny.

I was in the day room playing records when a nurse came in and told me to turn down the sound. I ignored her and turned the player up even louder. Five minutes later, she came back and turned the record player down herself. She looked me straight in the eye and told me that I was being childish. I whispered, 'Get lost.' I could tell by the way she looked at me that I might have gone too far.

Nurse Alex is right: I am my own worst enemy. What gives her the right to talk to me like that? She has one red band on her hat, so she is only a first-year student, but acts like she owns the place. She stood with her hands on her hips looking cross. If looks could kill! I brushed past her and went to get some supper. I saw her again just before she went off duty. She was standing in the doorway of the staff room with another nurse, pointing at me as they put their capes on. I knew they were talking about me. I hope she doesn't report me to sister.

It was difficult sleeping tonight. Every time I closed my eyes I kept having flashbacks of getting drunk and cutting my wrists. I couldn't get the images out my mind. A nurse came and sat on my bed and asked if I was alright. She said I had been shouting out in my sleep. She asked if I wanted a drink before she left.

25th September 1980

It's been a horrible day. My head is spinning, my heart is breaking, and I am afraid. I am in despair. I don't know where to turn. The voices in my head urging me to harm myself have driven me to do something that has left me distressed. I have just come back from the railway line. I must write down what happened. I am shaking. I can barely hold the pen.

Without telling anyone, I left the ward and headed towards the main road. I got as far as the birdcages when I heard a nurse shouting at me to come back. I ignored her and started running towards the hospital entrance. Once outside, I ran along the main road and carried on walking towards the railway embankment. I kept shouting out how I hated all those people who had caused me pain and who had made my life such a misery. I am shaking. Tears are rolling down my cheeks, causing the ink to run. I must write down what happened, though. I need to remember.

As I approached the railway embankment I prayed to God, not even sure if He was real. I wanted answers as to why I hurt so much. I stood on the railway track watching a train approaching in the distance. It would all be over in seconds. 'Just don't lose your nerve,' I told myself. I could barely see, my eyes were so wet, stinging from the tears. As the train approached, my legs started to shake. I heard its whistle. I didn't move. I closed my eyes, gritted my teeth and hoped it would be quick. At the last minute, I changed my mind and threw myself onto the embankment.

The train whistled past. I thumped the grass with uncontrolled rage, my head buried in the grass. I yelled, 'Aunty Lindsay, don't abandon me now. I need you so much!' I lay motionless for what seemed like ages. I got up shaking. I had nearly killed myself. I returned to the safety of the hospital. Writing my actions and thoughts down horrifies me. God! If I hadn't changed my mind at the last minute! Hell, I scare myself sometimes. What do I do now? Enough writing, it's depressing. I think I will go to the day room and play some records.

I have just come back from the day room. I have been listening to records, songs about love, with tears streaming down my face. I had been looking out of the window at the gardens. They looked so well kept compared to the shabby buildings. I am trying to take my mind off the train incident. If only I had seen a psychiatrist straight away instead going on a bloody waiting list, I might not have cut my wrists.

My sister kept ringing the doctors to find out where I was on the list. All she kept getting was excuses. Social services didn't want to know either. They brought me here from the city hospital, dressed only in my pyjamas, at the beginning of August. When I saw the bars on the windows, they literally had to drag me from the ambulance. It looked more like a prison than a hospital. The garden tried to give an image of normality but nothing is normal. What is normal? I am too sedated to care. Someone turned the record player off and interrupted my thoughts.

A young girl I had not seen before stood over the record player. I started to walk over to her. I wasn't happy that she had turned the player off and I intended to tell her so. Nurse Alex, who had come in with the girl, grabbed hold of my arm and pulled me to one side. She told me that I mustn't take any notice of this new patient because she was vulnerable and depressed. I got emotional and angry, and shouted at Alex. I told her that I had damned near killed myself by throwing myself under a train. Alex looked alarmed. She pulled me into another room, closed the door and asked me what had happened. I started crying. She pulled me towards her and held my head on her chest. Sobbing away I told her what had happened. Nurse Alex was sympathetic but firm and said it was her duty to report this incident to sister. Forcing my head into her bosom, she held me tight and said, 'We will see it through together.'

She made me feel special. Tears were streaming down my cheeks. She lifted my head, forcing me to look at her. I took that moment to say sorry for my recent behaviour and to confess that I had become dependent on her. She told me not to worry and then gave me a big hug before she got up to go. I asked her when she would be on duty again. 'Saturday,' she said and told me to hang on until then and not to do anything silly. I sensed a threat in her voice that made my stomach flutter with butterflies.

26th September 1980

I didn't sleep too well last night – despite the medication I couldn't get to sleep. Every time I closed my eyes all I could see was that bloody train coming towards me. After breakfast, I just wanted to lie on my bed, but the ward sister told me to get off the bed. She is always saying it's not part of my treatment to lie on the bed. Stupid bloody rule if you asked me. Sometimes, I am too depressed to fight the rules. It's easier to do as you're told. It's a lot less hassle that way. Besides, any resistance to treatment usually results in an injection and being placed in a padded room.

Most of the nurses are sympathetic to us. You get the odd one, like Miriam, in occupational therapy, but then she is not a proper nurse. She thinks she is but she isn't. The night staff are what they call 'auxiliary nurses.' They don't have the same training as the day nurses. I find the women auxiliaries a lot more sympathetic than the men. I don't like that big fat Irish man, the one that clocks on at eight o'clock then clears off in his taxi at half past eight, picking up fares half the night. The other nurses only cover for him because they're scared of the big ugly brute. He doesn't treat Sandy or me with sympathy either. I think he gets a thrill out of holding her down and baring her bottom to inject her. Pervert!

My head hurts and my stomach churns. My inner demons torment me and the voices continue. I can't shut them out my mind. Such hatred and self-loathing floods my thoughts. I am wicked and dirty and don't deserve to live. I should tell someone about the abuse but I feel too ashamed, too unclean, so I continue simply to focus on Aunty Lindsay and my love for her.

Whenever I play one of ABBA's records, I remember Aunty Lindsay taking us to see *ABBA the Movie*. I couldn't take my eyes off her in the cinema. Every song just made me feel so emotional. She got so cross with me when I caused a scene. She didn't know that I was upset because I had fallen in love with her. She just thought I was difficult and rebellious. That was the afternoon I ran away and she came looking for me. I remember she found me in the park, sitting on the swings. It was snowing at the time. She had wrestled me to the ground when I ran away from her. I know I hurt her when I kicked out and caught her shoulder with my foot. Boy, did she let me have it, slapping me across the back and calling me a silly boy. Even as she was lashing out at me, she looked so beautiful in her woollen hat, with the snow falling around her. I couldn't have loved her any more than I did at that moment. I am depressed just thinking about it; I miss her so much!

I just wanted to escape from it all today. I wasn't in the mood for mixing with others, so I ignored them. The new girl, whose name I still don't know, is quiet and sedated at the moment. It doesn't take long for patients to become like zombies in this place. The medication takes the fight out of you. Some of us try to avoid taking our tablets, but we have to open our mouths to prove we have swallowed.

The new girl's name is Carol. She came up to me and asked me if I wanted a 'jump.' I didn't know until later she was asking me if I wanted sex. George said 'jump' is slang for sex. She must be desperate, asking me. I have never had a girlfriend, never mind sex.

I went to the hospital telephone box to phone my sister. Sandy turned up and started talking to me. She hid behind the telephone box when she saw a nurse coming towards us. The nurse asked if I had seen her. I said I hadn't. After the nurse left, we went for a walk. Sandy confided in me about being raped. I think she is beginning to trust me, which makes me feel good, because she doesn't trust men.

27th September 1980

I had to wash the dishes with Sandy today. I tried to comfort her, but she shrugged me off and ignored me. Her moods change like mine – both of us are subject to extreme mood swings. If it wasn't for the medication I am on, I think I would be far more aggressive.

My sister visited me today. Still no letter from Aunty Lindsay, and I told her that I will kill myself if I don't hear from her soon. My sister became upset and started crying. She told me not to do anything silly and reminded me that people do care – she cares. Deep down I know my sister cares, I just don't care enough about myself. I hate myself. I hate my life. I feel so alone and isolated, locked within this world of torment, darkness and self-imposed exile.

I keep having flashbacks to my time in the children's home. Some days I feel that I am still there. I want to be there, to relive those moments in the children's home with Aunty Lindsay and the other children. I remember her coming to the home and how I flirted with her on Bonfire Night, pinching her hat and throwing it to the other kids, while she tried to get it back. And then I remember how such a great evening went so wrong when she slapped me around the face. I close my eyes and I am back there in the children's home, just wanting to say sorry to Aunty Lindsay for the problems I caused her. I wish I was back in the children's home rather than in this hell hole.

After dinner, I managed to escape the bed police and fell asleep on my bed. I was woken by George, who shouted at me through the open window. He reminded me that occupational therapy would be starting in five minutes and that I had better hurry, otherwise Miriam will be on my case. I told him that I would be along soon. I closed my eyes and I lay there for a moment. I became aware that someone was standing over me. I half opened my eyes. 'Aunty Lindsay,' I said but it wasn't her. It was Nurse Alex. She sat down on my bed and asked me again why I had stood on the railway track. I just told her that I was depressed and suicidal. I didn't tell her that voices in my head were urging me to harm myself. She listened but then, unlike the shrink, she always listens. She held my hand as she sat on the bed. It felt good. I asked her if I could still see her, once I was discharged from hospital. She told me firmly that she wasn't going to allow me to become too dependent on her, and that I should start to learn to stand on my own two feet. I felt hurt and rebuffed at her response.

She held both my hands, looked me in the eyes and started lecturing me on the importance of getting well. I turned my head away from her gaze. I didn't want to hear what she was saying. The ward sister came into the ward and asked Nurse Alex if she had a minute. Alex told me to wait until she came back so she could continue her chat. I didn't – I left the ward. I didn't want to chat any more with Alex. It was too distressing for me. Suicidal thoughts ran through my mind. I will kill myself rather than face a life without love. That's how I feel.

Sandy found me wandering the corridors and asked me to come and see some kittens she had discovered at the back of the gym. We had to climb a fence into the boiler room, but we managed and, just like Sandy had said, there were four kittens in a box. She picked up one of them. Its mother went for her and she dropped it. The mother picked it up in her mouth and jumped over the fence. Sandy and I climbed back over the fence and chased after the mother cat. Having cornered the damned cat, I took my coat off and tried to throw it over her. She dropped the kitten and ran off across the garden. Sandy and I laughed. The cat provided a little light relief from being in a mental hospital. I had skipped occupational therapy. I knew I would be in trouble.

Later that evening the ward sister called me to her office and told me off for not going to OT. She said that she saw little point in my being here, if I wasn't willing to stick to the programme. I felt like a naughty child. The sister dismissed me and I went back to the dormitory and lay on my bed. I couldn't help but think about the chat Nurse Alex had had with me today, about standing on my own two feet. How do I do that? I wish that I had a proper mum and dad to help me in life. It's scary being 18. Why had Nurse Alex said those things to me? I think maybe sister has told her not to get too involved with me. It might be my imagination, but I think Alex has been keeping her distance.

That big Irish nurse has been tormenting me again. He made fun of me and accused me of wasting the hospital's time. I wanted to hit him, but he is bigger than me and Irish, with a temper to match. He handed me my pills and made sure I swallowed them. He made a remark about them keeping me quiet. I retreated to my bedroom.

That dark cloud descended on me as the tablets took effect. I felt like I was floating. I couldn't keep my eyes open and drifted off to sleep.

I woke in the early hours of the morning and went to the toilet. None of the nurses heard me as I walked through the day ward. They were asleep in their chairs. The Irish nurse wasn't among them. He had gone driving his taxi for the night.

28th September 1980

I couldn't move this morning. I couldn't feel my body. I think it was the drugs – they mess with your mind and your body. Once I did get out of bed, I stumbled and fell on the floor. A nurse helped me back to my feet and asked if I was alright. I said that I was fine, but I wasn't. I felt so dizzy. I feel detached from my body. I am writing, I see the words, but they appear so far away from me, like looking down the wrong end of a telescope.

I fainted after breakfast, so they sat me down and made sure I ate more than one piece of toast. I have the morning off occupational therapy to rest and to see the shrink. Despite feeling ashamed I did try, this time, to tell the doctor about the abuse I had suffered as a child. He wrote it all down in his notebook but, as usual, there was little eye contact with me. I asked him to reduce my tablets because they make me feel detached and not with it. He refused and said that I needed them for my own good. Nurse Alex stood with the doc as he examined me. She gave me a reassuring glance. I ignored her. I was still mad at her for knocking me back.

The doctor asked me how I felt about Aunty Lindsay. I told him again that I was in love with her and couldn't let her go. He muttered something then scribbled something in his notes. He wanted to know if I were still having suicidal thoughts. I said, 'Yes.' In that case, he said he would consider electric treatment. I told him that my sister wouldn't agree to that. He said that he didn't need her permission if he felt that it was in my best interests. Nurse Alex walked me back to the ward and tried to reassure me that electric treatment was safe and would help cure depression. I am worried, having seen other patients have that treatment. I don't want my brain fried. I had better get to occupational therapy. I don't want to go, but I have no choice.

I have just come out of occupational therapy; a nurse escorted me back. They are not happy with me. I have caused a scene. I walked over to the sawmill and stood for what seemed like ages, watching the blade running at speed. George seemed oblivious to me. The voices in my head told me to place my hand in front of the blade. I had started to move my hand towards the blade. I could feel it, I was that close! A nurse grabbed my shoulders and dragged me away. She shouted at me, wanting to know what the hell I was thinking, her face red with anger. George tried to defend me. She told him to go away and mind his own business. Now I am sat outside sister's office. Hell! I close my eyes and try to imagine that I am anywhere but here.

I have just come out of sister's office. She went mad with me, shouting and waving her arms around, like a chicken flapping its bloody wings. I didn't know what to say. I just sat in the chair opposite her desk and took it. I thought, as I sat there listening to her, that she wasn't that bad-looking. I think I like women in uniforms! Don't ask me why, I just do. Mind you, Aunty Lindsay never wore a uniform, only an apron over her jeans, dress or skirt, but not a uniform. I wonder what she would have looked like in a uniform.

After the telling off from sister, I escaped from the ward without an escort. I went back to the railway. This time I lay down on the bridge and listened to the train coming. I could have rolled off onto the passing train, but instead I lay there with my eyes closed. I went back to the ward at six o'clock and had missed tea. They had been looking for me and were about to report me missing. Sister shouted at me again: 'That's twice in one day.' Bloody hell, I can't deal with this!! I am ill, depressed, suicidal and all they do is yell at me! Why won't they listen? What does it take? I didn't feel like tea after that.

I lay on my bed. To hell with the rules! I wanted to talk to Nurse Alex, but I didn't know how to approach her. I think she is avoiding me because I am becoming too dependent on her. I don't care. She is just like everyone else. She pretends to care, but she doesn't. She is only doing her job. I am just another patient.

Later this evening I decided to ask Nurse Alex if she was busy. She said that she wasn't sure. I told her it didn't matter, but I think she sensed I needed to talk, so she came and sat down next to me. I told her how I couldn't let go of the past and that I am afraid of the future. She spoke firmly. She said that I was living too much in the past and that I needed to move on with my life. I knew she was right, but I couldn't help it. I lived for Aunty Lindsay. I desperately wanted to go back and change the way I had treated her in the children's home. I had wasted so much time battling with her, that I had missed the opportunity of sharing my true feelings.

I would sell my soul to go back to November 1978. I knew Alex was right, but I had no answer for her. I asked her if I could hold her hand again. She said I could if it would help. I didn't know if it would help or not, but I held her hand anyway. Her hand felt so warm. When she squeezed mine I started crying, the tears rolling down my face. Alex lifted my chin and made me look her in the eyes. She told me that I must not transfer my feelings for Aunty Lindsay to her. I wished she had not made me look her in the eyes. She reminded me so much of Aunty Lindsay by her actions.

I am tired. It's late. I have written enough for today. Alex went off duty hours ago. I loved holding her hand. I didn't want to let go. In that brief moment I felt loved. The tablets make me drowsy. I will have to stop writing and lie on my bed. I hope tomorrow never comes, so I can remember forever how it felt holding Nurse Alex's hand.

29th September 1980

I like writing in this diary. It helps me express myself and share my feelings without anyone judging me. Everyone keeps asking what I am writing. I tell them, 'Everything that happens in this bloody hospital.'

'Everything?' they ask.

'As much as I can,' I say. That will keep them guessing, wondering if I am writing about them.

I will be 19 tomorrow. What a way to spend your birthday – in a mental hospital. The way I feel, I hope tomorrow never comes. I am more depressed now than I was when I first came into hospital. Those drugs are supposed to help me, but they don't. All they do is make me feel detached and spaced out most of the time.

Went back to occupational therapy today, but they wouldn't let me have any chisels to work on my wooden duck. How the hell am I supposed to sculpt a duck without chisels? Miriam is angry over what happened yesterday. I knew she would be, once she heard. She said I am not allowed near any of the sharp tools. Oh, well, that puts paid to this bloody duck – back to drawing trees.

'You're wallowing in self-pity. You're not putting your family first, and you don't care about their suffering. You're a selfish, self-centred, spoilt teenager.' That's what the ward sister said to me yesterday. I can still hear her voice echoing in my head. She kept telling me to look at her when she was talking to me. Talking, I thought, you're yelling not talking! She was making me feel sick. My head was spinning that much. I thought my 18th birthday was bad enough, but my 19th is going to be worse. I wish I could go to sleep and never wake up. My future is bleak. I cannot see past one day to another. It's my birthday tomorrow. The way I feel, I don't think I will be around to see it.

Nurse Alex is right, I am going to have to accept that Aunty Lindsay isn't going to love me in the same way I love her. I was just one of her charges, just another mixed-up kid she tried to help. Nurse Alex has tried to convince me that I have my whole life ahead of me – marriage, kids, etc. Don't make me laugh. Who will want to marry me? I am damaged and unlovable. I hate myself. I hate life. I don't want to live any more. I will show them. I will show them all. I am listening to *Puppy Love* by Donny Osmond. Those lyrics are so powerful. They express exactly how I feel and Donny sings it with such emotion. As I sing with him I close my eyes and just want to scream, 'SOMEONE HELP ME, HELP ME, PLEASE!'

30th September 1980

It's my 19th birthday today. It should be a day of celebration, but I don't feel much like celebrating. I had a few cards, some presents and a cake that Shene brought to the ward. The nurses sang 'Happy Birthday' to me at breakfast. Nurse Alex gave me a card and a small gift – a pen set – just what I need to write this diary.

Group sessions today – I hate these sessions. Everyone sits in a circle while the nurses try and encourage us to share how we are feeling. Sandy and I usually just sit quiet and withdrawn, not wanting to take part. I use this occasion to write in my diary. Writing helps me express how I am feeling. Right now I am feeling suicidal. I cannot see the point of going on living. Aunty Lindsay hasn't written back to me. I might not hear from her again and that is heartbreaking. What does the future hold? I am 19 today and I feel so low, so depressed. My sister did her best to make today special with the cards, gifts and cake. I just wasn't in the mood. I hate this bloody group session. Why do people use it to sound off at each other? The whole group sang 'Happy Birthday' out of tune, like a cats' choir. I hated it – bloody basket cases!

I have sneaked out of the hospital grounds without an escort. I have bought 100 aspirins. I am listening to ABBA. I have the aspirins in my pocket. I hide them until I decide when I am going to take them. I am going to the day room to play some records.

All I could think about as I listened to ABBA was Aunty Lindsay and my love for her. I kept remembering the few good times we had had back in the children's home, when I wasn't avoiding her or battling with her. I loved her so much! No one ever tried to understand me like she did. The other house parents and social services were not sympathetic, not even after I tried cutting my wrists. They said I was seeking attention. It was Aunty Lindsay who bullied me into eating after my hunger strike. She took the time to take me seriously.

If I close my eyes I can see her so clearly coming into the bedroom with a tray of food, sitting on my bed and telling me to eat. She was in no mood for my dramatics that day. Aunty Lindsay didn't know that I had fallen in love with her. I don't know what she would have done if she had known the depth of my feelings towards her. I might have scared her off. She was only 24.

Not long after trying to cut my wrists, they sent me away. I hate them all. I am stuck in this bloody mental hospital and social services don't give a damn. They never did. I blame them for the abuse I suffered. They should have protected my brother and me.

I am sat in the day room listening to my records. I am getting upset. I can't go on like this and I am hurting so much. Images from my past flash before me. I see Aunty Lindsay's face so clearly. If I close my eyes I can hear her voice, loving, kind, but firm. I can't see to write, I am crying too much, and ABBA isn't helping.

1st October 1980

It's 1st October. I am in the city hospital. I don't feel so good. I need to write down what happened yesterday. It's important that I record my thought and feelings.

Yesterday, I got myself into a state listening to ABBA. I walked into the kitchen. Someone had left the tap running, so I opened the aspirins I had bought and swallowed the lot, holding my head under the tap. I sank to the floor and held my knees to my chest. Sandy came into the kitchen. She knelt down beside me and asked me what was wrong. I ignored her and continued to hold my knees close to my chest, with my head buried in my arms. Sandy became annoyed with me and forced my head up to look at her. My face was wet with tears. I kept saying I was sorry. She asked me what I had done. I could see the alarm in her face. She looked at the floor and saw pills scattered around me. 'Oh God!' she shouted. 'What have you done?' She forced my hand open so she could see what I had taken. She yelled at me and called me a 'bloody fool.' She shouted for a nurse. Within seconds nurses were with me, asking what I had done. The ward sister came in and took charge. Helping me to my feet, she told two nurses to walk me around.

Sister then went back to her office and phoned for an ambulance. I felt faint, but two nurses held me up to prevent me falling. I accidentally knocked one of their hats off. An ambulance took me to the city hospital, where I had been taken after I cut my wrists. They put me in a wheelchair to take me to the ward. A doctor was asking me questions. I felt drowsy. I remember being in a room surrounded by medical equipment. 'Hold him down,' the doctor said to the two nurses. The doctor forced my mouth open and pushed a long tube down my throat. It felt like I was choking. I kept coughing and struggling, but the nurses were too strong. I felt the tube going down my throat. The doctor kept telling me to swallow and then warned me that if they didn't get the tube into me and wash out my stomach, I could die. I didn't care. I wanted to die. I must have passed out, because I don't remember what happened next. I woke up on this ward.

My sister Shene has been to see me this evening. She is upset at what I have done. She was tearful. I held her hand because I didn't know what else to do or say. She said that she had telephoned our mum and dad, but apart from calling me a 'silly bugger,' Dad hadn't said much. My sister said Mum was too busy talking about herself and her latest boyfriend, and wasn't interested in hearing about me in hospital.

I wish that I had proper parents. I envy those kids who grow up in loving stable homes. They don't know how lucky they are. If I had had loving parents I wouldn't have gone into foster care or a children's home. I wouldn't be in a mental hospital and my future wouldn't look so bloody hopeless. Poor Shene. I know that she's upset, but I can't help how I feel.

Shene also told me that Lincolnshire Social Services had written to her, to tell her that I am no longer their responsibility. I wasn't surprised. They washed their hands of me years ago when they sent me away from the children's home. Shene has been trying for two years to get support for me, but they have never responded to her letters or her phone calls. It's been a long day. Shene went hours ago. She told me not to do anything silly and to try and get well.

Some student nurses came to see me later this evening. They sat on my bed and chatted for a while, that is until the ward sister came along and gave them one of her looks. The doc said I'll be returning to the psychiatric hospital tomorrow morning. He has warned me the ward sister will want a chat with me.

2nd October 1980

I am now back at the West Cheshire Mental Asylum. How depressing this ward is compared to the ward at the city hospital. The ambulance came for me after breakfast, around nine o'clock. As I left, another ward sister had a go at me. She said that she had better not see me back here again. If she did, she would clip my ear! All these older women want to mother me. I would love any one of them to be my mother.

The ward sister had her little chat with me and it wasn't as bad as I thought it would be. I was worried that she would yell at me and give me another lecture. She was kind and sympathetic. She even smiled, which made her look even more gorgeous than usual. She reminded me that I was in hospital to get well and that she was here to support me. Her door, she said, was always open if I wanted a chat. That made me smile, because she scares me most of the time. I would be too nervous about knocking on sister's door. Every time I have been in her office recently she has been scolding me. I would rather talk to Nurse Alex than the ward sister. It made a change for sister to be sympathetic instead of yelling at me.

Well, I knew it was too good to last. While the ward sister was sympathetic to me, Nurse Alex, on the other hand, was cross with me and didn't hide her annoyance. She came to sit by me in the day room. I reached out my hand to hold her hand and she slapped it. She then asked me whether I had any idea just how much pain I had put my poor sister through, by taking an overdose. I must admit, I didn't know what to say. I had expected more sympathy. Instead she gave me the lecture I thought I would have had from the ward sister. Then she left me in the day room to think about what she had said. Sandy overheard much of what Nurse Alex had said to me, and said I had deserved the rollicking. That's rich coming from Sandy!

I had been on my own, sitting on the table in the dining room, when Nurse Alex came in and asked if anyone knew I was there. I ignored her. I still haven't forgiven her for slapping my hand the way she did. She was persistent and stood with her arms folded, tapping her foot until I gave her the courtesy of a reply. I told her that Ian, the male nurse, knew I was here. Then I said that I would like to talk to her. She became abrupt and told me that she couldn't devote her whole life to one patient. I felt hurt by her remarks. I wasn't demanding anything. My heart sank. I had pushed Nurse Alex too far.

My sister came to see me this evening. She was still upset over the overdose, but listened when I pleaded with her to write to Aunty Lindsay for me. She said she would. She stayed for a while and we chatted in the dining room. Well, I say 'we' – my dear sister did all the talking. My brother-in-law, Graham, came to collect her after visiting time. His mother came with him to see me. She told me that she had been an auxiliary nurse in this hospital years ago. It was bleak then, she said. She called me a 'silly sausage' and hoped I would get well soon, then she gave me a card with some money in it and some fruit. Graham's mum is nice. I like her. His sister, Jill, is lovely, very attractive and sexy. I wish she were my mother.

I have spent most of my time around her house since coming to Chester. It's handy having her and her family living around the corner from my sister's. I hope she will forgive me for bleeding over her carpet when I cut my wrists. After cutting my wrists at home, I managed to get to Jill's house before passing out on her living room floor. The next thing I knew I was in the ambulance. My sister told me that Jill had telephoned her at work to come to her house as quickly as possible because I had collapsed. She didn't tell her on the phone that I had cut my wrists.

It's late and it's been a difficult day. I am so depressed. I have made such a mess of things and I still feel suicidal. I am glad that my sister will write to Aunty Lindsay, but can't wait any longer. I am going to telephone her mum and dad once I have got the number from directory inquiries. I still have Aunty Lindsay's parents' address from when she gave it me, so I could send her a Christmas card. That's what I will do. I will ring her mother and ask her to ask Aunty Lindsay to get in touch with me.

The medication is kicking in, I feel drowsy, the room is spinning and I think I am going to pass out. I had better stop writing.

3rd October 1980

I woke up this morning lying over my diary. It's those bloody tablets. I wish they would take me off them. The shrink has told me that he is asking his colleagues and others about shock treatment. I hope my sister doesn't let them. I keep hearing those voices in my head telling me to harm myself. Are they voices or just powerful thoughts? I don't know. I am not sure about anything any more. Some days I wake up confused and remain confused for the rest of the day. I am told the medication can have that effect on you.

My sister had a meeting with the psychiatrist today and asked him why I wasn't getting better. She told him that she thought I was getting worse. He told her it was simply a matter of time, medication, plus sticking to the programme the hospital has put me on. They have told her that electric treatment may help in the short term, but long term I have to try and help myself and focus more on the present than the past. Despite what they say, my sister won't give her permission for shock treatment. They told her that I am not schizophrenic and the overdose was not a serious attempt at suicide, but they are watching me to make sure I don't do anything like that again. I think they were trying to reassure her that they are doing everything they can to help me. My sister blames herself. It's not her fault. She gave me a home when I left care and didn't know anything about Aunty Lindsay, until I tried to commit suicide. She was upset and shocked to learn of the real reason social services sent me to live with her. I have been asked to put my notebook away and take part in the discussion.

I walked out of group therapy. I didn't like it that my overdose was the topic of discussion. Some of the patients said I was attention seeking, others just wanted to know if I wanted to die, while others just made a noise for the sake of it. The nurse leading the group tried to get me to say why I felt depressed. How can I share about Aunty Lindsay in a group session? I couldn't take any more of the barrage. The nurse leading it lost complete control and everyone started to have a go at me, so I left. To hell with them!

I went and sat on the grass by the birdcages. It was a bit chilly, but peaceful. A nurse from the group who had followed me came and sat down next to me. She didn't say anything at first, then she started talking to me. She was okay, just doing her job. We chatted, then she asked me to come back with her to the group. I think it was when she said that sister wouldn't like it if I didn't join in that I decided to go back with her. I stayed for the rest of the session, but didn't say much.

I have been in hospital a while now and, in many ways, it's like being back in the children's home. I am told what to do and when to do it, even when to have a bath which is supervised by a female nurse. They are discreet – they don't stand over you – but I know they are in the bathroom. It's embarrassing, just like it was in the children's home. I am pleased that Aunty Lindsay never stood over us while we had a bath. I think she was as embarrassed as we were at the practice.

One of the night nurses just told me to go and have a bath before my supper. Like I said, it's just like being back in the children's home. I just hope the student nurse who has come and told me isn't supervising me.

4th October 1980

Alex is on duty, but I can't bring myself to approach her. I saw her in the dining room at dinner, but she didn't come over to me. She seemed too engrossed with her paperwork. After that I saw her with a group of other nurses leaving the ward. I think they had gone for lunch. I am lying on my bed writing, but I cannot keep my eyes open.

I don't know how long I was asleep, but I was woken by Nurse Alex. I lay looking up at her for a moment. She must have just come in from outside, because she was wearing her cape. She told me Peter, a neighbour and a friend from church, had come round to see me and that he was in the day room. She didn't hang around. After reminding me that I was not supposed to be lying on the bed, she left. I think she was avoiding getting into conversation with me. I didn't care. I didn't want to talk to her anyway.

It was good to see Peter. We went to the hospital canteen, but didn't stay long – it was too depressing. Peter suggested that he take me for a spin in his car. I had to ask the ward sister's permission. She seemed hesitant until Peter reassured her that he would look after me and make sure I was back before tea.

I was only ten minutes late back for tea. No one noticed. I just sat down and joined the rest of the nutters. Nurse Alex wasn't on duty, just as well. I wasn't in the mood for talking to her.

I must stop writing. Something is going on and its sounds serious. What a commotion. A nurse had discovered Sandy with a plastic bag over her head. She got it off her, then Sandy ran away. George and a male nurse are looking for her. I am going to see if I can help.

After I left the ward, I ran towards the hospital entrance where a male nurse with a bad leg had stopped to get his breath. I asked him to let me go and look for Sandy. He waved his arms for me to continue, so I ran off in the direction of the railway bridge. I found Sandy sitting on it. I put my hand around her shoulder and told her to follow me. We went down the embankment and started walking along the track. Sandy was upset and crying, but through her tears she confided in me.

She told me that she felt that she couldn't continue any more with her pain. She felt violated and ashamed. No one would believe her about the rape. I asked her if she thought it was her father who had raped her. She wasn't sure any more. She said she was too confused to think straight. She told me that she didn't want to believe it was her father, well, her stepfather. We walked a short distance then we sat down on the embankment and talked for what seemed like ages. Sandy said that she was beginning to trust me. It felt good to be trusted and needed. She placed her head on my lap and lay there for a while, crying. I stroked her head and tried to comfort her. When she was ready I held her hand and we walked back to the hospital.

A nurse met us at the gate and escorted us back to the ward. That evening she got upset again, and had to be held down by three nurses, and given an injection to stop her hurting herself.

5th October 1980

My sister Maxine came to see me today. She had driven from Boston on a Sunday specially to see me. She said it was a mercy dash to try and talk some sense into me. We went for a walk in the hospital gardens and reminisced over the mischief my brother Paul and I got up to, when we used to go to her house for the odd weekend. We chatted about our time in care and shared our disastrous childhood memories. Maxine was sympathetic. She had been in a children's home run by some nuns. Her experience, like mine, on the whole, had been good. I talked to her about Aunty Lindsay for ages. She wanted to know why I had fallen so in love with her. I told her everything, how

Aunty Lindsay reminded me of my favourite actress, Lindsay Wagner, how gorgeous she was, how she reached out to me, disciplined me and just made me feel so special.

Maxine listened to me and understood the depth of my feelings, but felt it wasn't worth killing myself over someone who could not return my love. I asked my sister if she had ever felt like killing herself. She said yes, she had. She told me about the abuse she had suffered at the hands of our deranged mother and how Mum had treated her when she found out she was pregnant. From the way Maxine spoke, I don't think she will ever forgive our mother for what she did to her. I cannot say I blame her. It was horrible listening to what mum did to Maxine. No wonder Maxine liked being in care. The nuns treated her well and I could tell by the way she was speaking that she loved them. Maxine stayed all afternoon. I was sad when she finally had to leave. She told me to forget Aunty Lindsay, to try and put the past behind me, and get well. I wish I could, but it's hard.

I asked Maxine before she left if Jenny, my other sister, would be coming to see me. She reminded me that Jenny never leaves Boston and so it's unlikely that she would come all this way to see me. I don't know whether Maxine was trying to be diplomatic, but she said that she was sure Jenny would be thinking of me. After Maxine left, I returned to my dormitory to put up some posters of Lindsay Wagner that Shene had sent me. Why am I tormenting myself further, putting up a poster of the one person who reminds me the most of Aunty Lindsay? Her character, Jaime Sommers, was and still is, my fantasy of Aunty Lindsay. I don't know why I am tormenting myself. Who cares? I am in love with Aunty Lindsay and I love Lindsay Wagner.

I have been reading all of Aunty Lindsay's letters that I have saved. I still have the first one she wrote to me dated December 1977. She had left the white envelope propped up on my bedroom window so I would see it when I came home from school. The night before I had sat down and written her a letter to say I was sorry for ignoring her. I explained that I had been hurt on Bonfire Night because she slapped me on the coach in front of the other children and, although I deserved it, I had hated her for humiliating me. I wrote that, having ignored her for so long, I didn't know how to talk to her. I had pushed the letter under her bedroom door before I had left for school. She was lovely and kind in her reply to me. She said how delighted she was to receive my apology, that she forgave me and had regretted slapping me so hard, and hoped I would forgive her. She said that we could start again after Christmas, a fresh start, her letter said, signing it 'lots of love, Aunty Lindsay,' with a kiss. I have cried as I have read her letters. It doesn't help listening to ABBA. It seems like I am determined to make myself miserable. God, I am depressed.

We're not allowed to leave the hospital grounds without a nurse. They had relaxed that rule, but they are enforcing it again. Nurse Alex cornered me and forced me to sit and talk to her. I felt in a rebellious mood. I told her that they didn't have the authority to physically stop us from going out of the hospital grounds. She told me they did and to stop being silly, then she wanted to know why I had been avoiding her. Good question, why? She is not Aunty Lindsay, but in my fantasy world she becomes Aunty Lindsay. I wasn't listening to Alex. She was lecturing me on how rude it was to ignore her, and how I wasn't helping myself by being difficult. My mind wandered. All I could think about was life in the children's home, and those final few months with Aunty Lindsay. I don't know how long Alex talked for. I wasn't really listening. She eventually had to go and write up some reports and left me alone with my thoughts.

A patient has just had a right go at me. She called me 'disgusting' because the end of my red belt was dangling down the front of my jeans in front of my flies. She said it's rude. The silly cow – doesn't she know it's the fashion? Bloody idiot. A nurse not much older than me came and stood between me and this nutter to stop her pushing and shoving me and trying to grab hold of the belt. The mental case went back to the day room and left me alone. The nurse commented on how good-looking I am. That made me feel good. She doesn't look too bad either, short dark hair, slim with a great figure, long legs, black tights, looking sexy in her uniform.

I rang Aunty Lindsay's mother. She was kind and sympathetic but didn't say if Aunty Lindsay had received my letter. It was a short phone call; I sensed that she didn't want to stay on the phone. I asked her to ask Aunty Lindsay if she had received my letter. She said she would pass on my message, then she put the phone down. I was shaking. I had been nervous phoning her. She was my last hope of trying to get Aunty Lindsay to get in touch with me. If she doesn't, then I don't care any more. I will have nothing left to live for. I need to talk to Nurse Alex about the phone call to Aunty Lindsay's mum, but she is off duty.

I have been lying on my bed looking up at my poster of Lindsay Wagner, remembering my time in the children's home, and the fantasy I had built around my heroine and Aunty Lindsay. How similar in looks they were to me. I couldn't believe it when Aunty Lindsay came to work at the home. I noticed the likeness straight away. It hadn't taken me long to form an attachment, then fall in love with her. The legacy of that forbidden love has followed me around for the last two years. I cannot or will not let it go.

A few weeks ago, I stood and watched a train coming towards me and had looked death in the face. Then I took an overdose – another failed suicide attempt. I am beginning to think I can't get anything right. I should have made a better job of it two years ago. Maybe I would have done if Aunty Lindsay hadn't wrestled the blade out of my hand. Perhaps the ward sister is right. I am selfish and self-centred, wallowing in self-pity. I cannot help feeling depressed or suicidal. No one knows or understands my pain. I want to feel normal but I don't know what normal is. Nurse Alex thinks I should be out clubbing and dating, not stuck in this mental hospital. I cannot change who I am. I don't like being like this. I hate myself so much. I wish I could be anyone but me. I had better go. It's time to queue for the happy pills.

I got fed up of queuing for bloody tablets and walked away. A nurse stopped me and told me to get back in the queue, but I refused. Then she threatened to put me over her knee. I am sure she was joking, but it embarrassed me when everyone started laughing. I almost dared her to.

6th October 1980

It's eight o'clock and the day staff have just come on duty. No sign of Nurse Alex at breakfast, I hope she is on duty today. It's hard to avoid someone when you need to speak to them. It's time for tablets. I hate queuing for them and then having to open my mouth to prove I have swallowed them.

I am still thinking of last night when that nurse threatened me. It reminded me of the time that Aunty Lindsay had threatened me. I had lost my temper and thrown a hairbrush towards her. The bloody brush bounced off the bedroom wall and nearly hit her. Picking it up, she then threatened me with it. If I am honest I was willing her to discipline me to prove she cared. Some of the events on this ward are similar to my time in the children's home and maybe that's the way I like it, because it makes me feel secure.

I had my session with a new psychiatrist today. He is just like the other shrink, obsessed with sex. I have never had a girlfriend, I have no experience of sex, I am still a virgin. I didn't even know what 'a jump' was until George explained it to me. I have not even kissed a girl. Nineteen, and I haven't even kissed a girl. I have fantasies, who doesn't? Mine are about dominant women. That bothers me. I think that's because I have been brought up by dominant women. I used to like it when Aunty Lindsay was firm with me. I guess that's why I like Lindsay Wagner. Her character, Jaime Sommers, is a strong woman – in control. I know that whenever Nurse Alex is firm with me, I like it, even though I sulk. When she dragged me back to the ward a few days ago, in a strange way, I enjoyed the tussle. She was in control and dominant.

I don't tell these shrinks anything in case they think I am weird or something. The doc wanted to know what I wanted to do when the time came for me to leave the hospital. Would I want to live in a hostel with other ex-patients, or go back to live with my sister? It's the first time anyone has mentioned the possibility of me being discharged. I hadn't really thought about it. I knew Shene would want me to live with her, but I told the doc I would rather live in a hostel. I don't know why, I just did. I cannot imagine life outside of this hospital at the moment, so I don't want to think about it.

I enjoyed going to the hospital gym today. Gordon the ex-army sergeant major is the remedial gymnast. He has got me interested in weights. I like Gordon. He cannot stand Miriam and all those occupational therapists who work with her. He thinks they are a waste of space. Gordon told me that going to the gym would be of more benefit to me than basket weaving, and to ignore Miriam. I get the impression he doesn't like her, so I am in good company. The women who help him in the gym wear white tunics with blue trousers. They don't look as sexy as those nurses on the ward who wear dresses, aprons, black tights and hats.

I had been lying on my bed after lunch just dozing when Dennis, a black nurse, woke me up and told me to get off the bed. I ignored him. Half an hour later he came back and told me to get off again. I ignored him again. The third time he told me, I knew that if I didn't do it this time I would be reported to sister, and I didn't want to cross her. I still had some time before OT so I went to the day room and sat in the chair listening to *A Modern Girl* by Sheena Easton. She is that Scottish teacher who became a pop star through a television programme, *The Big Time*, that Esther Rantzen does. She is only two years older than me. I bet she will be famous. I wished she had been my special needs teacher at school, instead of old Ma Barker. She was a tyrant.

It's that time again. I had better get to afternoon occupational therapy. I am reduced to basket weaving, because I cannot finish my duck without a sharp tool.

Someone has thrown the television through the one window without bars, just because another patient changed the bloody channel. That flipping nutter is now in a padded room where he belongs. This is a nut house! Someone is always screaming, shouting, or throwing their weight around or thinking they own the place and trying to throw you out, like one old lady did with me. She kept telling me to get out of her house and prodding me with her bony finger. Other patients just wander the corridors, shuffling along and moaning. What the hell I am I doing here?

I think Sandy is anorexic. She has started to make herself sick after she has eaten. Sometimes she refuses to eat and has to be forced. I think sister is losing patience with her. Jack still ignores me and George is due back in court. I don't know what he has done, but it must be serious to be sectioned by the courts. Lee is treating this place like her own private hotel. I think she has a bit of money. Well, she says she does. If that's true, why isn't she in a private hospital instead of this dump?

Nurse Alex is still not on duty. I wish she was here. I need to talk to her about my phone call to Aunty Lindsay's mum.

I have just phoned an old school friend. He was sorry to hear of my problems and wished me well. I asked him about another friend of ours – Fram. I haven't heard from him since he went off to Lincoln College of Art. I think he might have gone to live and work in America, in New York – he has some relatives out there. We met at primary school not long after I arrived at the children's home in 1972. As I got older his favourite trick was getting me drunk on his dad's home-made wine. I used to phone my mum from his house while drunk, then she phoned social services, who then phoned the children's home and I would get into big trouble. They put a stop to me going around to his house and drinking wine if his mum and dad weren't there.

We had had some good times over the years. He was a good friend who made me laugh a lot. I remember the first time I introduced him to

Aunty Lindsay. He kissed her hand, the charmer! The superintendent of the children's home had allowed me to call at his house to say goodbye on my way to the railway station, the day I left Spalding for Chester. I haven't heard from him for two years. I miss my old buddy. He was a good old boy. He will do alright for himself. He wants to be rich and no doubt he will be.

Nurse Alex hasn't been on duty all day. I have heard rumours that she is going to be moving to Scotland. I hope not. What will I do without her? The thought of someone else leaving me, that I have grown attached to, makes me feel so depressed. I hate it.

7th October 1980

It's 1.15am. I have just gone to the loo and, to my surprise, there are no nurses on the ward, no one asleep in the chairs, no one in the staff room or the office. I have a good look around, but I can't find anyone. I wonder where they have all gone. I couldn't sleep so I decided to go to the women's dormitory and wake Sandy. We both went and looked around the ward, but still we couldn't find any nurses. Sandy asked if I fancied a walk. I told her that all the doors were locked, but she knew of a window that wasn't. We got dressed and made sure our beds looked like we were in them, then climbed out of the unlocked window in the day room.

We walked all around the entire hospital grounds without the security staff seeing us. It felt good to be doing something spontaneous. We even got the giggles hiding from security. We talked until the wee hours of the morning about our problems. We even discussed a suicide pact – jumping off the railway bridge together. Sandy looked at the scars on my wrists and I looked at the scars on hers. We hugged and took comfort in our solidarity. Lying down on the grass we looked up at the moon. I don't know how long we lay there, but eventually we decided we should climb back through the window, before someone noticed we weren't in our beds and called the police. As we climbed back through the window the night sister caught us. After reprimanding us she told her nurses to take us back to our dormitories. Sandy's mood changed. She became difficult and started raising her voice, challenging sister's authority and sister didn't like it. She had to be given an injection to help calm her. A good night had ended like this.

Well, the day ward sister gave us both another roasting, and also swatted Sandy on the bottom as we left her office. Judging by Sandy's reaction I think sister caught the spot where she had the injection. Sister has a soft spot for Sandy and treats her like her daughter.

We returned to the day room for group discussion. No surprises what they were discussing today – the great escape. Most of the patients, the ones who have their faculties, think it's funny. The others don't even know what day it is. Nurse Alex is on duty and, as expected, I did get a talking to. She says she feels responsible for me and takes my rebellion personally, as does the ward sister.

I didn't feel like any dinner today. I just picked at my food. I am thinking of giving Aunty Lindsay's mum another ring later if I don't hear anything this afternoon. I am going to try and sleep again to escape this nightmare. Jolly Jack is trying to build bridges, but I am ignoring him.

I slept until 1.15 pm then I made my way across the gardens towards the OT room. I stopped on the way to buy some Bar Six chocolate bars from the vending machine. I like Bar Six, a bit like Kit-Kat but looks like a bar of chocolate.

All the hawks (nurses) were hovering around, their eyes glued on me. Miriam had a go at me and told me that my exploits last night were typical of someone who was just using this place as a hotel. I looked down at the screwdriver. I wanted to pick it up and drive it right into her fat belly. I closed my eyes and held my head in my hands. She forced my hand away from shielding my eyes. I tried to push her off me, but she was too strong. She said that she had seen my type many times and had no sympathy for me. She said that if I was intent on killing myself, then I should go somewhere and do it and not tell anyone. The old windbag said I was attention seeking. I hate her. She pushed me down in the chair and walked away. I spent the rest of my time in occupational therapy, drawing and painting. I waited until OT was nearly over before choosing my moment to sneak out without an escort. I returned to the railway bridge and stood on it, waiting for a train to come.

I didn't have to wait long. I closed my eyes and leaned forward. Voices in my head told me to jump and end this torment. They echoed in my mind as I leaned forward. Again, I chickened out at the crucial moment. I threw myself onto the other side of the bridge, landing on the gravel road. I lay there for a minute panting, taking deep breaths. I screamed into the air, 'I hate you all!' I just lay there panting. I returned to the ward to write down what happened. A nurse asked me where I had been. I told her to leave me alone and that it was none of her business. She is not happy, but I don't care. What can they do to me?

I cannot wait any longer. I am going to phone Aunty Lindsay's mum. I need to know if she has read my letter and whether or not she is going to write back to me.

8th October 1980

I was too depressed to write anything last night. I phoned Aunty Lindsay's mum, hoping that she would have some news for me but, instead, she told me that I must not phone her again. She told me that I must put my feelings for her daughter behind me and move on with my life. She reminded me that I was a young lad with my whole life before me, stuff I had heard so often that I was sick of hearing it. She wished me well and then ended the phone call. I sank to my knees and sat crunched up on the floor of the telephone box. My heart was breaking. I was sinking even further into despair. I must have sat on the floor of that telephone box for ages, just crying and holding my head in my hands. Someone knocking on the window disturbed me. I looked up at this wee slip of a girl in her uniform and cape, protecting her from the night wind. She opened the door and asked if I was alright. I wiped away my tears, got up off the floor and told her I was fine. She reminded me that the doors of the ward would be locked at eight and to hurry along.

After I had my night medication I went to my dormitory and lay on the bed. At least they don't mind you lying on the bed in the evening. I lay there looking up at my poster of Lindsay Wagner smiling down on me, looking so beautiful. I couldn't get Aunty Lindsay's mum's words out of my mind. How do you get someone you have fallen in love with out of your heart? I am tormenting myself, but I don't care. I hurt so much. I wish the pain would go away. I am going to write Aunty Lindsay a final letter to say sorry and goodbye, then I don't know what I am going to do.

I just keep sinking deeper and deeper into this pit of depression. My heart is breaking. How can pills fix a broken heart and years of abuse? I should just give up and let them do whatever they want to do and, if that includes frying my brain, fine. I am so confused, so depressed, so afraid. I am hopeless. I wish I was dead. Maybe Sandy and I should do what we spoke about and jump off the railway bridge together.

This morning I did everything on autopilot. I wasn't sure where I was or what I was doing. I just wandered around the ward, dragging my feet behind me. I had tunnel vision. Everyone and everything seemed so far away. Falling to my knees, I started screaming. A couple of nurses came running to my aid, trying to help me to my feet. I was screaming and crying. It took two of them to restrain me and take me back to my ward. I was given an injection which knocked me out.

It is now late in the evening. I remember my sister coming to see me. She stood over my bed calling my name. I couldn't respond – I had no energy. I heard Nurse Alex telling my sister that I had to be sedated after I became hysterical. She seemed upset. Alex put her arms around her and then I drifted off again. Now I am feeling groggy – able to write, but not able to move far from my bed. My legs are weak and buckle under me whenever I try to stand. I can't write any more, I need to sleep.

9th October 1980

I saw the shrink this morning. He asked how I was after yesterday. I said 'fine.' I wasn't in the mood for talking much. The ward sister has also spoken to me over my hysterical outburst. She was very kind and sympathetic. Nurse Alex came over to me at the dining table and we had a long talk. She held my hand and tried to comfort me, but nothing could comfort me. Then she told me she was leaving and moving to Scotland in a few weeks' time. That news should have devastated me, but it didn't. I was too subdued, too depressed to care. All I knew was that Aunty Lindsay had rejected me – she had ignored my cry for help. Nurse Alex held me close to her and I just stared blankly into space until she had to go.

I must have sat for ages in that chair after she had gone, just staring. I was aware of others around me, but I didn't respond to any of them. I heard one or two comments saying, 'Leave him alone, he is not here.' No, I wasn't. I was elsewhere.

I have been to town with some other patients, accompanied by a student nurse. She must be in her third year of training – she has three red bands on her paper hat.

I couldn't cope with the noise in Woolworths. I felt my head spinning. Voices echoed in my mind. I was breathing fast and becoming upset. The nurse looked alarmed and asked me to sit down. Instead, I ran to the restaurant balcony and leaned right over it. She came running after me, pulled me back and told me to move away from the balcony. I was conscious of other people looking at us, but was in too much of an agitated state to care. The nurse took control and managed to calm me down. Good job she was a third-year student and not a first-year one. Waitresses at Woolworths brought me a glass of water. The nurse said she would have to report the incident to sister, but nothing's happened yet. Spoke too soon – she has just had words with me, asking me if I have been taking my medication.

After tea, I went to the day room to play some records and write. I looked around for Sandy, to see if she wanted to go for a drink with me before they locked the doors. So long as we can find a member of staff to go with us we should be okay. I couldn't find her. She has been spending more and more time alone these last few days. She told me that she might be transferred to a private hospital. Her rich parents are unhappy with her lack of progress in this dump and think she would be better going private. I asked Carol to come with me for a drink instead. I think I am safe now since she asked me if I wanted sex on her first day on the ward. She is a lot calmer now, but then most of us are when we take our medication.

Sister allowed us to go to the pub opposite the hospital with some other nurses who were going with a couple of older patients. I could not believe it when the bloody Gestapo walked in, Miriam of all people. I think she was off duty because she wasn't in her uniform. She came over to us and asked if anyone knew we were out of the hospital. I pointed to the nurses who came with us. I felt obliged to offer her a drink. She refused my offer but, like an idiot, I insisted. I felt uncomfortable sitting there with her breathing down my neck. Carol kept giggling, pulling faces and kicking me under the table. I think she was flirting with me. She's an attractive girl, so I didn't mind. Miriam didn't stay long with us, thank God. She went and joined some people at the bar. We finished our drinks and then made our way back to the hospital, pushing and shoving each other, making fun of Miriam and laughing. I think it's the first time I have laughed in a long time.

I am keeping away from Nurse Alex. I don't want to talk to her. Now that I have had time to think about it, I am too upset that she is moving to Scotland. Why does this always happen to me? Every time I get close to someone they move away from me and I feel abandoned.

Aunty Lindsay has abandoned me. My sister tries to reassure me that she might not have, but after all this time and still no reply to my letter, what else can I think? Her mother put the phone down on me, after telling me to not bother her again and forget her daughter. That says it all, doesn't it? What is it about me that makes me so unlovable? Why do people, women in particular, cause me so much pain?

If I hadn't met Aunty Lindsay, if she had never come to work at the children's home, I would never have fallen in love with her. Why did she have to be so beautiful? There was never any danger of me falling in love with Aunty Freda, God forbid. She wasn't as good-looking as Aunty Lindsay, or sexy. She had been at the home for years, a former nanny, well into her forties, but Aunty Lindsay was sexy, beautiful, and intelligent, who reminded me of my favourite actresses, Lindsay Wagner. I feel bad that I ignored her for the entire length of the firemen's strike because of that one slap across the face which, if I am honest, I deserved. Now I am avoiding Nurse Alex, giving her the silent treatment. I know it's childish, but I have to protect myself from further pain. It's too much. I am going to write Aunty Lindsay my final letter this evening and post it tomorrow.

10th October 1980

I was distraught as I tore up all of Aunty Lindsay's letters to me, which I had kept. I have written my final letter to her to say sorry for all the trouble I have caused, and that I didn't mean to fall in love with her. I thanked her for her kindness and for helping me in the children's home, and that I would always love her, even if she couldn't love me in the same way. I told her I was sorry for phoning her parents and asked her to forgive me. I wished her and her new husband well and hoped they would be very happy. I signed it *Love, Mark x*

Once I have posted the letter, all I have to do is plan my suicide and make sure I do a better job this time. What do I have to live for? What hope is there for me? I won't even have a job if I leave here. My old boss has kept my position open at Foster Menswear, but he is retiring and the area manager, the skinny little weasel, hates me. He has always made things difficult for me. He wants to get rid of me. He feels that, because I am in this place, I should not be mixing with the public. I don't care. I hate him and if he pushes me too far, he'll regret it.

My manager has told me that he has asked everyone in the shop to write negative things about me. How cruel can he be? I am here because I am ill and now he wants to sack me while I am in hospital – heartless bastard! He won't have to sack me; I'll be dead before he gets rid of me. I like my old boss. When he interviewed me, I told him about my life in care and he gave me the job. But that heartless bastard of an area manager, the skinny runt, has picked on me from the moment he took over as area manager. He thinks he's tough. He had better not come near me while I am in here or I'll set Doug from the gym on him.

Alex is on duty. She said, 'Good morning,' but I ignored her. I don't like giving her the silent treatment, but I have to if I am to prepare myself for when she is no longer here. She has been so kind, so understanding and patient with me these last few weeks. I have not made it easy for her at times, but she has stuck with me and now she is going to disappear from my life for good. Every time she hugged me, held my hand or fought with me or told me off, I felt good, I felt loved, I felt secure.

Sandy and I are close, but only because we are two tormented souls who find comfort in sharing our problems, but she is leaving too. She is going to be transferred to a private hospital outside of Chester. I like Carol and, as much as she flirts with me, she scares me, because I think she is sex-mad. I have never had a girlfriend. I don't think I am capable of having a relationship with someone my own age. I keep falling for older women who I want to mother me. What does it matter, when I am thinking about taking my own life?

So that's it. I have done it. I have posted my last letter to Aunty

Lindsay. Unless she writes back to my sister I am going to have to accept that she has rejected me. I think her mother and father would have told her not to get involved with someone from the children's home.

11th October 1980

Nurse Alex is not happy with me for avoiding her. She has confronted me with what she calls my juvenile behaviour. She has told me that if this is how I treated Aunty Lindsay, then it's no wonder we nearly came to blows. She said that she had felt like walloping me, but she didn't want to jeopardise her career. She said that if I had been her son she would have done that a long time ago. Just hearing her say that embarrassed me, but also gave me butterflies in my stomach, wishing I was her son.

I wish I hadn't told her so much about Aunty Lindsay and myself now. She uses it against me. I told Nurse Alex that I was upset because she is leaving. She had another go at me, saying that I was making her last few weeks miserable. I felt sullen afterwards and sulked, but I knew she was right. Why do I do this? I can't help it. I always sulk and withdraw into myself and fail to see the hurt I cause others. When I withdrew with Aunty Lindsay, I knew that my actions were hurting her. Every time she confronted me, it always ended up with me being sullen and her becoming angry and walking away.

I could tell that she wanted to slap me. As much as I was willing her to, she just walked away, leaving me feeling so helpless. I used to get tongue-tied every time I tried to open my mouth to speak. If only I could have told her that I didn't hate her – I loved her. After she wrote to me, we did start again and it was wonderful. She didn't treat me any differently from the other children. She still told me off and she still expected me to do as I was told, but we had some laughs as well.

I remember walking back from church with her one evening. She had a dress on and the wind blew it up and exposed her thighs. She battled to keep it down, looking so beautiful with her long hair blowing in the wind. I only went to the evening service because Aunty Lindsay went. I was more interested in her than God. I loved her singing. She had such a lovely voice. It hurts to remember, because I miss her so much. I am sorry I have made Nurse Alex miserable; I haven't meant to. I know I have withdrawn. It's the only way I know of trying to protect myself from being hurt.

Shene and Frances came to see me this evening. We sat in awkward silence. It's not because I don't want to communicate, it's that I don't know what to say. I know Shene loves me. She always has, but I can't see beyond my pain. I cannot cope with her. Frances is a dear. She kept patting my hand and telling me that it will be okay. Graham's lucky to have her has a mother.

I hate my mother. All she did was give birth to me, then abandoned me. I didn't ask to be born. I would have given anything to be part of a loving family. The only decent set of foster parents my brother and I ever had, and then the bloody social services kidnapped us from school one afternoon and took us away to the bloody home. How lucky Sandy is to have two parents who care for her, who love her. I used to tell people at school that my mum and dad were dead. It was easier than trying to explain that I was in care because they didn't want me.

How can I make these doctors and nurses understand what it's like to feel so desolate, so lonely and unloved? I feel like rubbish because I have been made to feel like rubbish. I have been called a juvenile delinquent and backward, and now people will think I am mental because I have been in this place.

Apart from my manager, no one else from Foster Menswear has been to see me while I have been in this hospital. At least he came the first week I was here, to reassure me that he would keep my job open for me, and to not worry about that. I have worked for Foster Menswear for two years and now that bloody area manager wants to get rid of me. I hate them all. What do I care? I don't need them.

I don't need anyone, except Lindsay. But hell, she can go to hell too. No, I don't mean that. God knows I love her. I will always love her. No one can take the love I feel for her away.

Today has been hard. Some days I feel the pain will never end. It's late. I am lying in bed remembering how it used to be, those carefree days of the children's home. I did like living there, until the last few months when everything when wrong. I only left two years ago and now I am here, forgotten by social services. What do they care? Lying here in bed I can hear patients calling out in their sleep. Some are just howling. They frightened me when I first came into hospital, but you get used to them and this place.

I have this feeling of drifting in and out of the past, with my mind whirling with memories. I remember sexual, physical, and mental abuse from people who were supposed to protect me. It is so disgusting, so horrible and so painful that I can't talk about it. It's a terrible thing to be abused, to be rejected – is it any wonder I build a brick wall to protect myself? I tell these shrinks about Aunty Lindsay, but I won't tell them about the abuse, well, not in any detail. The truth is I don't trust them. Both shrinks I have seen have been obsessed with sexual questions.

I still cannot understand why I had to strip naked in front of Nurse Alex to be examined, when I was first admitted. I felt just as embarrassed as I did in the children's home, when we had to stand naked in a bowl of water for a wash, when we were on holiday. I was still being supervised while having a bath at age 16. Aunty Lindsay was always discreet. She never came anywhere near the older children at bath time.

It seems like every waking moment I am thinking about Aunty Lindsay and my time at the children's home. I am finding it so hard to let go of the past. It's not just while I am awake, either. Some of the nurses have reported me shouting out Aunty Lindsay's name in my sleep. I did that in the children's home and was told by one of the other house parents to control my feelings, otherwise Aunty Lindsay might leave. I feel like I am floating – must be the medication. I had better stop writing. Good night.

12th October 1980

With the ward sister's permission, I have been back to my sister's house today. Peter took me to pick up more of my posters of Lindsay Wagner and a few more personal possessions. I discovered a few more letters from Aunty Lindsay that I had not destroyed. I also found a photograph of a group of us in the children's home, taken around a giant chocolate Easter egg donated by Woolworths. It was the last photo I had taken at the home before I left. I am standing next to Aunty Lindsay. I am all smiles, I am in love, and life feels good. Aunty Lindsay has her hair tied back. I never liked her hair like that and always used to pull her ribbon out. It was my favourite trick, as was undoing her apron. It's a pity Brian's big head got in the way. I can only see half of Aunty Lindsay's face.

I stood for ages just staring at the photo. I remember it being taken. Aunty Lindsay had just sent me back to clean my school shoes. They hadn't passed her inspection. She had her tight jeans on that day and her stripy top, and her bottom looked gorgeous. Memories came flooding back to me as I stood in my sister's room. I remembered the first flutters of love, those innocent feelings, and the butterflies in my stomach every time she walked past me, looked at me, smiled at me, or even told me off. When she held my hand to comfort me or hugged me I was in heaven. Peter put his hand on my shoulder. He could see I was tearful. I looked around my old bedroom. For two years it had become my prison. My brother-in-law has stripped all the wallpaper off, ready to decorate for my three-year-old nephew.

I am wondering if I have done the right thing, saying that I will not go back to live with my sister once I am discharged from hospital. I don't know when that might be or if I will live that long. I am still trying to find the courage to commit suicide. I have put some more posters of Lindsay Wagner up. Some of the nurses have commented on them.

I couldn't concentrate on the television this evening. I had just taken some medication and was feeling dizzy. I slumped to the floor and started crying. A nurse ushered me into the office, gave me a drink and then suggested I go to bed. So here I am in bed writing my thoughts and feelings down and wondering if I will ever get out of here. Yet, even as I think that, I know that the thought of being discharged scares me. It's horrible here, but at least I feel safe. I am thinking of taking another overdose and have been saving a few pills. Carol has given me some of her tablets at a price. I had to kiss her while she passed them into my mouth from her mouth.

I am smiling for a change. Being surrounded by so many nurses reminded me of the time that my brother and I had gone to Maxine's for a short break. I had to have my ingrown toe nail removed at the Pilgrim Hospital in Boston. The nurse who looked after me asked what it was like living in a children's home. I told her it was okay, except for this new house parent, Aunty Lindsay, who was horrible, bossy, always shouting and telling us off and threatening us with the slipper. I made her sound really nasty. The nurse appeared sympathetic, saying that Aunty Lindsay sounded like a terrible person and poor me. A few days later Aunty Lindsay confronted me and asked me why I had been saying such horrible things to a nurse at the Pilgrim Hospital, who just happened to be her best friend. She was so cross with me. I told her I was only joking with the nurse.

Time for me to put this notebook away and go to sleep. I hope there is not a repeat of last night's screaming.

13th October 1980

Big John, the auxiliary night nurse, was out with his taxi again last night. He signed on at eight o'clock and went straight out in his taxi until eleven o'clock. I saw him come back. He only stayed for a short while and then went off again. I don't care what he does, so long as he leaves Sandy and me alone. I have noticed, though, that he only goes off in his taxi when sister isn't on duty. None of the other auxiliaries will drop him in it. They're too scared of him.

I approached Nurse Alex today and said sorry for making her miserable. I explained that I was sad that she was leaving and that I didn't want her to go. She gave me a hug and said she forgave me and that I should just try and enjoy having her around for a little while longer, rather than sulking in the corner. I would have liked to have asked her if I could write to her, but I knew she would say no, so I didn't. Instead, I spoke to her about my visit to my sister's yesterday and how I felt. She wasn't being so hard on me today. Perhaps it's because I am being more sensible and more co-operative than usual today. She wouldn't have been so nice to me if she knew that I had saved quite a few pills and was planning to take them all at once.

Nurse Alex is leaving in a few weeks, before moving to Scotland in the New Year. I wasn't going to ask her about keeping in touch for fear she would say no, but I changed my mind. I wish I hadn't, though. She said it would be unprofessional and that she could get into serious trouble for writing to a patient. Her reaction upset me and hurt my feelings. I am so depressed at the thought of her leaving. Even though I have tried to distance myself from her, I can't stop wanting or needing her.

The first day I came into this hospital I looked so pathetic and frightened, dressed only in my pyjamas and dressing gown. Nurse Alex had held my hand, stroked my bandaged wrists, wiped away my tears, kissed my forehead and stroked my hair, to try and reassure me that everything would be okay. She had even averted her eyes to spare my embarrassment when I had stood naked in the doctor's office. I knew from that moment that I would form an attachment to her, because she reminded me of Aunty Lindsay. I know I have been difficult with her at times, testing her, pushing the boundaries just like I did with Aunty Lindsay, and now she is leaving and my heart is breaking again.

No letter from Aunty Lindsay in the morning post – every day the same. I keep hoping and praying that there will be a letter for me. My sister hasn't received a reply to her letter either. I feel sick, depressed and angry. What more can I do? Queuing up for happy pills, it seemed ages before I got mine. It's these old people. They stand around asking bloody silly questions, moaning about how they never sleep. I didn't sleep much last night, but I don't stand around complaining about it. The reason I couldn't sleep was because I didn't take all my pills and no one checked, but I wish I had done. All that flipping snoring kept me awake. God, I hope I am not like that if I ever reach fifty.

I went to the gym after breakfast. I would have stayed all morning, but someone from occupational therapy, noticing I wasn't there, came to get me. Gordon the gymnast tried to get them to let me stay, but they said no. He made some rude gestures behind their backs as I left, which made me laugh. I don't know why I cannot spend more time in the gym. It's doing me more good than bloody OT.

The black male nurse stood watching me in OT. His eyes were glued on me. I felt intimidated but you get used to that in this place. Everyone is watching you, even when you think they are not. I was using a saw to try and carve out my duck because they still won't let me near the chisels. It didn't go so well. I made a mess of the duck and threw the saw down in frustration, which didn't please Miriam. I gave up in the end and just sat doing some artwork. I could have finished the bloody basket, but I didn't feel like it. I didn't wait around with the other patients to be escorted back to the ward for dinner. I went ahead of them.

Sandy was up when I got back, but still in her dressing gown. You could tell she was drugged up just by looking at her. I tried to speak to her, but she just looked at me with a blank expression on her face. It was like she didn't even know I was there. I kissed her on the forehead and stroked her arm, but still no response.

Dinner was tasteless – I left most of it. Tried to get Sandy to eat something, but she wouldn't or couldn't. She just sat there and made no attempt to feed herself. I couldn't finish my dinner. I wasn't feeling too well, my stomach hurt and got worse as the afternoon went on. I was asked if I had taken anything, but I hadn't. I am still saving the pills. They are in a good hiding place. The doctor examined me, pressing my lower stomach. I think he thought it might be my appendix. He gave me an injection to ease the pain and I have slept most of the afternoon.

It's late evening now. I am still in bed, recovering from whatever caused the pain. The nurse brought me some toast because I missed tea, which was nice of her.

14th October 1980

I was in physical and emotional pain last night, crying myself to exhaustion while listening to those inner voices, urging me to take my own life. My dreams are so vivid that I am always thankful to wake up from my nightmares, even in this place. It's only when I dream of Aunty Lindsay that I never want to wake up. I see her face, I hear her voice, I feel her touch. I can even smell her hair. I had such a dream last night, and woke up with a tear-stained face and wet pillow.

This morning, I dragged my aching body out of bed. I looked in the mirror in the bathroom. I looked terrible; dark shadows under my eyes and my hair could do with a wash. I looked so pathetic. I hate myself. I hate my life. I thought if I closed my eyes long enough I would open them and be standing in the bathroom at the children's home and all of this would have been a horrible dream. A student nurse came in the bathroom and asked if I was alright. I screamed at her to leave me alone. She left, but told me to hurry up because they were handing out the medication. I didn't move. I just kept staring at my pathetic face in the mirror. Moments later Dennis, the male nurse, came in and asked me to go and get my tablets. I ignored him and continued washing my face, then returned to my dorm to write in my notebook.

With still no letter from Aunty Lindsay, I am beginning to think that she has turned her back on me or she doesn't know what to say, so she is saying nothing. I wish I knew what she was thinking. I just hope she doesn't hate me. I couldn't bear that. I am so depressed, I think I will take those pills today and end the torment, end the pain. I cannot go on like this – wondering, hoping, praying that I might get a letter. Death will be a welcome escape from the torment and despair that I feel. I don't know how I would get through the days without medication. I used to think it was cruel to keep us drugged up, but now I welcome it. I don't want to face reality. It's too painful. At least the happy pills help a little. Talking of happy pills, I'd better go and get them before Dennis comes back.

My day got worse when I discovered Sandy with her suitcases, sat in a wheelchair, waiting with her parents for an ambulance to take her off to a private hospital. I tried to talk to her but she was too sedated to respond. I held her hand and squeezed it. She didn't respond. She just sat staring into space, tears in her eyes. Then a nurse came and wheeled her away. I watched as they put her into the ambulance and then drove away. I went to occupational therapy with a heavy heart. The one person my own age who I could relate to was gone. I really am on my own now. Carol is nice and she is good looking, but she is also scary. I think she is in here because she is sex-mad. I don't want to get too close to her.

During occupational therapy, I was asked to go back to the ward to see the doctor. I wondered what he wanted. However, it wasn't the shrink who wanted to see me but the hospital social worker. He was an old bloke, about fifty. He seemed alright, but I hate social workers. Apart from one, all of mine have been a bloody waste of space. He didn't seem that interested in why I was in hospital. He just wanted to know if I still wanted to live in a hostel once I am discharged. I don't know what will happen to me if I am not successful in taking my own life. Maybe if I survive they will lock me up for good and throw away the key, like so many of the poor sods in here wandering the corridors. I cannot imagine life outside of this hospital. I am scared of death and I am scared of living. I am anxious and depressed. What should I do? I must speak to Nurse Alex. She is always reassuring.

15th October 1980

I am in big trouble. One of the other patients told a nurse that I had been hiding tablets and she went to my locker and found them. She did go mental. I have never seen her that angry. I thought she was going to hit me. She has told me that if I don't take my medication they will give it to me by injection and make sure it bloody hurts. I can't believe she swore at me. Is that the effect I have on people? Then she told me to get out of her office and go and think about what she had said. Sod them, they can do what they bloody like to me. I hate them all. I am angry and upset. I can't believe she spoke to me like that – no sympathy, no understanding. I feel better now. I have just grabbed the first thing that came to hand, a chair, and thrown it across the bloody ward. It smashed against the wall, narrowly missing another patient.

I have been sedated for most of the day. All I can remember is two nurses holding me down while they stuck a big needle in me. I tried to fight them off, but they were stronger than they looked. I didn't have time to be embarrassed at having a needle shoved in my bare bottom. I just went to sleep.

Sister is right. I am my own worst enemy and the only person I am hurting is myself. Aunty Lindsay said that to me more than once. I guess there is a part of me that presses the self-destruct button and to hell with the consequences. I am hopeless and pathetic. I don't know how to change. I want to but I don't know how. I wish someone would help me to be different, to be normal. It's been a horrible day. Sister is right. I am rebellious and uncooperative and what sympathy people do feel for me will start to diminish if I don't help myself. She has warned me that if I don't start to cooperate then there is little point in my being in hospital.

Oh, God, I am so sorry for the mess I have made of everything. I have screwed up again, just like I did in the children's home in my last year. The superintendents said I had changed beyond recognition from the nice mischievous lad I used to be, to a rebellious and manipulative love-struck teenager. They warned me that I had to control my feeling towards Aunty Lindsay. I tried, but I couldn't help it. I know it's stupid, but I used to imagine that she was Jaime Sommers, the Bionic Woman. I guess I had a thing about Lindsay Wagner long before Aunty Lindsay came to work at the children's home. She just brought my fantasies to life. Even the scalpel blade incident could have come right out of an episode of *The Bionic Woman*.

I remember the superintendents telling me that nothing like that had ever happened in the children's home before. They made me feel such a bad person that I hated myself. I became angry, fearful, suicidal, and withdrawn. I only threatened to cut my wrists with the scalpel blade because I was desperate. I wasn't thinking. I just held it to my wrists and warned Aunty Lindsay not to come any closer, otherwise I would cut myself. If she hadn't fought me to get it off me, I might have been more successful. She was very brave. I might have hurt her in the struggle. I wish she had been tougher on me and not allowed me to manipulate her so easily. Only once did I get the kind of reaction from her I had been wanting, and it frightened me that I had pushed her too far. I wouldn't have blamed her if she had hit me, I would have deserved it. She walked away, though I remember it as if it was yesterday.

The ward sister frightened me today. I pushed her too far. I got a reaction alright, but it scared the hell out of me. I am so sorry for my actions, sorry for causing people so many problems. I feel so tired and my bottom hurts where they stuck the bloody needle in.

Now I have to go and have a bath and wash my hair. I know they are discreet, but I wish a nurse didn't have to be in the bathroom with you. I always use loads of bubble bath to cover my body in the bath, just in case.

16th October 1980

My session with the doctor this morning wasn't comfortable. He had a go at me about yesterday. He said that I was putting my family through a difficult time, by appearing not to be cooperating with my treatment and contemplating suicide, by saving those pills. I wasn't in the mood for a lecture, but I had no choice other than to sit and listen to him and the ward sister. Both of them were having a go at me. Nurse Alex sat in the corner listening. The shrink said that if it hadn't been for my sister refusing to give permission for shock treatment they would have done it by now. He reminded me that it was in everyone's best interests if I cooperated fully with the programme while in hospital. The doctor read a report from occupational therapy, who were recommending that I should start domestic training with a view to becoming a day patient. The shrink says that he is going to reduce my medication and review my case in a few weeks' time.

He strongly advised me to cooperate with the programme, with a warning that, with or without my sister's permission, if I tried to commit suicide again they would shock me. I wanted to get up out of my chair and tip up the table in a rage. Instead, I gripped the arms of the chair so tightly that I thought it would break them. He just went on and on and on until I just snapped and retaliated the only way I knew how. I exploded into another one of those blinding rages. I shouted at them to get off my case and accused them of being hard and uncaring. I shouted at them both, but they didn't respond. They just asked Nurse Alex to show me back to the ward. I leapt to my feet so quickly that I tipped the chair backwards. I stood motionless, shaking, but still they sat unimpressed with my outburst. Sister just said that if I wanted another injection it could be arranged, so I had better calm down. Nurse Alex took me back to the ward and told me that next week would be her last week.

Another hell of a day – first Sandy and now Nurse Alex, and still no word from Aunty Lindsay. Life sucks and I don't feel like writing any more.

17th October 1980

Nurse Alex told me last night that she was very disappointed in me for hiding the tablets, and that it had been foolish, childish, and downright thoughtless. She said that I deserved the roasting I got from the sister. She wasn't being very kind to me and I became upset. Forcing me to look her in the eyes, like she has done on many occasions, she told me that she was being tough on me because she cares about what happens to me. She reminded me that she had come to the end of her training and that she was leaving the hospital and moving to Scotland in the New Year. Tears rolled down my face. She hugged me before telling me that I really did have to start helping myself. Then she had to leave to go off duty. Why do people always say that I have to start helping myself just before they are about to walk out on me?

First, they tell me to trust them and then they get me to share my feelings, promising to help me and then, when it all gets too messy, you cannot see them for bloody dust. That's the story of my life. Is it any wonder I am beginning to feel that there is no one I can trust? God, I am depressed, so depressed. God help me. That's a laugh! He only helps those who help themselves and according to everyone, I am not helping myself, so why should I expect any help from the Almighty. What has God ever done for me? Where was He when I was being abused? Where was bloody God when they sent me away from the children's home? I'll tell you where He bloody was. He doesn't exist, so He wasn't anywhere. I don't believe in God any more. I don't know if I ever believed in Him. I only went to church because everyone in the children's home went. Sod God, sod the church, and sod Aunty Lindsay.

OT has told me that I will be starting my domestic training soon. I want to get out of this place, but it's scary. At least I feel safe here, well, most of the time, anyway. I am not sure if I can cope living on my own outside this hospital. It's a scary thought. I guess some would say I am not coping on the inside either, so what's the alternative?

Well, I know that I am losing the will to even try suicide. I could try, but if I fail, then they will shock me and I don't want that. Maybe I am just a coward, frightened of dying and frightened of living. I don't know. I am confused, hurting and depressed. Life looks bleak at the moment. I have no future that I can see. I have given up my home with my sister. Where will I live? I don't know. I don't care. I am just too damned depressed to give it much thought. Just getting through each day is enough at the moment. I feel very close to the edge today. I swear if anyone even looks at me in the wrong way I'll fly for them.

I went for a walk on my own without telling anyone. I stood for ages on a bridge in the freezing fog, watching the river swirling beneath me. I was reminded of James Stewart in the film *It's a Wonderful Life*. I had watched it a while ago and had enjoyed it. I tried to imagine what it would have been like for people around me if I hadn't been born. The truth is, I wished I hadn't been born. I wasn't wanted from the moment I left my mother's womb. Why she had another boy two years later, I don't know. We both ended up in care. I miss my brother Paul. It was such a wrench being separated two years ago – we had never been apart.

I must have stood watching that river for ages. More thoughts of killing myself, not by a train this time but, like Anna – jump and drown. It was tempting. A few people passed me and joked, saying, 'Don't do it, lad.' If only they knew how much I hate this bloody life.

On this ward I am surrounded by middle-aged and old people. I am the youngest here except for Carol. Well, she is quite old, in her late twenties or early thirties, I think. I don't really know. I wish Sandy was still here. At least she was the same age as me. The second post has been, but nothing. Why do I put myself through this torture? Every day's the same. I am watching and waiting for a letter that isn't going to come.

18th October 1980

The discussion group was bloody horrible, chaotic, with everyone screaming and shouting and throwing tantrums. I spent the entire session imagining that I had a machine gun, shooting them all before turning the gun on myself.

I have just discovered Nurse Alex isn't coming back to work here. She has some holidays to use up. She has taken them now rather than work until next week. How am I supposed to feel about that? I can't believe that she has simply left without saying goodbye. I am hurt and upset. The last thing she said to me was that I should start to help myself. She knew she wasn't going to see me again. That's why she was being so tough on me. I am numb with shock on hearing this news.

I have grown fond of Nurse Alex. She has been lovely. While I have been in hospital she has put up with my mood swings, my irrational behaviour and tolerated my deviance. She has reprimanded me, threatened me, been there for me just like Aunty Lindsay had been, and now she is gone as well. I am going to cry, I am so upset. Alex, I am so sorry. You were right, I have to start helping myself. I am sorry, I am sorry, forgive me. Please forgive me, oh God, Alex has gone. The last thing she did was hug me, and then she went off duty, never to return. What I am I going to do now she has gone? Life is so cruel. Oh God, I am so distressed, what do I do? I can't breathe. I want to die. Please God take me, I don't want to live. My heart is breaking. I cannot stand this pain. Alex, please come back. Don't leave me here. I need you. I need you so much.

I have wandered around the hospital grounds in a daze. I just can't think straight. I know Nurse Alex was concerned that I was becoming too dependent on her, but I had backed off when I knew she was leaving. I have bared my soul to Nurse Alex and she has gone. I don't deserve this. It's bloody horrible. Did she care or was I just a job to her, another patient – not just any patient – but a mental patient? That will be a stigma I will carry with me for the rest of my life, just like my mother did after her time in a mental hospital.

The regime here has been as regimented as it was in the children's home. The only difference is I am not a child any more and have rebelled against it. To be honest, I have found the group sessions difficult and have not always been as open with the shrink about my past as I could have been. I have not shared with him the issues that I have struggled with. I don't want the shrink or anyone else thinking I am weird or kinky.

I should tell the shrink about my childhood abuse but he won't believe me. I have focused so much on Aunty Lindsay, rather than talking about the abuse I suffered as a child, that if I start talking about it now, he will think I am looking for sympathy.

The drugs I have been on have not worked. They have not cured my depression, just suppressed my emotions and made feel detached. That's why the shrink keeps talking about shock treatment. I don't want electric treatment. I have walked through the ward after people have had that done. It's not a pleasant sight; all of them lined up on beds in a row, still with the rubber bit in their mouths to stop them biting their tongue. My sister has not given her consent for shock treatment, but if I try to commit suicide again they will do it without her consent.

It's been a distressing day. I have tried to sleep for much of it, curled up on my bed. I haven't had much of an appetite. I have just picked at my food. I miss Nurse Alex. I wish she had come and said goodbye before leaving. I don't know what I am going to do without Alex around to talk to. I am going to go to sleep now and hope I never wake up.

19th October 1980

Nurse Alex has gone. I am distraught, depressed and heartbroken, but I must conform or I am out according to Miriam. I have spoken to Dennis, the male nurse, and he says it's not up to her to say when I am discharged – the doctor will make that decision. The dark-haired petite nurse has said she has taken over from Nurse Alex as the senior student nurse and that if I have any issues I should talk to her about them. She can go to hell. I don't trust any of them. She is only the same age as me and she threatened me a few weeks ago. From now on, I am talking to no one. Whatever dark secrets have been unlocked while I have been in this place will remain secret. I will take them to my grave before I trust anyone enough to reveal them. It's too risky. I don't trust anyone any more; to hell with every single one of them.

A new girl has come to our ward. Her name is Shannon. She is very nice and the same age as me. She is small and dainty with curly auburn hair and a lovely soft, sexy Irish accent. I think she likes me. Norman from the next ward started crying during group discussions, as tomorrow will be a year since he lost his son. I feel sorry for him, as he hates his own sense of helplessness. He cries all the time. Then we started talking about death and one of the patients said, 'I think we should make the best of this world and thank God we're still alive!' God again! Why the hell should I thank God for being alive? Living sucks! Someone then said that it doesn't matter if you're discharged from a mental hospital because the people outside still think you are mental. Then, the religious nut from the next ward agreed and said the smell in the hospital was awful, and she was going outside to breathe in God's clean air. I sat there shaking my head, wondering what the hell I was doing here.

I have become more depressed since they reduced my medication. These group sessions become dafter every week. I couldn't help but notice Shannon staring at me and doing things with her hair all the way through the session. I think she was flirting with me! Maybe she's impressed with my red belt that I wear hanging down in front of my jeans. At least I am fashionable, not like some of these squares.

My future is bleak. I can't see from one day to another. I really do wish I could go to sleep and never wake up. The doctor has spoken to me about being discharged into the care of the local psychiatric nurse and becoming a day patient. They have kept me drugged up for weeks, threatened me with electric treatment, sedated me when I have got out of hand, and now they talk about kicking me out. I don't want to live in a hostel any more. George told me that the hostel is a doss house. It's all very scary and rather worrying. What's going to happen to me? I am really scared and feel so alone.

20th October 1980

With the number of student nurses being reduced, no one noticed, or maybe they didn't care that I left the hospital grounds and went back to the railway bridge. Now I am sat here on this bridge with my feet dangling over, looking down at the track. How often I have been here just contemplating jumping into the path of a train. Why did I chicken out last time? If I had only had the courage to stand my ground, my pain, my torment would have been over in a second, a lot quicker than death by an overdose, which I now know can be slow and painful. Voices in my head are telling me to jump. I can't jump now. I would only succeed in breaking my leg. I have to wait for a train. I am sat here writing in this bloody book, contemplating taking my life. It's surreal. I can hear a train approaching. I can see it.

My head is in bits! I can't think straight. I hardly slept last night. I didn't take the sleeping tablets they gave me. It feels like, once again, I am being abandoned because I have become too much trouble. No one knows what to do with me in here any more. I remember my last night in the children's home. I was packing my case to go on holiday to my sister's. I will never forget that evening. The superintendent sat me on the bed, held my hand and then told me that it would be in everyone's best interests if I didn't come back from Chester. With tears running down my face and numb with shock, I begged her not to do this to me. I was in a state of panic and now I am in a state of panic again. I am to be discharged from hospital once I have finished my domestic training. Nothing's changed. I am still hurting, still depressed, and still suicidal. The shrink said that there is nothing more they can do for me and, to put it bluntly, he told me that they needed my bed. I am not even going to be a day patient. The community psychiatric nurse is to be responsible for me once I am discharged. I am hurting, I am emotional, I am frightened.

That train could end my pain and show all those bastards. There are so many mixed-up crazy thoughts going through my mind. I am crying so much I can hardly see to write. I'm shaking. No one will be able to read my writing. Oh, how I want to jump to end this bloody horrible life of mine. I am 19 years old, I hate my life, and I can see no future whatsoever. Why do I keep doing this? What am I trying to achieve? I am a coward. I tried, but chickened out again. With my legs dangling over the bridge, I leaned forward as the train approached and caught my legs against the stone brickwork. I felt myself slipping. I cried out to God to help me and a wave of terror came over me as I heard the train draw closer. As it passed under me, I managed to grasp hold of the top and hurl myself up from the edge back onto the top of the bridge. Hell, I am scared! I almost did it. If my leg hadn't got caught I would be dead now.

When I got back to the ward I shared with Shannon what I had done. She took me in her arms to hold me and kissed me on the forehead. My head rested on her breasts as she held me. It felt good. The unexpected happened. Shannon moved down from kissing my forehead and put her lips to my lips and started to kiss me. I couldn't believe it. I still can't believe it. The kiss turned into a full-blown snog. I have never been kissed like this before. It was a new and pleasurable experience. She started to touch me and I felt so aroused that I got carried away myself. We were interrupted by Nurse Rachel who told us that our behaviour was inappropriate. She sent Shannon back to her ward and reprimanded me. I am confused as to why Shannon did what she did. Does she fancy me or is it because she is a nymphomaniac? I have been told that she is an 'alcoholic, nymphomaniac, manic-depressive' by the nurse. I have been warned to keep away from her for my own good. I don't think she is going to be here long. She is being transferred to the alcoholic unit, an old army barracks a few miles down the road. If she is transferred I am going to go and see her. I didn't even know what a nymphomaniac was. I have had to look the word up in a dictionary.

News travels fast in this hospital. It seems like everyone knows about the kissing. George says he has known Shannon for years and that she has always been a man-eater, very mature for her age, even at 13. He further added that she keeps a white wedding dress in her trunk. So now I am the butt of everyone's jokes. They are saying I am Shannon's toy boy, because she is well into her thirties and I am only 19. I had enjoyed the kiss and the fondling. It made me forget all about the train and being discharged.

21st October 1980

I was surprised yesterday when a Methodist minister came to see me. Peter had asked him to visit me. He was nice, sympathetic, and caring. He laughed when I told him that four of us kids from the home had been asked to leave the Methodist church because we were disruptive. He asked me if I had been upset about that. I told him, 'Not really.' It meant that I got to go to the Baptist church and join the Boys' Brigade. When he left, he said that he would remember me in his prayers and suggested that I prayed. I don't know about all this God stuff. I haven't been to church since I left the children's home, and I only kept going then because Aunty Lindsay went to the same Baptist church. Peter's minister was alright. He has got me thinking about God again. I am not really sure if God exists or not, but I think I'll write Him a prayer just in case.

I have decided to write a prayer: *'Dear God, I don't know if you are real or not, but if you are, then please listen to me. I am totally and utterly depressed and desperate. I cry night and day, but my tears go unnoticed. I feel so lonely. Life sucks and I hate myself, and I hate all those people who have caused me so much pain. I am sorry God, but sometimes I want to kill them. I know that it is wrong and I am not proud of how I feel. I love Lindsay so much, but she ignores my cries for help. Some days, I find myself hating her. I have never felt such pain before. Some days, I would give anything for it to stop. I cannot think straight. I cannot function. I just exist in this horrible place, hoping that things will change, that I will start to feel different. I feel that it would be better to die than to continue to live with the pain I feel. I have tried to take my life but have been unsuccessful, and now I feel too afraid to try again. I have cried and yelled out to you, oh God, but if you do exist, why do you remain silent. WHY? My sister Shene does her best but I am unable to respond to her love. I am so wrapped up in myself. I cannot see past my own self-imposed isolation. What can I do? I have failed and thrown everything away. Oh God, if you're listening, give me hope. Give me a future. I don't know what to do any more. Help me. I beg you, help me! Someone help me please!'*

I rang the Samaritans, but they didn't want to get involved once they discovered I was a mental health patient. Instead they suggested I talk to the doctor about my depression and suicidal thoughts. It feels like I am beyond help. Even the Samaritans don't want to know.

The ward sister has been showing a new student nurse around the ward. She said hello to me as she walked past. I nodded my head but didn't say anything. I went over to the hospital gym where I met two new nurses working with the gymnast – a young girl called Jackie and a male nurse called Derek who's a homosexual. He is a bit on the funny side, but he seemed nice enough, so who cares what he is.

Went to the OT room, took my duck's head off and re-glued it. Still unable to finish it properly, with no chisels. I have had to saw it and sand it. An OT nurse has just asked me to make a list of things I need to buy for lunch for domestic training. I ignored her and continued sanding my duck. She came back after ten minutes and told me again to make a list. I told her that I knew what I wanted without making a bloody shopping list. She told me to watch my language or she would wash my mouth out with soap and water. I think she was serious too! They used to do that in the children's home if you used bad language, or slipper you, as Aunty Freda did when she heard me say 'Shut the bloody bedroom door.'

This afternoon Miriam told me to go with a young lady in a white coat, who would be supervising my domestic training. I thought she was a doctor so I didn't say anything to her. I just dutifully followed her. Once outside she spoke to me. She asked me if I recognised her. I told her I didn't. Then she reminded me that she had met me at the general hospital after I had cut my wrists. She seemed nice so I chatted to her. It turns out that she is a trainee occupational therapy nurse. She told me that she suffers from depression herself and that she couldn't stand Miriam either. We got on well. It was nice being with her as she helped me cook my lunch. I was sorry she had to go after dinner. She told me that she was only on placement as part of her training, hence the white coat. Before she left, she kissed me on the cheek and wished me a speedy recovery.

22nd October 1980

I started my domestic training today. I had to go into town on the bus with a nurse to buy some food to cook. Miriam stood over me in the little kitchen and didn't miss the opportunity to taunt me and remind me that they would be discharging me, as soon as I had found somewhere to live. With a parting remark, she said that once I was discharged it wouldn't be long before I was back because my sort, she said, always came back, unless I killed myself first. I lost my appetite and couldn't eat what I had made. I scraped the chips and burgers into the bin and sat for ages just resting my head on my hands, looking out of the window across the fields.

More bad news – I have been sacked from my job at the menswear shop. The area manager came today with the new manager. They felt that I could no longer work with the public because I had been in this mental hospital. I didn't say anything. I was too desolate. I just sat staring into space. I didn't even notice that they had gone until someone tapped me on my shoulder to inform me that the pills were being given out. What's the use of trying? Everything is against me, no job, no home, no qualifications, no Aunty Lindsay, no hope. I am a lost soul. I have spoken to student nurse Rachel about how I feel.

She was disgusted at how I was told that I had lost my job from the menswear shop by the area manager, after my old manager had kept it open for me. She said to come to the hospital and sack me was like something out of Victorian times. She suggested that I take them to an industrial tribunal. I might just do that.

I spent the evening just sitting and listening to records in the day room. Shannon came and joined me. It wasn't long before her hands and lips were all over me. I was quite relieved that she was asked to go back to her ward. She has told me that she is being moved down the road to Moston Hall, an old army barracks which is now a hospital, in a couple of days. I like Shannon, but I am pleased she is moving to another hospital. She worries me with her sexual appetite. I have been avoiding her for the last few days; well, avoiding being alone with her. My sister has arrived – I'd better go and see her.

I can't sleep so I will write until I feel tired. I have been thinking about my time in this hospital. It has not been a pleasant experience locked away, for the most part, from the outside world. It really does feel more like a prison than a hospital. Some patients are here instead of being in prison and I am put here with them – it's horrible. Apart from Sandy, who has left, there are not many people my own age. I am the youngest at 18 – well, 19 now. I was 18 when I came in.

I have to say most of the nurses are in their twenties and look quite young, apart from Miriam, who looks like an old witch. There are quite a few student nurses on this ward. Some of them are very pretty. Mind you, I have noticed that a uniform makes those who wear it act superior and bossy. It's like being back in the children's home on this ward. I am 19 and I am treated like a child most of the time, especially by the ward sister. I wonder what will become of me.

Shene has told me that my brother, Paul, is going to join the navy when he leaves the children's home next year. I wish I knew what my future was going to be. I don't suppose Aunty Lindsay is going to be part of it. It's been so long since I wrote to her. I don't know why she has not replied, but my heart is broken thinking that she has abandoned me. I think my letter has frightened her off and who can blame her? Donny Osmond's song, *Puppy Love*, describes exactly how I feel. My tears have all been in vain and no one will ever know how a young heart really feels. I am emotionally exhausted. I must accept that Aunty Lindsay, like Lindsay Wagner, was only a fantasy, nothing more.

They are going to kick me out of here because they can no longer help me, and they told me they need my bed. At the same time, I am told that I will be back, because my type always does. What does that mean? My type? I have discovered over these last few weeks that there is very little sympathy for a teenager in love who has tried to take his own life.

My sister has been informed of the hospital's decision and she is upset and unhappy. She had a row with the ward sister, saying that she was worried about my safety. Even Lincolnshire Social Services don't want to know. My sister has had a flaming row with them on the phone.

Shene has demanded to know from the social services what happened in the children's' home between the house parent and me. They would not comment on what they considered was the inappropriate behaviour of a teenager in their care. They told my sister that Aunty Lindsay had not encouraged me in my affections and had acted professionally. They told her mistakes had been made and new policies were in place to ensure it didn't happen again. They hoped I would soon recover and wished me well. Briefly, they spoke about Paul to Shene and informed her that he would be going to live with my other sister, Jenny, in Boston for a short while, before he goes into the navy. I think she was disgusted with their attitude. She had expected more support from them.

Shene mentioned to me the possibility of going back to live with her when I am discharged, rather than live in a doss house. I have spoken to my brother-in-law, Graham. They would be more than happy to have me come back and live with them. I feel that it is very nice of them, considering the problems I have caused over these last few months. I am feeling tired now. I will stop writing in a minute. I told Shene that Aunty Lindsay had no idea that I had fallen in love with her. She thought it was just a teenage crush. I wanted my sister to know that Aunty Lindsay didn't encourage me at all in my affections. It was my fault – I manipulated her. I am tired now. I can't write any more.

23rd October 1980

The day I have been living for, but dreading, happened today. Shene came to see me. When she said that she had had a letter from Aunty Lindsay, I froze and just stared at her. I couldn't speak. My heart was pounding and my legs felt like jelly. I have been waiting for over a month for her reply to my letter. I had begged my sister to write to her and now all I could do was stare at the white envelope Shene was holding in her hands. She handed me the letter. I sat down. Shene left me to go and get a coffee whilst I opened it. I was shaking. Aunty Lindsay hadn't let me down, I thought. However, as I started to read it, my heart sank. Aunty Lindsay started saying how sorry she had been to hear that I was in hospital.

She then went on to talk about her husband and how they were looking forward to a new baby. It was all general chit-chat. She said nothing in response to my letter to her. I could not believe it. I had poured out my innermost feelings to her on paper, made myself vulnerable, shared my love, my pain and now she replied with chit-chat. What could I do, but just sit there in disbelief and shock.

Shene returned moments later with a cup of coffee. I showed her the letter. She just held my hand and tried to comfort me. I asked my sister if she also had received a letter from Aunty Lindsay. I could tell by her hesitance that she had. She had left it at home, but nothing could have prepared me for what she told me. I still can't believe it.

Aunty Lindsay had been disturbed and alarmed to hear that I was in a psychiatric hospital and had phoned the hospital wanting to speak to me, but they wouldn't let her. The one person who could give me reassurance and hope, and now my sister has told me that Aunty Lindsay had phoned the hospital wanting to speak to me. I would have heard her voice for the first time in two years. What a difference that would have made. For my Aunty Lindsay to have spoken to me lovingly and reassuringly, and even firmly, would have made all the difference to me. And what does the hospital say to this person on the phone, the one person in the whole wide world that I want to hear from, speak to? They told her that I was very ill and that it wouldn't be in my best interests for her to speak to me. It was the day after I had taken the overdose that Aunty Lindsay had phoned.

When my sister told me that, I was horrified and very angry. I wanted to scream! I stood up from my chair so abruptly that I sent it crashing to the floor. Grabbing the table, I was about to tip it over, but she grasped my hand and begged me not to kick off. She said that they would only sedate me again. She picked the chair up and got me sat down again. I flopped, exhausted, back on to the chair. I was beaten. You cannot fight the system. They win every time. How can you fight the system? Once I was calm, Shene went and spoke to the ward sister.

The ward sister would only say that it was a joint decision by the whole of the medical staff responsible for my wellbeing. They felt that I needed to identify the root cause of my attachment to the house parent and that any contact she made with me would prevent me from doing that. It was a risk, she told me, but a risk they felt was worth taking, because they didn't think I was serious about taking my own life. They admit now that this was probably a wrong decision based upon the overdose and the train incident, which Nurse Alex had reported. Shene told me that they still think it would be better to continue my treatment on the outside, because they feel that I have become institutionalised and that isn't aiding my recovery. So what now? Who cares?

24th October 1980

After my sister left yesterday, I wandered around in a daze. I was fuming. Just to have spoken to Aunty Lindsay would have made all the difference. It would have given me hope. Or would it? I don't know. I am so mixed up. I cannot think clearly. It was difficult sleeping last night, so many things going on in my mind. Haunting images from my past dominated my thoughts. Every time I closed my eyes I saw Aunty Lindsay, I saw the children's home. I imagined myself back there – the sights, the sounds, the smells seemed so real. Maybe it's because I so desperately wanted to be back there. I replayed in my mind events leading up to my brother Paul and me going to Ivy Cottage.

I tried to shut the thoughts out, but they were too powerful. Sweat was pouring off my forehead as I tossed and turned. Why were we snatched from school one afternoon by social services? Without warning, suddenly to be taken from a foster home that for two years had become the only stable home we had ever known, seemed cruel and heartless. I wept as I remembered Mr and Mrs Tait, our foster parents. What had become of them? My lasting image of Mrs Tait was her seeing us onto the school bus. What a lovely spring morning that was. Paul and I were so looking forward to the scouts' football match that evening. Everything appeared normal. We had no idea as we sat on that bus that morning that, by evening, our world would be torn apart and we would never see our foster mum and dad again. God knows. Why? Why? What had we done to deserve this?

As I recall my thoughts from last night, it's hard not to want to scream and yell and kick off. I simply cannot get these images from my past out of my mind. Some would accuse me of wallowing in the past. I could not argue with them. I am wallowing because I don't know how to move forward. I don't know how to let go. I am scared, vulnerable, weak and helpless.

I couldn't lie in my sweat. I had to get up and wander into the day room. There were no nurses around; well, not in the day room. I saw the glimmer of light coming from the office, but no one noticed me standing at the window looking up into the night sky. I don't know how long I stood there. Silently I prayed, which surprised me. All I could do was ask God to help me move forward with my life and to deal with the pain I was feeling. I don't know if God is real or not. It seems so long ago since I was last in church. I used to love going to church with Aunty Lindsay. Just looking at her as she sang made my stomach churn. Walking back with her from the evening service, well, was just out of this world. She never looked as lovely as when she wore her woollen hat with her long hair dangling down. Damn, why did they treat me so unsympathetically? Couldn't they see that I was in love and hurting?

I drifted back to my ward and again just closed my eyes trying to sleep. I wondered how long I had before they would throw me out of this hospital. What would I do then?

25th October 1980

I am sat in the day room trying to make sense of my feelings. No one bothers much about me these days. Nurse Rachel is friendly but doesn't make any effort to talk or engage me in conversation. It's as if I am just being left alone now. I get the feeling that they have decided I am not worth bothering about because I am soon to be discharged. The nurses don't say anything about me lying on the bed these days. As long as I go to OT for domestic training they are happy enough to leave me to wander around the grounds.

My weekly visit to the shrink doesn't last more than ten minutes now. I am less drugged up these days and, as a result, I am becoming more aware of my environment, and realising just how horrible my ward is. It looks and feels like something out of a Charles Dickens story. I am still depressed, though. The wounds on my wrist have healed nicely. I can still see the scars though, a reminder of my suicide attempt while I was drunk.

We had a ward meeting today, which was unusual for a Saturday, so I knew something was going on. I was right – the ward is closing for refurbishment. It doesn't affect me, though. I am being discharged at the end of the month into the care of the 'care in the community' psychiatric nurse. Some of the other patients are upset that they are having to move to other wards and are creating a right noise about it.

I returned to my ward and lay on the bed for a while. I had been looking up at my poster of Lindsay Wagner, just imagining what she might say to me, and then she spoke. It wasn't the comforting words I had hoped for. She scolded me, reminding me that a lot of people cared for and loved me and that I had a lot to live for. It was all in my imagination of course but, nonetheless, real. I didn't like being told off by my hero and tried to shut her voice out of my head, but the more I tried the angrier she became, until she was shouting at me. I shouted at her to leave me alone, telling her that she was just like everyone else. I stared at her poster and it seemed to come alive. She was moving towards me, hands on her hips, leaning over me, still scolding me. I recognised the scene from an episode of *The Bionic Woman* where she was threatening a troubled young girl she was looking after, but in my mind, I had replaced the young girl. I closed my eyes and covered my ears, shouting at her to leave me alone and go away.

Someone shaking me brought me back to reality. It was the ward sister. It was the first time that my fantasy had taken a sinister turn. I was relieved to be shaken out of it. I looked up at the poster of the *Bionic Woman* looking down at me, her smile warm, friendly and comforting again. We had nearly come to blows and perhaps in my fantasy, like with Aunty Lindsay, that is what I had longed for, hoping someone would love me enough to discipline me.

I have been walking around the fields most of the afternoon. It has been wet and windy. I am drenched and shaking with cold. I only had a zipped casual jacket on. I didn't care, though. I hoped I would catch pneumonia. I sat down under a tree, took out Aunty Lindsay's letter and re-read it. I was hurting, reading her words that didn't offer me any hope or reassurance. I screwed up the letter and threw it away.

The wind took it. I sat there for ages. The tree offered little shelter. My face was dripping wet with the rain, merging with my tears. I felt so alone, sat under that tree trying to shelter from the rain.

I am back on the ward but still no warmer. At one time I wouldn't have been allowed out of the hospital grounds without an escort, but these days no one notices when I slip away. Shene thinks I am worse now than I was before I came into the hospital, as a result of them digging into the abuses of my childhood. To be honest, I have been reluctant to go into detail about the abuse I have suffered. The doctor asks, but I avoid answering his questions. It's too embarrassing and painful.

I have returned from my wandering in the country, wet, sick and dizzy. I have struggled to stay in control. I feel like a time bomb is ticking away. I have lined up for my tablets. I don't take as many as I used to, just enough to take the edge off my depression and keep me calm. I am shivering so I have climbed into bed and pulled up the covers. A nurse has just asked me if I am okay. I just said, 'I don't feel well' and she seems satisfied with that. Hell! I am shivering. That's nice! The nurse has just brought me a hot drink. So they do care! Well, she does. One ring around her hat – first-year student. It won't be long before she becomes just as hard and detached as all the others. That's one thing I have noticed in this bloody place. The first-year students do seem more caring, more touchy-feely than those who have three rings, or fully qualified nurses with no rings. The male nurses wear grey suits with name badges and look like prison wardens.

To tell you the truth, I have not shown much interest in the male nurses. Who cares what they are? I much prefer the female nurses. Most of the students are stunners. If I was a normal 19-year-old, perhaps I could see myself dating one of them. But then, I am not normal. Well, at least I don't feel like a normal teenager. I have never had a girlfriend and the only kiss I have had was off Shannon, the alcoholic, manic-depressive nymphomaniac, who wouldn't leave me alone. Thank God she has gone to Moston Hall.

I sat up in bed with my hands around the hot drink, grateful for it after shivering in my bed. I am tired and feeling unwell. I am going to go to sleep.

26th October 1980

I sat in the doctor's office waiting for him to return. While he was away I had a look at my notes which had been left open on his desk. I don't understand what he has written, but he mentioned sexual issues and fantasy a lot. He has written that my emotional difficulties are caused by maternal deprivation, which had disrupted normal personality development. It's all mumbo jumbo to me. He also wrote something about sexual immaturity and delayed puberty. I don't understand a bloody word. I must record it in my diary before he returns.

'I understand that Mark's only psychiatric history is of a breakdown in the Spring of 1978 while he was a resident of Ivy Cottage Children's Home in Spalding, Lincolnshire. Mark developed an inappropriate relationship with a house parent. This was pure fantasy on Mark's part. The speed at which this developed caused some concern with social services. The children's home did their best to address the problem, believing it to be nothing more than a teenage crush. The situation was judged to have become serious after Mark tried to cut his wrists with a scalpel blade, which he had taken from school. The written record shows the house parent put herself at risk to disarm him, which resulted in Mark receiving a serious cut to his thumb which needed hospital treatment. Soon after this Mark went on hunger strike, forcing social services to act for the good of the children's home. It was decided by Lincolnshire Social Services that it would be better for Mark to leave the children's home sooner rather than later. It was while Mark was a patient at this hospital that he wrote to this house parent in the hope that she would respond to his cry for help. The records show that she phoned the ward soon after she received Mark's letter. She was advised by the ward sister that it would not be in his or her best interests to talk to Mark in his present fragile state.

My impression of Mark is that he is suffering from clinical depression.

He has not responded well to treatment. We would have considered electric treatment but his sister was against that course of action. Mark was kept sedated to keep him calm and to prevent him injuring himself. Mark's fantasy relationship with his house parent has remained a controlling influence over his life since he left local authority care in 1978. It's a fantasy that he has been unable or reluctant to let go of. This has prevented normal adolescent development from taking place. Mark is now aged 19, but his behaviour while a patient in this hospital has been consistent with that of a rather naughty, if not rebellious, stubborn, sullen 13-year-old.'

I am not writing the rest – it's embarrassing. They are just talking about my overdose, even my attachment to Nurse Alex, and saying that I wanted to be disciplined by her. It's not nice reading this. They are saying that I have become institutionalised and that they cannot do anything more for me. The rest is background information about my mother, father, sisters and brother, etc. Hold on, what's this last paragraph saying? I must be quick, otherwise I'll get found out.

I almost got caught. I just managed to read a bit more before the doc returned. I don't know how I feel about reading about myself. It does make me feel rather uncomfortable and angry reading what Shene had already told me, that Aunty Lindsay had phoned the ward wanting to speak to me and they wouldn't let her. Bastards!!! I bet my notes from social services would make interesting reading but, then, I am never likely to see them.

Spent the afternoon in OT. Almost finished that stupid duck. It has taken me ages without chisels. The ward is almost empty, with most of the patients transferred to the temporary ward. Nothing feels the same any more. I am frightened of what life is going to be like once I am discharged.

I have noticed that George and Jack seem to be getting on better together. I am still wary of Jack, but not scared of him. He tries to make conversation, but I am just not in the mood these days. I keep myself to myself, spending most of my time lying on my bed or wandering around the hospital grounds. I am just waiting to be told when I am being kicked out. Shene is redecorating my bedroom, ready for when I return home. I will have to share with my nephew until I eventually find somewhere to live.

27th October 1980

The days seem long and pointless at the moment. No one has yet made a decision as to when I am being discharged. I wish they would make a decision one way or the other. It's not a very nice feeling, not knowing what they are going to do with me. Shene wants them to transfer me with the others to the smaller unit. She isn't convinced that I am stable enough to be discharged just yet. I am not sure I am either, but that doesn't matter to them. Once I leave here, I won't be given a second thought. Within a day I will be forgotten. The ward has become spartan, even the furniture is being moved. Talk about desolate. The ward looks like how I feel. Ever since I heard from Aunty Lindsay, I have just closed down completely, emotionally, as far as she is concerned. It's strange how I have gone from being completely obsessed with hearing from her, even my very life hanging in the balance, to feeling indifferent. I love her and when I think of her it hurts, but I don't have the desire any more to want to hear from her. She has gone from being all that was good, to all that is bad. It's that love-hate thing again.

Her letter was such a rebuff after I revealed the depth of my innermost feelings for her. To have not acknowledged anything I had said, I don't understand. It's not Aunty Lindsay's fault. The doctor's report is right; she was just someone who I could pin all my feelings of rejection on.

I had a rare conversation with Nurse Rachel today – I say rare, because we haven't really spoken much recently. She came and sat down by me in the almost derelict ward. She asked how I felt about being discharged. I told her that I was scared. She understood and said that it was only natural to feel apprehensive after being in hospital for so long.

I shared with her about Aunty Lindsay and her letter to me, and about the hospital not allowing me to speak to her when she phoned the ward. She seemed a bit taken aback by that, but didn't comment. Then she said something which made me think, and reinforced what I had read in the doctor's notes. She said that Aunty Lindsay probably only brought to the surface feelings that would have appeared, one way or another, as I grew up. Nurse Rachel added that the need for a loving and supportive relationship is such a basic human need, that anyone who had shown me care would have filled that gap. I was a little embarrassed when she mentioned Nurse Alex as an example. She told me that sister had reminded the nurses about getting too involved with their patients and cited me as an example of a vulnerable person, who would latch on to anyone who showed affection. I asked her why she was sat talking to me then. She thumped me on the shoulder and told me not to be silly and that no one had been told not to talk to me, just to not get too involved.

She told me she was moving to another hospital soon and didn't really care whether or not she was seen talking to me. Another time, another place, perhaps we could have been friends. She wished me well and went off duty, and that was that. It was nice talking to her and she had given me food for thought. No, I couldn't blame Aunty Lindsay. It wasn't fair to pin all my pain on her. That doesn't mean to say I am not deeply hurt by her inaction, it's just that I am trying to understand why she didn't acknowledge my feelings. I wonder if I will ever see or hear from Aunty Lindsay again. I do love her so much, despite the feeling of anger towards her at this moment.

It's been a boring day. Apart from my brief conversation with Nurse Rachel and yet another wander around the hospital grounds, I haven't done much. Shene came to see me this evening and told me that my bedroom is nicely decorated, just in case they kick me out sooner rather than later. After she left, I just lay on my bed feeling depressed and sick in my stomach again. With few patients left on this ward it's becoming very lonely. A skeleton staff look after the few that remain.

28th October 1980

Tonight, I went to see Shannon at the hospital down the road. I know it was risky but I thought 'what the hell!' She had been nice to me while she was on the ward and, despite her sexual advances towards me, at least she had given me my first snog. She hates it at Moston Hall. She is very depressed. I thought this Victorian workhouse was bad enough, but hers is even worse, an old broken-down army barracks. We sat and spoke until half past seven. It was when I put my arms around her to comfort her that she hugged me so tight that I thought I was going to burst. I could hardly breathe. I had to prise myself away from her. She is really a nice girl but she scares the hell out of me.

When I got back to the ward, the doors were locked. So I climbed through the same window Sandy and I had climbed out of, the night we went for a walk around the grounds. It had broken again, but with the ward deteriorating on a daily basis, broken windows had not got fixed.

I am losing the will to write. Having recorded so much, there doesn't seem any point now. Everything is coming to an end, even this diary. I wonder how I will feel in years to come, reading back these entries. Will I be any different? Maybe I won't even be alive and someone else will be reading it.

This morning I cooked an apple pie and a few scones in the occupational therapy room. I was quite pleased with the way they turned out. In the afternoon, I visited my old workplace, Foster Menswear. No one wanted to talk to me. They have been told that I have been sacked. They were too embarrassed or ashamed after writing so many negative things about me to the area manager, which justified him sacking me while I was in hospital. They all questioned my mental state prior to being admitted to hospital. It had been good of my old manager, Mr Beddows, to have kept my job open for me when I initially came into hospital. He had always shown me kindness and understanding. The new manager and area manager are bastards. How heartless, sacking me while I was still in hospital and coming to the ward to do it.

If he hadn't retired or been asked to retire, I would have a job to go back to. Now these people who I have worked with for two years don't want to know me. The stigma of being in a mental hospital will follow me around. I'll be lucky to get another job. No one is going to want to employ me after being in a mental hospital. Not only that, I don't have any qualifications, I don't think CSE Art grade 1 will count for much. Thick and mental, what hope do I have? A love-sick teenager whose efforts to take his own life ended in failure. I couldn't even do that right. Some would say I have made my bed, now I have to lie in it. And so, here ends another day. I am going home in a few days – I have just been informed by the ward sister, just the paperwork to sort out. I am so scared of the outside world. At least in here, I have felt safe, secure, and protected, even if it is horrible. I think they are right. I have become institutionalised, just like so many in this place have.

29th October 1980

I am sat in the day room thinking and writing, wondering what my time in this place has achieved. Nothing – and now I am to be thrown out. It's obvious to all that I am still very depressed. I had at least hoped for some counselling while I was in this place. I don't feel any further forward than I did when I was first admitted. What was the point of it all? I wish I knew. I wish someone would explain it to me. I have nothing to look forward to. Most teenagers of my age are either in jobs or at university. I really don't know what is going to become of me. My future seems blacker now than it did. What will people say when they find out that I have been in a mental hospital? I have no qualifications, no job, no hope.

I looked back on my school days and realised that, having been to so many different schools, my education was hit and miss. How can I forget old Ma Barker at Gleed Boys Secondary Modern in Spalding? I laugh when I remember having to go to her special needs classes when I first went to secondary school. I could barely read then. She made my life hell when it came to doing joined-up writing. I told her that I didn't like doing joined-up writing. That four-foot nothing of a woman rose to her feet, almost doubling in size, and bellowed that she didn't like teaching me and made me join up my letters. It's funny now, but at the time it wasn't.

Must go, a nurse has told me that I have to go to OT to complete my domestic training. I am being discharged in two days. I have resigned myself to the inevitable, no point in fighting it. At least Shene and Graham have agreed to take me back, which was nice of them, after what I have put them through.

Occupational therapy was a waste of bloody time today. I didn't do much, no cooking anyway, just sat around, chatting and drinking coffee. Miriam made a snide remark about them throwing me out. 'And about time!' she said. I didn't retaliate. I just ignored the fat cow. I won't be sorry to see the back of her. She has made my life a misery whilst I have been here. How do people like that end up working with the vulnerable? I hate her.

Five patients left on the ward now – the others have moved, women to another ward and men to the smaller unit.

30th October 1980

I had a longer session with the shrink today, because it's my last. He wanted to know how I felt about my time in here. I told him that I didn't think anything had been resolved. I am still depressed, not so suicidal, but still depressed. He felt that was progress. I didn't. In order to want to die, you have to be alive. I don't feel alive. I feel dead and empty within. I have just given up even wanting to die because I am dead already. Inwardly, there is nothing.

I stare vacantly into space wishing that I was somewhere else in time, anywhere but here. The doctor told me that the community psychiatric nurse will be writing to me to arrange an outpatient appointment within the next few weeks. Meanwhile, I am to continue on the anti-depressants and sleeping tablets. I nodded but didn't really say much. What could I say? When you're beaten, you're beaten. You wave the white flag and surrender to your fate, whatever that may be. I don't have any fight left in me. I have retreated into myself and I am going to build a wall around my emotions, and no one is going to penetrate it.

The doctor has spent a lot of time scribbling in his notes again. We covered a lot of old ground. I didn't respond. I shrugged my shoulders once or twice. He didn't notice. He was too busy humming and writing. Just as well – I don't think he would have appreciated the faces I was pulling. He spoke about the failure of normal personality development, which will affect all my relationships. He was just reading what I had already read.

He said that I would need to keep working at the implications of such a difficult start in life. He warned me about forming attachments to perceived authority figures, particularly females. I switched off at that point. I knew that what he was saying was true, but what can I do? I need someone to love me. I have this need and I know that anyone, particularly a female who shows me affection, I will latch on to and even fall in love with. I know that's why I fell in love with Lindsay. I know that. But just knowing that doesn't help me deal with the pain I am feeling. Oh God, how can I change? How can I be different? The doctor is right. I am flawed, damaged, probably damaged beyond repair. He has told me what the problem is, but what is the solution? God! I wish I knew. Bloody hell. Damn! Damn! Damn! Is it so wrong to want to be loved? It seems like I have always been a problem. I was a problem at the home, a problem that got out of hand, and that's why they sent me away.

There are times when I even blame myself for my brother and me being pushed from pillar to post by social services. Maybe if I had been more loveable someone, somewhere, would have wanted us. We were rejected by our parents and rejected by foster parents. Who the hell wants damaged goods? This bloody teddy of mine was also thrown on the rubbish heap, that's why I rescued it. Well, someone rescued it for me. But it reminds me of myself. I wonder what it would have been like to have two parents who loved you and wanted you. What would it have been like to have been hugged as a child, to have had a story read to you, to have been tucked up in bed at night with a kiss? Aunty Lindsay gave me a little of what I have always wanted: affection, warmth, love, even discipline.

Who would have thought that to be deprived of those basic human needs would have resulted in my having a mental breakdown? My parents, social services, they all have a lot to answer for. But they don't care. My mum and dad, neither of them have written, phoned or been in touch since I came into this hospital. Why do I allow it to hurt me so much? They have never bothered. My sisters have. Maxine even made a mercy dash all the way from Boston, but they haven't.

31st October 1980

I am sat in an empty ward waiting for my sister to come with a taxi to take me home. This place is now void of activity. The rest of the patients were transferred this morning. It's strange. I sit here alone with just a couple of nurses in the office. It's bleak. How I remember the busy-ness of this ward when I was first admitted. I was so scared then, wondering what I had done, scared of this place, the stories I had heard about it. I can't say I have enjoyed being in here, because I haven't. But it has given me refuge from the world and allowed me time to think. I have liked the banter between some of the patients, even the crazy ones. There was some comfort in being with them. It's only these last few weeks, though, since they reduced my medication, that I have become more aware of things and become more thoughtful. For the most part I was kept sedated, for my own good, apparently.

I lived in fear of having my brain fried, having witnessed other patients having it done. Then my greatest fear was realised. Aunty Lindsay, for whatever reason, didn't respond to my letter in the way I wanted, despite my pouring my heart out and declaring my love for her. She declined to comment. I will never know what she felt on receiving it. I had wanted to die, and the images of my standing on that railway track continue to haunt me and cause me to break out into a sweat every time I relive that event. What was I thinking of, slashing my wrists and taking an overdose? I don't know. Did I really want to die, or was I crying out for help, for someone to take me seriously? Again I don't know. So it comes to this, all my feelings and emotions exposed with nowhere to go. What do I do with this pain? How do I switch it off? Shene's here, I have to go.

A female nurse wished me luck as I climbed into the taxi, and handed me my case. No one else was around to say goodbye. It felt very lonely. I didn't speak all the way home. I hung my head. Now, I am sat here in my box room at my sister's, feeling very depressed and suicidal. I can't prevent the tears from flowing. Shene has tried to comfort me. She has shown me the letter Aunty Lindsay wrote to her

Mark aged 16, taken with school camera.

153

and I have sobbed my heart out reading it. She hoped that I would get better and be able to come to terms with the fact she could never be anything more to me than a friend. I still love her and always will.

The new carpet replaces the old one. Shene couldn't get the bloodstains out from where I slashed my wrists. What now? What do I do? Where do I go? How do I pick up the pieces of my life? I have more questions than answers. To be honest, I can't see beyond my pain, it hurts so much. Maybe one day things will be different!

CHAPTER 9

LIFE IN A MENTAL INSTITUTION – A REFLECTION

My journey into the mental institution felt very sudden and traumatic. It wasn't like the drawn-out continual rejection and upheaval of my childhood. It was quick and dramatic. Seeing my sister cry as I was taken to hospital and sectioned under the Mental Health Act was deeply upsetting.

I have so many memories of being told to 'snap out' of my depression, but I was definitely astounded to hear it in a mental institution. It's quite amazing when you think about it. These were the people whose jobs were to look after mentally ill people! And yet still they would tell me to snap out of it, as though it could ever be that easy!

I appreciate that it must have been frustrating to look after me. I recognise that often I was a pain, and that some of my behaviour was not down to my depression, but my immaturity and my tendency to baulk at authority. I would be lying if I made out that I wasn't also a little bit of a whippersnapper at that time. I was! I had an attitude and acted like a naughty boy. Often when someone told me to go to occupational therapy, I used to think 'Make me! Drag me there!' It wasn't entirely unlike the way I behaved with Aunty Lindsay.

But there were times when I was genuinely so distressed and so drugged up to my eyeballs that the last thing I wanted to do was go to occupational therapy and make wooden animals or play scrabble. It didn't help that I was dyslexic (though of course no one knew at the time – and I doubt that would surprise anybody). In school and the children's home I had been told I was thick and stupid. I had taken all that negativity in as a child. And all that time I was dyslexic, and of course nobody picked that up. As a result, I often went around telling people I was stupid. I genuinely believed it.

Occupational therapy was a strange concept to me at the time. Fair enough, it gave us something to do rather than lying on our beds all day. But people who ran occupational therapy at the institution I was in were old school. As you can tell from my diary entries, many of them had no patience for those of us who were suffering and playing up. And I truly doubt there was any vigorous training for the staff who ran it. If there was, would we still have been constantly told that we were a waste of space and a waste of time?

In my mind, there were times when I wasn't even in that psychiatric hospital. In my mind I was back in the children's home. And that's because I wanted to be, because that's where I'd felt the safest. I was always trying to recapture something from the past, because my present was so grim. It got to a point where I could lose myself in fantasy and transport myself back to the children's home – that's how vivid things were in my head. And I guess I never really lost that ability.

I do remember feeling guilty about Anna, the old lady who committed suicide after I spoke to her. I shouldered some of that responsibility. It was a tough emotion to cope with among all the others, and of course now I know that it had nothing to do with me. But at the time, when it's so close to you, and you have had contact with the person not long before they commit suicide, you can't help but point the finger at yourself. You question yourself – could I have done more? Could my actions have changed anything? But I suppose at some point down the road I recognised the fact that I had my own stuff to deal with; I was suffering with my own torment! I couldn't have changed the outcome.

At this stage I was clearly in need of real psychological help and yet I wasn't getting it from anywhere. And I was drugged up to the eyeballs with Prozac and things, and that didn't help because I didn't know what was going on half the time. I never, ever felt in control. No wonder I tried to rebel all the time.

It is one-hundred percent true that the psychiatrist constantly asked me if I had sexual feelings or fantasies about my mother. It sounds like something out of a sitcom – a mental health fraudster obsessed with spouting out simple Freudian theories! The very thought disgusted me, of course it did. But no matter how many times I protested or brushed him off, he kept asking me. It was a weird kind of obsession with him.

I would often be asked to share and unpack my story to get to the 'real reasons' behind my problems, but then I would be given more Prozac and tranquilisers which suppressed them anyway! I really don't know how that was supposed to help. The most frustrating and frightening thing was that when that didn't work, which inevitably it didn't, they would say 'If you don't get with the programme, we're going to give you the electric shock therapy.' And that was absolutely terrifying!

It didn't help, either, that you had to walk past the people who had received it in order to get to the ward to receive our medication. The curtains were drawn around them, as though they were something to be ashamed of, or as though they were something scary that needed to be hidden. I saw nurses with injections a few times too. And it wasn't like it is today in modern units, where people sometimes have their own room. It was a Victorian asylum with bars on the windows! You can see why this scared us so much, especially since we had no real understanding of it.

People do still have this treatment today. It's called Electroconvulsive therapy (ECT) and it's used for deep, severe, entrenched depression and other mental illnesses. So I don't want to paint a picture of it as this awful torture procedure. But at the time it was used as a threat against us, and without proper knowledge of it, we were of course terrified of it.

It's interesting to see now how I referred to the other people in the ward as 'the mentally ill', as though they were mentally ill and I wasn't. I didn't want to think of myself, at that point, as mentally ill, because stigma in those days had people believing that being mentally ill meant being criminally insane. Also, to be honest, I was different to them. Some of them physically looked like zombies and one man even dragged himself around, moaning loudly. We didn't know it at the time, but it turned out that he had Parkinson's disease. He was all disfigured and walked around howling. He was shoved into a psychiatric hospital because they didn't know how to treat Parkinson's at the time. It was seen as a mental illness. His name was Jerry, and he used to be an electrician. And here he was dragging himself around like Quasimodo!

And so of course I thought that they were crazy when they were howling like wolves, or when the women were cackling loudly and creepily through the night. Of course I wanted to separate myself from that, because I thought well they're clinically insane! I wanted to scream at people, 'Look, I'm not mental! I'm not mental! I'm just depressed!'

That didn't stop other people in there, and the staff as well, seeing me as crazy. But I was hardly Jack the Ripper! In those days though (that phrase makes me sound ancient!), everyone who was slightly mentally ill was painted with the same brush. If mental illness was ever mentioned at all, people thought of the criminally insane, of Broadmoor. And the institution I was in probably resembled Broadmoor to a certain extent – bars on the window, not allowed to go out past 8pm – and you couldn't go anywhere without an escort. No wonder people thought I was dangerous.

Okay, so fair enough I had had violent outbursts in the past. I appreciate that I had threatened my sister with a knife and that was in the forefront of their minds. But that wasn't the real issue.

The real issue was that I was struggling with maternal deprivation, I was underdeveloped psychologically, and I was deeply depressed. My cognitive functions weren't good enough. In many respects, I was a child trapped in a teenager's body, living in a fantasy world. They considered it to be 'not normal'. And they told me that it's irreversible unless you have the right environment around you. But I didn't have the right environment. I wasn't to find God for a while yet.

They kept saying I was having an emotional breakdown and that does make sense, looking back. I wasn't able to function well. And the worst part is that I wasn't really concerned about anybody other than myself. The nature of my depression was that, as Aunty Lindsay once put in a letter to me years later, I had no idea of the pain and suffering I caused other people. I was too absorbed with myself. I didn't understand the pain I caused my sister, and I wouldn't until years and years later. I had no understanding of it because it was all about me. It was all about my pain. And who cared about anyone else? I was the centre of the universe. That's the way some people become when they're depressed.

And that's what it was. Depression. And yet, I was put on a ward with a paedophile, a senile dementia patient, a criminal, an alcoholic, a schizophrenic, and an anorexic! I didn't know the word paedophile then, but I knew that the guy was one, and that put me on edge. The person with dementia kept trying to throw me out of the house. The wacky person who came from LA unnerved me a little bit. The girl who was a nymphomaniac made me feel nervous and emasculated due to my sexual inexperience. Then there was the alcoholic who had her kid's wedding dress in a trunk. She really freaked me out.

This was the world I was in! Constantly feeling fearful and under threat from those around me! I was living alongside those who have been in the institution for years and years. There was no differentiating us from each other, no tailored plan for individuals. There was no streamlining or 'young people's services', as such, then. We were all just lumped in together.

And nothing helped – nothing. All I was given in counselling was the third degree about my mother and grief about my suicidal tendencies. The other stuff didn't help me either: having to go to occupational therapy, doing stupid games, and going through art therapy where they wouldn't let me near a chisel to finish my wooden duck. I was aware that things were old-fashioned even then I suppose. It was containment, more than anything, rather than rehabilitation. It was all very regimented and so on some levels it was just like being back in the children's home. We were just going through the motions. What chance did I stand of recovery in there?

I did have some friends; I formed a camaraderie with some people in there. And for us, it was an 'us versus them' situation. I once watched *One Flew Over the Cuckoo's Nest* – perhaps you've seen it before. That film reminds me so much of the institution I was in. It was old, Victorian, with bars on the window. I watched the other people on the ward with me and I knew I was different. But I didn't know what was wrong with me. I knew I was mentally ill, because I thought, 'Why else am I here?' But I didn't know precisely what the problem was. Eventually I came to an understanding in the years to come. I never really received much of an insight into my plight while I was sectioned.

My closest friend in the institution was Sandy. Though it's obvious from the diary entries that the staff had no time for me or Sandy because we were the youngest people in the hospital, we formed an alliance as a survival technique. We had a kind of a reputation, and a rapport with each other. I guess we needed that in order to survive.

Clearly Nurse Alex leaving was yet another thing that strengthened my abandonment issues, formed already by my parents leaving me and breaking their promises to visit me. And they moved with me into my adult life. Some of the stories in my diary are classic examples of how big a problem stigma was at this time. In today's day and age, if someone sacked you for being mentally ill, there would be immediate outrage.

Not everyone was so discriminatory against mentally ill people at the time. In fact, when the original manager of the shop interviewed me, he hired me straight away, and that was after I explained my story and my struggles to him. I think part of him took pity on me because of my turbulent upbringing, and he wasn't scared of the impact that it had on my mental wellbeing.

But after I went into psychiatric care, that manager retired. The area manager had taken an instant dislike to me since day one, and so when brought in a new manager, they took the opportunity to sack me. The fact that they did it right in the middle of the hospital, so that everyone knew about it, was particularly callous. To tell me that they didn't think I could do my job or function normally in society was out of order. And to tell me my colleagues didn't want me back was just cruel.

As it happened, I did end up taking my sister's advice and taking my case to a tribunal when I left the home. Thankfully, I won. I got £800 in compensation, which was a lot of money back then. The judge was very much on my side. He said that sacking me because I had had a mental breakdown was draconian. 'You went straight to his hospital ward and sacked him, while he was still recovering?' he asked my manager, incredulous. 'You could have set him back months. He could have gone off and killed himself.'

I wish I could say that stigma isn't as rife today – but I'm not sure I believe it. Things are getting better. Much better. And hopefully, the more people tell their stories, the better it will get. But there is still so much discrimination and misconception around mental illness that I bet the story of my sacking probably won't shock a lot of people all that much.

What probably would shock people is Miriam's comment to me. Can you imagine if a nurse said that to a patient nowadays? Miriam worked in mental health, for heaven's sake! And yet there she was, telling me that things were never going to get any better for me.

Nobody liked her. She was a real piece of work. She hated me, and the feeling was mutual. Not one of my interactions with her was helpful.

I took Miriam's comment to heart and for a long time it made me feel like a complete lost cause. Had my mind been in a worse state at that point, it could have triggered me into trying to take my own life. It was a cruel taunt and it is so dangerous to speak to mentally ill people this way. Sufferers should be treated with kindness, compassion, and understanding.

The staff were a strangely mixed bunch of people, which made things all the more confusing for us. The ward sisters were very authoritarian, and wanted to rule everything. Nurse Alex was very good. She was a mature student, training to be a nurse. She had a bit of nous about her! She took no nonsense from me. She was, however, often in trouble for giving me too much attention. The psychiatrist / doctor who kept asking me about sexual fantasies about my mother was just completely draconian, and I didn't trust him as far as I could throw him. Dennis was okay, but the man who moonlighted as a taxi driver was a bully. He especially didn't have time for me or Sandy. I don't know why he was there.

How did these people end up working in that environment?

I'm glad things have changed for the better in this respect, but I do have a bad feeling that some people in society probably still treat the mentally ill in this way today. It's amazing to think that we're still so backward in some respects. There's a lot of work still left to do.

I do feel a little bit sorry for that young student nurse who had to deal with my meltdown in Woolworths. Bless her! She clearly didn't expect me to have a complete meltdown! I didn't know such a small person could shout so loud, but she had a good go!

I still remember that incident vividly to this day. I know the meltdown started because I was getting more and more worked up, but in all honesty, once I realised I'd gone a bit too far, I couldn't pull myself back anyway. Part of it was deep distress, and part of it, deep down, was a game to me. I knew everyone in the cafeteria was watching me. When it was over and I'd been told off, I smirked like a naughty boy. I had got a reaction, and that's what I'd wanted.

I recognise entirely that I never helped myself. I do get that. There was an evil side of me, smirking all the time, when I wasn't in deep anguish. There were two sides of me: the real, genuine victim and the cheeky little kid who just wanted to get the kind of attention that I craved. I had an attitude; I know that. I was playing the arrogant young lad. I played little mind games, seeing how far I could push people, and I did it deliberately. I got some kind of warped, perverse pleasure in it. I tried to create confrontation in order to recapture the experiences of my past.

That trait didn't leave me for quite a while, even after I left the hospital. I became good at manipulating situations to my advantage, and that came out of feeling a total lack of control in everything that had happened to me so far. It got to the point where sometimes I wasn't even aware I was doing it any more. It was a self-survival mechanism, but that doesn't make it okay. What I needed was someone to come along and give me a clip around the ear and knock it out of me!

When the hospital told me that they couldn't do anything more for me, that they needed my bed, and that they were worried that I was becoming too institutionalised, it was a nightmare scenario. It was a case of history repeating itself. This was the place that was supposed to help me, but they'd decided to throw me out and let me fend for myself. I felt like I had no one to turn to who could really help me solve my mental health problems. But just like every other time in my life, I had no control over what was happening to me. I had no choice.

It was time to tackle the world outside of an institution.

CHAPTER 10

FACING LIFE OUTSIDE OF AN INSTITUTION

Trying to climb back onto my feet after leaving the mental hospital was very hard, as you're no doubt unsurprised to hear. The first few months were rocky. Living in Shene and Graham's house was a lifesaver for me but it wasn't ideal, and I tried my absolute best to get back into employment. A couple of interviews for cleaning jobs and the like were unsuccessful, and my lack of qualifications and troubled past were just too much for anyone to take me seriously. As I said, stigma around mental illness was rife.

In order to keep myself busy I took up volunteering at the local hospital. I worked with geriatric and stroke patients in the gym. I bathed them, fed them and made their beds. It gave me a real sense of purpose and I really loved doing it. It was the first thing I'd felt truly good about in a long time.

A happy coincidence was that I ended up working alongside my old childhood friend, Lee. Now that we were older, and more mature (well, he was. I don't think I could ever call myself mature at this point), we got along really well. On one of our regular Sunday meet-ups, he told me that he'd become a member of the Chester Gospel Hall Mission and that the pastor there was looking for volunteers in his soup kitchen.

It was strange because at that time I felt religion had nothing to offer me. I had stopped attending church a long time ago. I couldn't cope with a God of love, because I had never experienced love as a child. Not real love. I baulked at the idea of a God who loved me and could bring healing into my life, because it just didn't ring true to me. If He wanted the best for all His children, why had He let all these awful things happen to me? Why had I not felt loved for my entire childhood?

Despite these feelings, though, I saw no issue with joining Lee at the soup kitchen. It was another chance to help people, and thank God I did! One lunchtime I followed him into the church hall, where there were long trestle tables on which bowls of soup were being served by volunteers. The most beautiful woman stood in front of me, ladling some soup into a bowl and placing a bread roll beside it on a tray. She had curly brown hair, a heart-shaped face, and a gorgeous smile, and introduced herself as Lesley.

'What do you do, Mark?' she asked me, ladling some soup into a bowl and placing a bread roll beside it on a tray.

'I, er … Well, I'm volunteering at the local hospital at the moment while I interview for jobs.' I deliberately kept things vague; I still felt slightly ashamed of my upbringing and lack of academic achievement. Besides, I had no idea what she would think of it. 'Are you a student, like Lee?'

'Yes, I am,' she smiled at me warmly. I felt a rush of attraction for her. 'I'm studying History with English.'

Throughout that day together we chatted amicably while providing more than 50 people with a hot meal and some tea. In doing this it struck me that I was lucky I wasn't homeless like these people, because in any other circumstance I could easily have been. It made the experience all the more rewarding.

'I go to the Gospel Hall Mission, too,' Lesley told me. 'Will I see you there with Lee?'

I nodded. 'Lee has been asking me to go with him,' I said. I didn't mention that actually I really didn't fancy it. And as it turned out, I still took some persuading.

And so it was that the next Sunday I accompanied Lee to church. There I socialised with his girlfriend, Karen, their friends, and Lesley. Lesley seemed keen to hang around, which I enjoyed. There were lots of young people there and that appealed to me, I must admit. I was, after all, still a kid in my head.

After the service Lee introduced me to Pastor Coombs. He was a friendly, slight, ageing, balding man with thick-rimmed glasses and a friendly smile. Immediately I warmed to him. 'Nice to meet you, Mark,' he said to me, grinning. 'Lee has told me a lot about you.'

Not too much, I hope, I thought to myself.

'Once you've settled in, I'd love a chance to talk to you and learn more about your story,' he said to me. I was flattered. He seemed like a great man and there were very few good people in my life who had been so interested in me, despite my mental health issues and dark past.

It was around this time that I got the letter from the employment tribunal, informing me that I'd won the £800 in compensation from the menswear shop. Enclosed was a cheque, and I smiled to myself, thrilled. Now I could take Lesley out for some ice cream!

Over the next few months, I had some very mixed fortunes. Courting Lesley was wonderful, and I was finally beginning to understand what it was like to be truly loved. However, at this time I was still suffering badly with anxiety and depression, and I struggled with the church and what it meant to me. I kept attending services and was keen to know more, but I couldn't stop myself from feeling as though I had been let down in life by God. As a result, I found it hard to truly believe that there was a real, consistently loving father figure in life. There had never been one in my life before; why should this one be any different?

It actually took Lee, Karen, and a few other friends to really get through to me. Pastor Coombs decided to do a sermon about suicide and how God truly loves everyone, even those who are troubled. It was difficult to hear because the very fact that I'd been suicidal, and that my life had been so atrocious up to that point, was the very reason I was having trouble accepting God. I remember that evening. My friends sat with me into the night as I cried. They listened to my story and read me passages from the Bible, telling me to give my heart to Jesus.

I knew that for a long time I'd been on the road to destruction. For so long I'd been in self-destruct mode, and being out of psychiatric care for some months hadn't helped. If drugs had been around me then, I probably would have drifted into drug culture. I would have taken drugs just to take the pain away. Someone once said to me that having depression is like having no skin. It's like all your nerves are exposed. That's the kind of pain that I felt. Mentally, things were still pretty bleak for me at the time. So I suppose when someone came along and told me that Jesus could help, I thought, I've got nothing to lose.

As a result, I finally took the plunge and made a commitment to God. On 27th July 1981, I was baptised, and over the next two years I worked as a volunteer alongside Pastor Coombs as a City Missioner. Pastor Coombs became my mentor. His love for people and his concern for their needs, both spiritual and material, was the motivating force behind everything he did. He greatly influenced me and was a brilliant man.

He was also very generous. He bought a house (he got a mortgage at 50-something, believe it or not!) and set it up for Lesley and the other students from the church to live there while they were studying. The idea originally had been for me to live there too, but because of the evangelicalism of some of the residents, they were against me living there as I was courting Lesley. They said to me, 'You shouldn't be living here because you're courting. You're not married.'

I could have lived with my sister, but I was trying to be independent and prove that I could do it on my own. My sister didn't know I was homeless, in all fairness. So in effect, I was homeless for a few months and had to sleep on the church floor. In theory, it was my official role to look after the night shelter, and so I slept in the office upstairs. But in reality, I was just as homeless as the others downstairs. This was only temporary while the pastor tried to find me a bedsit, but it still wasn't pleasant. I had my meals during the day at the house where Lesley lived, and slept in the old musty church during the night. I could get a shower and a wash and things like that at Lesley's, but I couldn't sleep there. That's the way it was.

Looking back, I wish it hadn't happened that way. It wasn't very nice being homeless. The night shelter was big. I was upstairs, but eventually the stench from the homeless people below would permeate upwards. It wasn't a proper hostel or anything; it was just somewhere for people to sleep rather than sleeping on the street. It was horrible really. Sometimes drunks came up the stairs when I was trying to sleep at night and started banging on the door, trying to knock the door down, because they were stoned out of their minds. I had to barricade myself in. It got rough. They were fine when they were sober! They were the nicest people you could ever meet.

There were some other big challenges for me while all of this was going on. One of them was meeting Lesley's parents, Elfed and Jeanette. I was incredibly apprehensive. Lesley came from a privileged middle-class family with a comfortable income and a stable family foundation. Her family was everything mine had never been, and as I walked through their house, with plush carpets and leather couches, I felt very aware of my frayed jeans and too-short jumper sleeves. Lesley had been so closeted in her own upbringing. Meeting me exposed her to a whole new world that she didn't even know existed. I believe God put me with the right person, though. If two damaged people are put together, it can be disastrous. In any good relationship, you complement each other. She appreciated me for what I was and it made me fall in love with her even more deeply.

I have to hand it to Lesley and her family – they never once showed any aversion to me or my background. They could have done. They could have turned their backs on me and decided that I wasn't good enough for their daughter. But they didn't. They welcomed me with open arms. And so it was that when I decided to propose to Lesley, she said yes with no hesitation whatsoever. It was one of the first moments of pure joy I had had in years.

Despite all this, my mental illness had far from abated. In fact, all I'd managed to do was repress my trauma while I was trying to find my place in the world. Around this time Paul returned home for a visit from the navy. He didn't think much of my involvement with the church. He told me that going away with the navy helped him get away from his awful past. I personally thought it was just escapism, and told him so.

I knew only too well that it wasn't as simple as literally running away from your issues. Terrible memories of abuse surfaced routinely. I often found myself collapsing into tears, and often Pastor Coombs had to hold me until the panic attacks subsided. My anger issues manifested themselves routinely too, and I often found myself lashing out when things were just too much. I remember once I threw a chair at Pastor Coombs in frustration one day, my fury bubbling over and victimising one of the first people in my life to truly look after me. My problem was the same as it had always been: Pastor Coombs exercised authority over me and I didn't like it. What a surprise!

Thankfully, he took no nonsense from me and reprimanded me when it was needed. He also always did his best to nurture me. I suppose it's no surprise, then, that he played an instrumental part in one of the biggest and best decisions of my life: to go to college.

It came about when I opened up to him about my desire to serve the community in a more official capacity. I told him that, quite frankly, it was beginning to feel like a calling. And being the wise man that he was, he suggested I test this calling by doing some Bible College training.

I felt unsure. The old feelings of inadequacy bubbled up to the surface again. I was useless and stupid, remember? I couldn't even write properly, or make a toy duck without screwing it up. I was a nobody who was destined never to have anything good in this life.

'Mark, you know that isn't true,' said Lesley, when I voiced my concerns to her.

'Do you really think I have what it takes?' I asked her, a flicker of hope igniting inside me.

'I really, really do,' she replied, kissing me. And with that my decision was made.

Meanwhile, my wedding day was looming. We were very excited. Lesley's parents, very generously, gave us gifts ready for our first home. I was still on the dole at this point, and times were hard financially, but we managed to find a one-room rented bedsit ready to move into after we'd married. Things really did seem to be looking up.

We were married in April 1984. My wedding day was the happiest day of my life. Lesley looked absolutely stunning in her white gown, and I beamed throughout. Every photo to this date shows me with a huge grin on my face. I couldn't believe my luck; or rather, that God had brought such a special person into my life.

Even if it wasn't Lindsay …

Our honeymoon was a couple of nights away in a hotel. It was the best we could afford, but we were happy with it. It felt like we had the world at our feet. I was married to an amazing woman. I was about to start a new adventure with my training. We had our own house to live in and had returned home alone to enjoy each other. Nothing could dampen our spirits that night.

Or could it?

A knock at the door interrupted our first night together as a blissfully happy wedded couple. Confused, I answered the door to a distraught Karen and Lee.

'We're so sorry to tell you this, Mark,' she said quietly, rubbing at her eyes with a tissue.

My blood ran cold. 'What is it?' I said.

Lee looked at me, swallowing hard. 'Pastor Coombs died of a heart attack yesterday morning.'

No.

At that moment, my world tipped upside down all over again. Grief ripped through me. Lesley did her best to comfort me, but it was all I could do not to howl in despair. Here I was, now a fully grown, married man, and yet again another father figure was being ripped away from me in the cruellest fashion.

Mark and Lesley on their wedding day.

I reacted horribly. In my anger at the world, I hurled anything I could grab across the room, smashing things up in my attempt to let out all the frustration and grief. Lesley and Karen screamed in fear, Lee yelled at me to calm the heck down. But years of uncontrollable rage and emotional breakdowns proved that I had no control over my reactions.

I stormed out of the house when messing up the furniture was no longer enough to let out my misery. I ran out into the street to get away from my friends, and wailed at the unfairness of it all.

When would the people in my life stop leaving me?

CHAPTER 11

BREAKING DOWN THE WALL

Weighed down with grief, but optimistic about the future, we moved to Dorset. I went to study for a two-year diploma in theology at Moorlands Bible College, the college Pastor Coombs had told me would be a good fit for me. Starting my spiritual training there felt like a fitting tribute to a wonderful man. I must admit that during my time there I had a bit of imposter's syndrome – I never felt quite qualified enough to train as a Christian. I had doubted God so much in the past. But I was determined to do my best.

Over those next two years I worked in an open Brethren Assembly, led Bible Studies with a boys' group, and ran activities for them. I really enjoyed working with children and worked as hard as I could while I studied. It took some time to get used to studying as I'd never excelled at it before. But now in all fairness I had fewer distractions. I still received letters from Lindsay a couple of times a year, and the depression would hit me and leave me in waves. But somehow tackling this new, exciting life that gave me purpose, with the love and support of my gorgeous, amazing wife gave me the strength to see things through. I tried not to think about my past unless I couldn't avoid it; I only spoke about it when I knew I could get something positive from it. Blocking it out was easier than constantly remembering all the awful things I'd been through.

I received my diploma in June 1986 and after college I was accepted by Kay Street Baptist Church in Rawtenstall, Lancashire as their new pastoral assistant. I really was thrown into the deep end, but I quickly became more confident as I threw myself into lots of different activities and aspects of Christian ministry. I was allowed to administer sacraments, officiate at baptisms and funerals and be involved in policy and decision-making. I almost felt like a fully functioning adult at last!

I had the opportunity to talk to people who had attempted suicide, which was both rewarding and fascinating for me. I worked in a drug rehab centre, and spoke to kids in the local children's home, telling them all about my experiences in Lincolnshire (except for the abuse, of course!) I felt good doing this. I felt like I was being my true, authentic self in a positive way, and I was good at it. Still I repressed the most horrific memories from my mind.

Yet all of this paled in comparison to two of the best things that had ever happened to me in my life: the birth of my son and daughter. Jonathan arrived in 1985 and Fiona was born in 1987. They brightened up in my life in ways I never thought was possible and made me determined to turn my life around for the better. Though things were hard as a young father on low pay, it seemed at that time that my family was complete; what a turnaround from the upheaval of my life in care!

One thing did begin to niggle at me, though. In 1987, I began to have horrific stomach pains and I could find no explanation for them whatsoever. I ate relatively healthily, and as far I was aware I wasn't allergic to anything in my regular diet. It got so bad that Lesley urged me to visit the doctor. The response I got from him was really surprising. He suggested that my issue was psychosomatic, not physical.

'The doctor thinks it could be past trauma that is causing my pain,' I explained to Lesley. 'All this repressed anger and resentment is affecting me physically. He wants me to see a psychiatrist. I can't think of anything I want to do less.' After all, what good had psychiatrists ever done me before? All I recalled was getting pills shoved at me and being told to be quiet!

'Well, there is another option ...' Lesley said to me, looking thoughtful.

'What's that, then?' I asked.

'There's a vicar in the local Anglican church who has a healing ministry,' she said. 'Why don't you go and speak to him? You might find that he can help you, in which case you wouldn't need to see a psychiatrist if it makes you uncomfortable.'

'I dunno,' I said to her, mulling it over. I was a little sceptical of healing ministries.

'It might be worth a shot. You can't lose anything, and it might just help you.'

It took me a little bit of time, but eventually I decided to give it a try. Lesley was right; there was nothing to lose. With this in mind I made an appointment to see Reverend Peter Haywood.

The following week I went to meet him. He was a lovely man, quite ordinary and approachable. I expected him to intimidate me but I immediately felt comfortable in his presence. I still felt apprehensive, though, about sharing my past. It felt counterintuitive.

His study was warm, inviting, and very unorganised and messy, but in a charming way. Peter's wife Jane served me tea and cake and cracked jokes with me. It helped me to open up to them and over the next couple of hours I poured out my life story to them. I had no intention of crying but at some points the compulsion became too strong. Sadness moved over me in waves as I recalled all the harm I'd come to over the years, both at the hands of other people and myself. By the end of it I felt exhausted and the pain in my stomach had returned. It was then that I finally became convinced that the pain might be due to stress after all; it had hit me hard when I started to remember the bad times again.

When I left, I agreed to see them again. I felt like I needed to. Opening up to Peter and Jane had been like picking at a scab and ripping open an old wound. I suddenly felt as though all my nerves were exposed. The guilt, abandonment issues, and heartache had all returned with a vengeance.

Oh, God, I thought to myself as I walked away from the Reverend's house. *I still love Lindsay.*

I shook my head and tried to fight this distressing thought, but there was no staying away from it now. Peter had told me that over the years since leaving the mental institution I'd built a mental wall between myself and my past. Now I was to start breaking it down bit by bit. He told me that God was helping me to deconstruct myself before I could build myself back up, this time with the right mental tools to deal with things.

'Identity, security, and worth comes from God, from within you,' Peter said to me with a reassuring smile. 'It's not easy, but we'll help you get there. Your happiness does not need to depend on your job, your circumstances or on other people's opinions. You don't need to change who you are – you just need learn how to think differently.'

As a man of faith, this meant a lot to me. But it also made sense from a humanistic point of view too. I came away from the session feeling hopeful but a little bit wounded. I'd opened up the floodgates I'd been so sure I'd closed for good. It was terrifying. I was going to need all the help and support I could get.

And so as I made my way back home I came to an unwelcome realisation. If I was going to try to face my demons head on and tackle my depression once and for all, I would have to tell Lesley the truth. I would have to tell Lesley that I still had feelings for Lindsay.

Later that night, we discussed whether or not I'd be returning to see Peter. 'I think I need to,' I confessed to her. 'There's some issues I thought I'd dealt with, but they're still there under the surface.'

'Is there anything in particular you haven't shared with me?' Lesley asked gently, holding my hand.

'I don't want to hurt you …'

She squeezed my hand, giving me permission to speak.

'I realised in the counselling session that I still have some issues surrounding … surrounding Lindsay, the house parent.' Lesley had heard about her briefly before, but had no idea.

'Do you still love her?' she asked in a small voice.

I realised I had to tell the truth, if there was to be any trust in our marriage. I nodded. 'I wish I didn't, because it affected me badly. I thought I was over her, but deep down I'm not.'

She thought about this for a few moments before saying, 'Do you still love me?'

I stared at her and felt a strong pang of guilt. 'Of *course* I do,' I told her. 'You and the children mean the absolute world to me. This is just something that's left over from my past, that I never got the chance to work through. I want to put it to rest, and forget about it for good.'

She nodded, tears welling up in her eyes. I swallowed hard, preparing myself for my next question.

'I know this is a lot to ask, but will you support me through this? I want to resolve things in my own mind, and tackle my depression too, for the good of our family.'

'Yes, I will stick by you,' Lesley said, and in that moment I loved her more than I'd ever done before. 'I want to be free of your past too, for our family's sake and for mine.'

The following months were incredibly difficult for me. I attended Peter's healing ministry a lot, trying to work through my issues. We discussed my abandonment complex and addressed my inability to forgive my parents up to that point in my life. I began to accept that the things that had happened to me were not my fault, nor were they a reflection of my true worth. Slowly I started to accept that there were many things in life that we could not control, but that didn't need to be a black cloud over my life. I needed to find a way to be okay with that to a certain extent.

But reliving physical and mental abuse was harrowing and traumatic. Many times I found myself breaking down and sobbing, remembering how unfair life had been to me. I told Peter about how I was sacked from the menswear shop, locked up in a cupboard, pulled away from every kind of family I'd ever had. We talked about my fear of it happening again. And while I can't say I felt an immediate difference to my mental health, slowly my physical symptoms started to fade away. The stomach problems became far less of an issue and my thinking patterns altered.

In many ways this felt like progress; in others, I felt like a failure again. No matter how much I discussed it with Peter, my obsessive love for Aunty Lindsay did not abate. I was so frustrated. When was I going to loosen this grip she had on my emotions? I resigned myself to the fact that not everything could be solved by talking therapy, but still I continued to battle with my own mind. Looking back, I think I would have benefitted from some kind of therapy that wasn't purely from a spiritual perspective as well. But hindsight is a powerful thing, after all.

At some point during that year, I realised that I couldn't keep looking backwards. This had always been a big part of my problem. I had been a pastoral assistant for almost three years now, and it was time for me to look ahead to the next step in my career. Spurred on by ambition, my faith in God and the local Baptist superintendent, I researched what I needed to do to become an accredited pastor.

But yet again I was to face crushing disappointment as, after a number of interviews for the post, I received a letter telling me I'd been unsuccessful. That old familiar rage flamed up inside me and I began storming about, throwing the letter around and yelling loudly in poor Lesley's direction.

'Yet another failure!' I fumed. 'Thrown onto the rubbish heap, again!'

'They're just concerned about your lack of qualifications and whether you're mentally fit enough to deal with a stressful job,' Lesley reasoned. 'Let's trust God to know what is best for us. There's nothing else we can do about it.'

If only I was as 'together' as Lesley was. If only it was so simple to accept it when bad things happened! There was a strong internal struggle in my mind as I tried to make my peace with their decision, in a way that would be considered healthy. It was so hard! I did my best to put into practice some of the thinking techniques Peter had taught me. It was down to me to remember everything I had to be thankful for in life and that a rejection did not make me worthless. But what was I to do in the meantime? I didn't want to stay a pastoral assistant forever, but there was no way of moving upwards!

I shared my frustration with Peter and my other friends within the Anglican Church. They encouraged me to stick in my pastoral job in the Baptist Church until God showed me the way forward. It was a true test for me and my impatience, but Lesley and I prayed for direction for a whole year. Then, in January 1989, Peter suggested that I apply for full-time ministry in the Anglican Church instead. He put me in touch with the DDO (Diocesan Director of Ordinands) for the Anglican Church in Manchester.

I was invited to interview a few times with the DDO, who told me that because I'd had no experience with the Anglican Church, the best thing to do would be to quit my job as a pastoral assistant with the Baptist Church and join their church instead. That way, I could get some real world experience of their denomination.

'But if I give up my job to join your church, what will I live on?' I asked the DDO, concerned.

'As it happens, Reverend Peter Haywood has a solution for you,' he replied, smiling. 'He's agreed to take you on as a pastoral assistant in his church, which will give you the right experience.'

'That's brilliant!' I said, thrilled.

'Yes, it's good news,' said the DDO. 'The only problem is, though, that job won't be vacant for a few months yet. So, you'll be unemployed for a bit. And when you do enter the job, it will only pay £40 a week plus benefits. I understand you have a young family to support, but go home and think it through.'

This was a tough choice. Giving up my job in the Baptist church meant that I'd have to give up the house that went with it, and of course a steady wage. Yet again, I had to pray on it, because I was aware that it wasn't just me I was dragging into this situation. Eventually, though, we decided together that I should just go for it and apply for the Anglican Church. We'd never had much money anyway, and I needed to move forward with my life.

My time as a key worker in the Anglican Church were tough financially. The Baptist church were kind to us, and allowed us to stay in the house they'd provided us with until I was officially transferred to the Anglican Church. I was always so bowled over by their generosity; without kind donations from them and the Anglican Church, we would have barely been able to make ends meet that year. Occasionally, we would get home to find anonymous gifts or cheques posted through the letterbox. I experienced some true kindness during this time, and though I'd had to put my counselling on hold for a while until I sorted things out, I felt truly blessed.

Soon I received some bittersweet news: I'd been accepted for training as an Anglican priest! The only issue, though, was that because I had barely any Anglican experience, I was told I had to take a two-year pre-ordination course first before I could take any job as a pastoral assistant. But I saw no easy way to do it! The Baptist Church were very kind and generous, but even they were unlikely to let me live in a house provided by them for two years while I studied to join another denomination.

The problem hung over our heads like a dark, black cloud – until something amazing happened. A local Anglican priest, upon hearing about my difficult situation, took it upon himself to use his authority and overrule the recommendation of the two-year pre-ordination course. Instead, I could apply straight away to St John's College in Cranmer Hall at Durham University. If I succeeded in my interviews, I could start studying for the Anglican priesthood straight away!

And so it was that I took my interviews and miraculously, it seemed, I was offered the place in Durham. To top it all off, we were offered a three-bedroomed house near the college! Praise the Lord!

It was time for me and my beautiful young family to head to Durham. I was finally on the road to ordination.

CHAPTER 12

REVISITING THE PAST

My first year at Durham University was demanding. The transition to the ordained Anglican ministry was to involve a lot of soul-searching and at times painful experiences. I had to adjust to rigorous academic study and I missed the open, informal worship of my previous church. But no matter how hard it was, I knew it was going to be worth it. Finally I was being recognised for something positive! I had been given the chance to prove myself.

The difficulty really started, though, when eight or nine months in we were asked to undertake self-assessment assignments. The assignment called for us to delve into our deep personal issues as a reflection of ourselves and our wider journey. There was no wonder I was apprehensive when my last stint of counselling had brought forth such dark emotions within me.

The whole class had been taken to a retreat in the Lake District for a week or so as we put together our assignments. I had fun there with my friends, and it was good to have time to socialise and relax a bit. But putting that assignment together did something to me. One morning in class as I opened my folder, I turned to a photo of all of us in the children's home. The photo showed me standing next to Lindsay, looking happy and carefree. I'd seen the photo many times before, but this time it sparked off a kind of panic within me.

I felt my entire body tense up as I stared down at the image, memories coming at me all at once. Suddenly I could almost smell Lindsay's perfume, the way her eyes lit up when she looked at me. I remembered the fury in her voice as she told me off for rebelling; I recalled the horrific scene as she tried to stop me from cutting my wrists. My breath quickened and my lungs began to feel tight. Sparks appeared in front of my eyes and my head felt dizzy and light.

'Mark, are you all right?' my university tutor John Pritchard asked me.

I closed my eyes and tried to regulate my breathing, but it didn't work. I hadn't felt like this in a while, not since I'd been in the psychiatric hospital. I heard John's voice somewhere around me, but it became muffled and distant. I wasn't paying attention any more.

I decided to leave the room until I could calm myself down. Nobody stopped me as I left the big beautiful Edwardian mansion we were staying in. I walked and walked and walked across the lush green field, desperate to keep myself moving and keep my mind from breaking down. I found myself walking beside the lake, the sound of the water rushing by and birds chirping up ahead soothing my anxiety. Eventually I found myself in a position to be able to stop completely and I realised that I'd prevented myself from having a full-blown panic attack. I breathed deeply, relieved but rattled and unsettled.

Why had that happened? I'd seen the photo before. It made no sense to me that I should have had this kind of reaction now. There seemed to be no rhyme or reason for it. I closed my eyes again, feeling the warm sun on my face, and tried to block out the negativity that had gripped me so powerfully.

I heard footsteps behind me, and John Pritchard spoke.

'I'm glad I found you,' John said to me in his warm, friendly voice. 'Do you want to talk about it?' He'd already read my self-assessment and knew about my issues. It was a relief to not have to relay the whole story all over again. Instead I just talked about my depression in general, and despair that I couldn't let go of my obsessive love for Lindsay.

'Mark, your other tutors and I think it would be a good idea for you to get some help for this once and for all. Help with your childhood traumas too. Would you be willing to do this?'

I told him that I would; after all, I'd been willing to let Pastor Coombs and Peter Haywood counsel me, and both had helped to a certain degree. They hadn't, however, been able to completely solve my issues and I desperately wanted to be free of them.

John put his hand on my shoulder. 'We also talked about the possibility of you meeting Lindsay face-to-face again, to talk through your problems again. How would you feel about that?'

I exhaled loudly, shaking my head. 'I really don't know. Do you think it will help?'

'I don't know for sure, but it's worth a try. You've come this far already.'

There was a short silence.

'Okay,' I said. 'I'm scared, but I'll give it a go.'

The last few days of the retreat were insanely hard. When I was around people, I just about kept things together. But one night just before we returned home to Durham, suicidal thoughts began to creep into my mind. What's the point in seeing Lindsay? My mind taunted me. She will just reject you. Like everyone else. You're a reject!

I started to shout out loud at God. 'Why won't you help me?' I yelled into the ether. 'Where are you, God?' I knew he was out there somewhere but I couldn't understand why he wouldn't listen to my pleas. Why couldn't I feel him with me?

Things with Lesley were strained when I returned home. I felt emotionally drained and troubled, and Lesley sensed it. Loud, vicious arguments broke out between the two of us. She told me she'd dreaded me coming home, because every time I started to become obsessed with Lindsay again, I made our home life miserable. Of course this was understandable, but in my current mindset I lashed out, accusing her of making things harder for me. Once again I'd become that self-absorbed kid who cared only about his own problems. Never mind that Lesley was feeling threatened. Never mind that she was feeling lonely. Never mind that she was stressed about our financial situation and our future. It was still all about me and how Lindsay was affecting my life.

John was true to his word and got in contact with Lindsay, who was now living in Scotland with her family. He arranged for me to meet her at the end of October. This both terrified me and excited me. I had no idea what to expect, no idea what I was going to say to her when I saw her. There wasn't any protocol for a situation as unusual as this one!

The weeks leading up to our meeting were a personal hell. I felt myself spiral into a pit of depression and uncertainty. I could barely eat and sleep was elusive. My birthday came and went, and it was a bittersweet day. I appreciated it so much that Lesley and the children were trying to make me happy, but it didn't quite work.

The day before the meeting brought our family some horrible news. My sister Jenny called me in floods of tears. Through choking sobs I managed to get it out of her what had happened. Our brother Paul had tried to commit suicide.

Feeling frantic, I called the hospital and mercifully I was able to speak to him. He had taken an overdose. He was okay, but even though he didn't tell me I sensed that he was feeling lonely, misunderstood, and helpless. He'd been institutionalised since joining the navy after leaving the children's home, and it sounded as though he'd been finding things just as difficult as I had. He assured me that he wouldn't do it again, and I got the impression that he'd been trying to make himself heard. I spoke to my other sisters, Shene and Maxine, later that night and they'd had the same reassurances from him.

I should have felt relieved at the reassurance and worried about his wellbeing, but in my current frame of mind all I could think about was how much of an inconvenience it was for me to deal with it when I had a meeting with Lindsay coming up. I felt disgusted with myself for feeling that way.

My family tried to make me happy, but I couldn't muster up a lot of enthusiasm. Help was seemingly at hand, though, because John helped me get an appointment with Rebecca, the university's psychotherapist. She told me that I was trapped in a time warp in my mind, that part of me was still an adolescent longing for someone to discipline me at the same time as showing me love. Perhaps that's why I formed such close attachments to Pastor Coombs and John Pritchard. They always knew when to be firm with me, and didn't let me get away with any of my bad or petulant behaviour.

October 31st came slowly, but I still felt completely unprepared when John Pritchard picked me up from my house and drove me to Lindsay's house in Scotland. I was quiet for much of the journey, the energy seemingly sapped out of me. I couldn't muster up the energy, couldn't articulate anything into words. Memories attacked my senses as we drove along; I could smell her perfume again, I could see her beautiful face clearly in my mind's eye, hear her laughter.

Imagine how bizarre it felt for me when, a few hours later, she opened her front door and greeted me in person for the first time in fifteen years. My reality and fantasy worlds collided. There was the object of my years of obsession, right there in front of me.

The years had put some grey in her tawny hair, some lines around her eyes. She carried a little bit of extra weight, the weight of having had four children over the years. But in every other sense she was the exact same Lindsay. Her smile was as beautiful as ever when she recognised me and ushered me into the house.

'It's so wonderful to see you, Mark,' she told me once John and I had shaken hands with her husband Geoff, a jolly-looking man with a full head of hair and black beard. She hugged me and I felt like a 15-year-old again.

The next hour was utterly surreal but lovely as Lindsay pulled out a scrapbook filled with photos from the children's home. It was great looking back on old times over tea and cake, but I was desperate to speak to Lindsay alone. There was a big elephant in the room and I was itching to address it. Eventually we got the opportunity when John offered to help Geoff with the washing up, and Lindsay and I went outside for a walk.

I couldn't stop myself blushing and stumbled over my words as we made small talk. Lindsay knew all about my issues and my obsession with her, and I wondered if she could sense my nervousness. I was taller than her now and I found that really weird. Internally I willed her to kick-start the conversation we knew we needed to have. Every time I opened my mouth, no sound came out.

'I'm so pleased you could visit us,' Lindsay said. She turned to me and looked me squarely in the eyes. 'But be honest with me. How is our meeting making you feel? Is it hard for you being here, talking to me?'

I gulped. 'Yes.'

'Let's talk about it.'

'Where do I start? I haven't been able to think of a single thing to say to you for weeks. And yet there's so much to say.' I sighed, and there was a short silence. 'It all began that night when I accidentally hurt you, and you slapped me.'

She frowned. 'I don't remember slapping you, Mark. It doesn't sound like something I'd do.'

'I think it was an accident. But it shocked me, and convinced me that you didn't care. Just like every other adult in my life at the time.'

She nodded without saying a word. 'But the fact is, I was still in love with you. Completely obsessed, in fact. And every time you showed me a bit of attention, I craved it more.'

'I was told I gave you too much time and attention, actually,' she said. 'I knew about your crush, but I had no idea how to handle it. And you were, if I may say so, the most difficult, demanding, and manipulative kid I've ever worked with. I really had my work cut out for me.'

I chuckled along with her. I had nothing to say against that. I was well aware how much of a nightmare I was.

She put her hand in mine. 'Mark, you know that we have to have a different kind of relationship now, if we want to keep in touch. I'm flattered that you felt so deeply for me, but the teenager in you needs to let this go. You get that, right? We're both adults with families now. The dynamic has changed. We can be good friends, but that's all it will ever be.'

A pang of pain shot through my heart. She was right. I knew she was right. But how was I supposed to let her go? She'd meant so much to me for 15 years. As strange as it was, I didn't know how I was going to live without this … this problem that had defined me for so long.

'This isn't a rejection, Mark,' she said softly. 'You will always mean a lot to me. But this obsession isn't healthy. You need to let it go.'

CHAPTER 13

THE LONG, HARD ROAD TO ORDINATION

If John Pritchard thought that my meeting with Lindsay would fix me right away, he was to be strongly disappointed. The whole encounter sent me into a spiral of decline. It took me a long time to understand why, but I now know that I was going through a mourning period. My mind was having to come to terms with letting go of something hugely important to me, and the trauma of it sent me headlong into a mental breakdown.

I didn't realise what was happening at first. I got through Christmas and New Year okay, though there was a mental fog around my brain that wouldn't lift. I went on my first trip to abroad to Taizé in France with the university, which kept my mind occupied for a while. Over the spring and summer, Lesley and I made the conscious effort to spend more time together. The arguments had been explosive and sometimes physical, and we worked hard to heal our marriage as best as we could. We spent time with and without our children, who were growing into boisterous kids with their own distinct personalities. Things still weren't great between us, but it was alright, at least until I signed up for a placement with the local social services over the summer holidays.

Shadowing Sue, a social worker, I went to visit children from broken homes. Some were drug users, some were alcoholics, and some were school leavers and unemployed. I worked with Sue to help the kids access programmes and resources to get the skills they needed to progress with their lives, something I really could have done with myself all those years back. Their living situations seemed to mirror my own: often the kids had been in care, or in small houses on battered council estates.

A couple of cases still stick in my mind today. One of them was the case of a three-year-old boy whose mother had pushed him out of the house and into Sue's arms because she was angry at social services' interference. He had screamed and cried in distress as Sue had carried him away. Hearing the story brought back all kinds of horrible memories for me, but it also kind of put things into perspective. Perhaps social services weren't as evil as I'd made them out to be in my mind. I still believed the system had failed me massively, but clearly there were social workers who wanted to do good and protect innocent children.

The second case touched me deeply and acted as a catalyst for my breakdown. Sue took me to a high-rise car park, and told me the story of a girl who had died there. She had taken herself to the highest floor and thrown herself off it.

For the longest time, I couldn't get the image of this girl out of my mind. She had almost the same background as me, being moved from care home to care home, and struggled badly with rejection. She couldn't find a job and it all got too much for her. She was the embodiment of what could have happened to me if I hadn't been luckier. It distressed me far more than I expected it to and over the following months I broke down.

Lesley tried to help me and suggested I go to visit The King's House, a team of counselling, teaching and listening staff based in an old vicarage near Gateshead. Dr Peter Ward, a GP, and Reverend Anne Black had set it up with their respective families and they were surrounded with a team of volunteers who helped people with depression, bereavement, and abandonment issues. John had first suggested it and Lesley was keen on the idea, but I was tired. I was so, so tired of just regurgitating my story over and over again to new people. Nothing ever came of it. My mental health never seemed to improve. I promised Lesley I would get in touch with them, but then forgot about it for a while.

Meanwhile, my behaviour at home and at university became bizarre and erratic. The tiniest things sent me into a meltdown and I was seemingly angry all the time. In losing Lindsay I felt lost, and so I began to form unhealthy attachments to some of my friends and staff around me in university. I plugged into them and relied on them far too heavily. At first people didn't think anything of it, but after a short while it became obvious that I'd lost the plot completely. In order to cope with the grief of losing Lindsay I walked around half the time picturing myself back in the children's home in Spalding. I had totally regressed! I started acting like a petulant little teenager again, throwing tantrums, spacing out for long periods of time, getting worked up over the tiniest thing, crying at unusual things. My appetite disappeared and I became pale and ill-looking as I lost night after night to insomnia.

To the onlooker, it must been very weird. I don't think anyone understood that I was having a breakdown. Some people became convinced that I was hearing voices and that I was schizophrenic. But of course, I wasn't. I was just struggling to comprehend what was going on in my own mind.

Eventually some people got scared and had to withdraw from their relationships with me. I understand now why certain people felt they had to take flight from me at this stage. Understanding when to step back in these situations is just as important as understanding when to stick around and give your support. Providing support has to be done in as safe an environment as possible for everyone, otherwise things can become troublesome. Today there are safeguarding practices with vulnerable adults, as well there should be. But back then, losing more people because of my mental state felt like another cruel blow. A betrayal.

At this time Lesley bore the brunt of my fury. One day I came home from university to find that she and one of my classmates had taken it upon themselves to book me an appointment with the counsellors at The King's House. Though a kind and loving gesture, the child in me reacted badly. I swore, I screamed, I raged at her, telling her I didn't appreciate people going behind my back and taking my decisions into their own hands. Poor Lesley was terrified, constantly on edge.

Nevertheless, I didn't seem to have a lot of choice in the matter. My tutor John had spoken to them and agreed that it was something I needed to go through if I wanted to move on from training and become ordained. He believed in me and my vocation, but I was in the second and final year of my studies now. If I didn't pull myself together and pass it, I would be finished.

A fair few people at the university wanted my head on a platter. Some people higher up than my tutor John wanted me to withdraw from training. I was hard work and they clearly weren't interested in that. But John believed in me. As a man of faith, I truly believe that he is one of the key individuals that God placed in my life. Not everyone looks at these things from a faith perspective, but that was genuinely how I saw it. He did everything in his power to stop me being withdrawn from training, and put his neck on the line for me. And he should be commended for that.

Despite my reservations, my first appointment with Peter and Anne went well. Peter was a tall, thin fellow with black hair. He seemed very laid back and relaxed, which put me at ease. Anne was small, attractive, with long brown hair and an inquisitive smile. Just like I had with Peter and Jane Haywood, I sat down and took the time to tell them my story in detail. They were very understanding, and very forgiving of my anger with God. They asked me if I was willing to make a gesture for my own mind, and write a final letter to Lindsay, in order to let go. I wrote one then and there, pouring everything into it that I should have said in person. They then gave me a match and allowed me to set the letter alight. It felt cathartic. It felt like closure.

I began to visit Peter and Anne on a regular basis. As a form of counselling their methods seemed very effective in helping me understand myself. It also brought back memories I never knew I had. There were a number of sessions that left me sobbing with anguish as images of abuse during foster care resurfaced, clearly repressed for all these years. I remembered one foster mother telling me, with a snarl in her voice, that baby Paul was my responsibility and that it was my fault he'd wet the bed. I remembered her whacking me, hard, on the bottom and the backs of my legs, punishing me for crying. I remembered being terrified that she would hurt Paul and the pressure of this responsibility made me constantly tense. I wept at the sense of the injustice I felt for myself as a toddler.

Some days were more positive than others. Some days were dark, and hollow, and depressing. Suicidal thoughts still crept their way into my mind whenever my guard was down. There was one harrowing incident, I remember, when I left college early for the day, skipping class. I remember standing not far from the college looking over the flyway. And I wanted to jump off that bridge and onto the tracks below. I stood there for ages thinking that my life was over. I thought I'd ruined everything with this breakdown. I thought I'd scuppered my chances of becoming a priest.

'There's no future,' I whispered to myself, in tears. 'There's no hope for me. I've wrecked everything.'

Somehow I managed to pull myself back long enough to call one of my university friends on the nearby payphone. I told her, through heaving sobs, what was going on. She tried her hardest to calm me down. But her voice wasn't getting through to me. Instead the only voice I could really hear was the one in my head. 'Kill yourself,' it told me. 'You're worthless. You're never going to be a priest. Go on, do it, do it, do it!' It was so powerful.

And then I thought about my two young children and my wife. Jonathan and Fiona. Lesley. They meant so much to me. Weren't they worth fighting for? Despite all the rejection and abandonment issues I had, surely I still had them? After the hell that I had put my beautiful family through, they were still there with me. Soldiering on through the storm. If they were willing to do this for me, shouldn't I have been willing to live?

I was to have more suicidal thoughts in the months to come, but Peter and Anne slowly helped me to fight them. During this time my marriage was strained, and sometimes I would catch Lesley crying when she thought she was by herself. And yet through it all, she protected Jonathan and Fiona from the turmoil and the pain. She told me over and over again that she wouldn't let me give up, even if I felt like it. She was, and still is, an amazingly strong woman.

Christmas was bittersweet, but I got through it okay with the help of my family. I still wasn't well, and I had to keep attending counselling while somehow managing to keep on studying. The following months were a very rough time for all of us. Both my wife and my counsellors had to deal with my short fuse, and I became irritated easily. I would lash out at them when I felt that they were speaking down to me, or accuse them of thinking they knew me better than I knew myself. The nightmares returned in full force as I continued to unpack my past and uncover repressed memories.

Though counselling was a slow and painful process, slowly but surely I began to notice my thinking patterns changing. Sometimes there were short gaps between my counselling sessions as I had to force myself to keep returning. Things felt different now. I was facing my demons without being medicated like I was in the children's home, and so retraining my brain was a harder fight. At the end of each session we prayed, and though God often felt elusive to me, when we prayed I felt Him trying to protect me.

I absolutely dreaded going back to university after the Easter break. I was totally convinced that I had failed my exams. Imagine my relief and delight to learn that I had passed with reasonable grades! My relief was short-lived, however, when John told me that it would be in my best interests to complete a third year at university, in order to consolidate all of the academic and personal work I'd done. I admit I was devastated, as I hated the idea of all of my classmates moving forward to ordination without me. Hadn't I weathered the storm enough?

But when John showed me his report on my progress, I felt uplifted. *Mark is particularly good at listening and talking. He is a fascinating man, full of passion and self-doubt. His love of God, his certainty of God's hand on his life, and his commitment to the Gospel, will give him a purpose in ministry which will be appreciated by many ...*

It is clear that given the right environment and encouragement, Mark will flourish in his ministry. If the Church nurtures his vocation, it will be richly rewarded.

After endless weeks of turmoil, John's words touched me deeply. I decided to put my trust in him, and my trust in God, that this was the right path for me. Besides, I was still recovering from an awful mental breakdown. I still wasn't completely okay, and this would give me time to work, in counselling, on forgiving key individuals in my past and reaching a mentally healthy place. If I could do this before I became ordained, perhaps that was for the best.

As I worked through my final year at Durham, I had to jump through an awful lot of hoops to convince the university and our bishop that I was worthy of being ordained. I continued with my counselling, which was productive but emotionally draining. It also became less frequent as I found myself becoming stronger and less fragile. I worked hard on learning how to forgive.

I had to have a psychiatric assessment and psychiatric profiling organised by the college authorities too, which was then to be reported back to the university. At the time I resented that, though looking back I can completely understand why the university felt the need to make sure I was psychologically sound. They had witnessed some very strange, non-cooperative behaviour from me in my time at Cranmer Hall. But nevertheless the decision process was long and drawn out, and John and I often felt frustrated at how long it took them to make their final judgement. For me it was the biggest test I'd ever faced.

At some point I was aware of feeling mentally strong enough to make a conscious decision. I had to stop focusing solely on myself and looking inwards at my own pain. I had spent too long only really caring about what was going on with me and my own life, and I had neglected my wife, my children and my wider family. It was time to end the self-pity party. One positive to come from having a huge question mark hang over my head was that Lesley and I became closer. We supported one another through the uncertainty. Things weren't perfect; the silences were longer than they'd ever been before and physical contact felt less natural. But slowly we began to find some kind of peace with each other again.

Thankfully I was to be rewarded for my hard work and perseverance. The psychiatric report came back and confirmed that the university deemed me fit to finish my academic studies and go on to be ordained. I was delighted.

CHAPTER 14

THE JOY OF ORDINATION

Mark Antony Edwards will be ordained deacon in Carlisle Cathedral, Sunday 2nd July 1995 at 10.30am, read the invitation. He will serve as Curate in the Parish of Ulverston in St Mary's, Cumbria.

Remember Lesley, Jonathan, and Fiona as they share in the joys and pains of ministry.

And what a joy it was! It was a scorching hot summer's day, made all the more bearable inside this beautiful cathedral, with rainbow colours dancing on the floor as the sun shone through the stained-glass windows. I sat quietly on one of the pews as I waited for friends and family to show up outside at the entrance.

I felt a mixture of elation and worry. My counselling had finished for good now as I was moving on to pastures new, but there was still obviously that old feeling of self-doubt niggling away at the back of my mind. What if I just wasn't cut out to be a priest? Perhaps all the grief I'd endured over the years was a sign that this wasn't really the path that had been set out for me?

I didn't have a long time to think about it, however, as family and friends began to file into the cathedral and I went outside to begin the proceedings. I was dressed in long black robes and worried that I would do something daft and trip over them during the ceremony.

Nevertheless, I proudly joined the procession led by the archdeacon, walking along in time with bishops, clergymen, and others who were to be ordained along with me. The organ played loudly and I felt a strong sense of peace and achievement grow from within me. *This is it*, I thought, a huge smile plastered across my face.

As we walked towards the altar I looked sideways and saw Lesley, Jonathan, and Fiona dressed in their finest. All of them smiled up at me, Fiona and Jonathan clearly amused at my outfit. Jonathan was ten now, and a beautiful young man. Fiona, now eight, looked utterly adorable in her Sunday best. I made eye contact with Lesley and we smiled at each other shyly. Over the past few months we'd fallen head over heels in love with each other again and I was incredibly proud of my beautiful young family.

I spotted some other familiar faces in the audience but they didn't quite register with me in my nervousness. Butterflies fluttered around in my stomach as I sat down in my designated seat. The enormousness of my achievement was overwhelming but in a good way. As we began to sing hymns my doubts washed away and I basked in the joy of the moment. It had been a long time since I'd felt so happy.

Following the service the other newly ordained deacons and I began to administer communion to the congregation. One by one they lined up to receive the bread I handed to them from a golden plate. 'The body of our Lord Jesus Christ, broken for you ...' I said in a low voice to the bowed head in front of me.

'Amen,' the man replied. *I recognise that voice*, I thought. The man looked up.

'Paul!' I choked, delighted and moved that he was here to worship with me. It was the first time we'd ever come together as true Christians and it was so lovely to see him looking happy and untroubled.

That wasn't the only pleasant surprise. After I'd finished the Holy

Communion I left the cathedral to find a big group of friends and family waiting for me. Peter and Jane Haywood were there, talking to Lesley and the kids. I really appreciated them coming all this way just to see me. I clapped Peter on the back and kissed Jane, turning away only to find John Pritchard standing behind me. I hugged him warmly. If it wasn't for him I wouldn't have been there and I felt so grateful to God for placing him in my life. But the biggest and most pleasant surprise was yet to come. As I was hugging my son and daughter, I felt a tap on my shoulder. I stood up to see who had done it, and found myself staring at a familiar face from long ago. It was Uncle Andrews!

'Uncle!' I yelled in joy at him, giving him an enormous hug. 'How are you? How did you know about my ordination?'

He smiled at me. His hair was greyer now, and he seemed shorter. But I guess I'd only known him when I was a boy. 'Your sister Shene told me about your ordination, and invited me up here.' His Scottish accent was as strong as ever.

'Is Aunty with you?' I asked.

'I'm afraid not,' Uncle replied. 'She died two years ago.'

I took his hand and squeezed it in what I hoped was a comforting manner. 'I'm so sorry to hear it, Uncle.'

'Thank you, Mark,' he responded. 'She would have been very proud of you.'

I shook his hand again, memories of the children's home flooding my mind. But as they did, a realisation hit me. I had not looked out into the crowd today, looking for a particular face. I hadn't craved her presence. She hadn't even entered my mind. After a lifetime of pain and obsession and torment, I had managed to let go of my love for Lindsay. I was finally free.

What an absolute joy it was to see so many of my loved ones mingling and chatting to each other. So many people I loved were all here together to celebrate my big day. Here were my friends and my family and people who had cared for me over the years. People who had stuck by me through incredibly hard times, and people who had nurtured me and looked after me with no obligation to do so. *Nobody's child? I hardly think so.*

I sighed deeply and looked down at my robes. My gaze wandered and feasted on the splendour of the beautiful cathedral before me. I said a silent prayer to myself as I watched my loved ones interacting and celebrating with each other in the beautiful sunshine.

A new feeling washed over me. It took me a moment to realise what it was, but when I did, tears sprung to my eyes. I no longer felt let down. I no longer felt rejected.

Instead all I felt was the strong, unconditional love of a Father.

CHAPTER 15

STILL FIGHTING THE STIGMA

The previous chapter reads like a brilliant, final happy ending. Of course, life is never quite so simple.

It wasn't all bad, of course. I absolutely adored the first six months of my curacy at St Mary's. I did some pastoral visiting, got involved in the local youth club and loved getting to know people. Lesley, Jonathan and Fiona were content and settled in our home. I had managed to become a Church of England Anglican curate despite so many years of adversity and hardship. Things really did look as though it was all going to be okay.

But all too soon, before I could really get into the swing of things, another problem reared its ugly head. This time, it was my physical health rather than my mental health that started causing me issues. It wasn't long before I'd started to lose quite a bit of weight. I was blacking out fairly regularly during services, which was embarrassing. I was also passing blood a lot and that was frankly terrifying.

It had been going on for weeks before I had it seen to, as for one reason or another I hadn't got round to getting it sorted. A small part of me was also petrified that it might be cancer. I'd heard of people having similar symptoms to mine who ended up having cancer and sometimes that scares you into inaction rather than action. Eventually, though, Lesley pushed me to see the doctor and I had some blood tests taken.

Seeing the doctor resulted in my being signed off sick for a few weeks, as I had to have regular blood transfusions until they found out what was wrong with me. It wasn't ideal as I was still so new to curacy. It was an added inconvenience on top of the number of blackouts I'd had during services.

My rector, the man I worked under at the church, was incredibly unimpressed and he never failed to show it. He made things awkward between us at every turn, and got angry with me whenever I had to call in sick. As a young and still mentally fragile man, this bothered me. I didn't want to feel victimised by someone who I was trying my best for, especially when I had no control over my physical health.

One day I called John Pritchard to vent my frustrations and concerns to him. He had been hearing things on the grapevine and warned me that my rector might be planning to fire me. Distressed, I headed over to the rectory to see what he had to say for himself.

'I've heard some things through John Pritchard, and I need to know what is going on,' I said to him.

'You'll hear from the bishop in due course. I can't say anything here,' he answered, slamming the door in my face. I just stood there for a few minutes, staring at the door, shaking.

But nothing was to be done. I couldn't get answers out of him if he didn't want to give me them. Instead, I had to just wait it out. My mind was a little distracted anyway, as shortly after that I was admitted into hospital for more tests.

In between hospital stays, our bishop visited us. He confirmed my worst fears: the rector wanted me gone. The reason was cited as 'a clash of personalities' and I'd always got the sense that the rector was unhappy with my background and therefore unhappy with who I was as a person as a result. This was a horrible mirror of what had happened to me in the children's home when I'd been given the sack: people were intimidated by my personal life and I bore the brunt of the stigma of it. I'm sure it won't be to anyone's surprise that I was feeling rejected all over again.

I wasn't to be suspended and I still had my licence, but what it meant was that I would have to restart my curacy somewhere else. I would also have to wait an extra year to become a priest. Yet another cruel case of history repeating itself!

Both Lesley and I were very worried, though we did our best to keep things hidden from Jonathan and Fiona over the next few weeks, who were now 11 and 9 years old. It was hard, though, because I was still very emotionally immature and my anger issues flared up with the stress of it all. My poor children had to witness me flying off the handle at times, throwing objects about and yelling. I still feel guilty about this now, but at the time it all felt out of my control. I understand now that rejection and being misunderstood were my triggers. Unfortunately, I'd had to endure a lot of these trigger events over my life and it seemed they were still destined to happen. And, admittedly, playing the 'victim' always felt easier than being the bigger person.

I understood why the rector didn't like me. He was uncomfortable with my past, but he also disliked the way I brought my personality into my worship. When I preach and teach, I like to be animated. I'm an orator. I like to use my voice and my hands and my body and my personality. I don't like to go off a script. Sometimes I'll go on for longer than intended, or on a tangent, but again I think this all feeds back to me wanting to be freer and less under the control of an external rule or force. It's precisely why I am a man of faith, but I don't like religion. I like to be as authentic as possible, rather than resorting to forced piousness. The rector clearly didn't like that.

The local community were outraged on our behalf too. Some wrote letters to Bishop Ian, some wanted to go storming round to the rector's house, and others just shared their sympathies with us. It was nice to know that they supported us, but it was no wonder we were feeling vulnerable as I was also due to go into surgery that July. I'd been diagnosed with a large intestinal diverticulum, and I went under the knife to have it fixed. Thankfully, it was a success and it was removed, with no sign of cancer anywhere. That was one thing off my mind.

Waiting for news about my new curacy was hard. At times I felt like giving up. In fact, I distinctly remember saying to myself, 'I'm giving God three months to turn this around, otherwise I'm giving up my holy orders.' That was how desperate I was at the time.

But I wasn't to be let down. Soon I received a letter from the bishop: I was to restart my curacy at St John's on Barrow Island under Reverend Ian Davies. My ordination would take place in December 1996. We would carry on living in Ulverston until a house became available to us. I knew I'd have to work hard to prove myself, but I'd done that plenty of times before. I was in a healthier state of mind now and I felt ready to tackle my obvious reputation as a 'problem' curate.

The rest of my curacy went well under Reverend Ian in terms of my vocation, though I still really struggled with my anger issues. I just couldn't get a hold on them no matter what I did. My poor kids really suffered on the receiving end of it and we'd often have blazing rows with each other. I would tell Lesley off for doing the smallest thing, and she took it all with calmness. I still don't know how she did it.

Sometimes I would take things out on Ian too. Once, we were playing squash and I lost my temper. I was in a bad mood anyway because I'd argued with my son. I threw the racket at Ian and nearly took his head off! He said, 'You need to calm down,' and I got angry. Has anyone ever calmed down after being told to calm down? I certainly haven't! He responded by putting me up against the wall until I'd cooled down a bit. He said to me, 'When you're in charge of your own parish, you cannot act this way. You've got anger issues, Mark, and you need to deal with them.'

I really am thankful that he did this for me. He nurtured me in the ministry, let me develop at my own pace and affirmed me. He pulled me up and reined me in when he needed to. He told me that he knew the stories that had been going around about me being a problem were untrue, and that he'd defied the local authorities who wanted rid of me. The man was a legend. He did such a great job that ten months into my curacy with him he wrote a report to the bishop recommending that I be allowed to take up priesthood early. He wrote about my passion for people, my passion for God and my good work in the local community. What's more, the bishop agreed. I was ecstatic!

And so it was that I was ordained as priest in Carlisle Cathedral in 1997. I began my priesthood with enthusiasm and I was very well accepted in Barrow. Things got off to a happy start, but I faced a confusing mix of emotions when I learnt that my mother had died. I hadn't seen her much over the years, except for one visit not long after I'd first been ordained as curate. It had been an awkward and upsetting affair, and none of us had been very comfortable. She'd reeked of alcohol and her house was a total state. She'd also gone parading me around the neighbourhood telling people proudly that her son was a priest. I remember thinking, *Well, hold on there. I got here on my own steam!* But all I could do was just stay quiet and let her have her moment.

Now she had died and despite my lack of intimacy with my mother, I still cried. Her death brought up so many memories and regrets for me. I found myself ruminating for days on end: how might things have been different if she'd have had it together? Would my life be much different if I'd had a proper mother figure in my life? Why was she so happy to let us all suffer?

Why was I still thinking about myself when she'd died? After a short while I began telling myself to stop playing a victim, as I'd vowed to do before. She was still my mother when all was said and done. Grieving became a more bearable thing to endure when I thought about Mum's death in different terms and somehow I didn't fall apart. Young Mark would have lost it completely and had a mental breakdown. Perhaps I really had matured emotionally in some way, over the years.

The following years passed fairly happily, though it came as a bit of a shock when I started losing my hair! Embracing the baldness was difficult at first, especially with my inability to take change very well, but soon I came to like it.

Getting used to Jonathan and Fiona becoming teenagers was harder. I really didn't want my little boy and girl to get older. I struggled with Jonathan being a teenager because he'd become so moody and sullen. No medals for guessing who he'd inherited that from! With Fiona things were difficult for different reasons. I hated it when she started replacing her dolls with makeup. It was never an easy transition for fathers anyway, but with someone as emotionally messed up as me things were far more complicated! It didn't help that they were changing so much physically too.

The teenage years were very stressful for Lesley. She was the only person of calm in the eye of a storm. I argued a lot with my kids and my temper never really abated. It was like a game of good cop, bad cop, and I was certainly the bad cop. While I still enjoyed time with my family and loved my wife deeply, the stress of the constant conflict at home was getting to me. I started losing my connection with God.

On the surface, I was a fully functioning vicar with help from Reverend Ian Davies. But something in me was changing and I kept it hidden from everyone. The problem didn't really surface until one day in the summer of 1999, Ian broke it to me that he thought I should take my own parish at St Francis's and St Matthews', two churches on the other side of town. The thought of going solo made me feel sick. I wasn't ready!

'I thought I had another year on my licence here?' I asked Ian. I'd probably surprised him somewhat with my lack of enthusiasm.

'You do,' Ian replied with a smile. 'But you've done brilliantly on Barrow Island. You're the best priest I've ever known. I fully believe you're ready to have your own ministry.'

I took the compliment, but the sickened sensation I had in my stomach didn't abate. I broke the news to Lesley later that night and she was thrilled for me, jumping up and down in her excitement. I couldn't match her enthusiasm. Instead, I curled up into the foetal position in my office and barely moved for days. I had regressed.

There's nothing more disappointing than having depression hit you like a tonne of bricks again, especially when you thought you were over it. But I guess something deep down inside me still detested the idea of being uprooted against my will. As well as being terrified, I was seriously frustrated. Was this going to happen every time something in my life changed? Would my relationship with God always be hindered when something negative happened to me?

I spent days on the sofa in my office, curled up like a baby and only coming out for food or toilet breaks. Lesley, as the wonderful, patient, amazing wife that she is, looked after me every day. She reassured me that God had not abandoned me. Reverend Ian would still be there to mentor me, only at the other side of town. Jonathan and Fiona were fine with the move, she said, as was she. It wasn't much further for her to go to work or for the kids to walk to school. We would have to wait until the vicarage near St Francis was renovated anyway, so it would be a slow and gradual change. And besides, this was far better than having to move to a new city completely. It wasn't that big a transition at all!

Slowly but surely she lifted me out of the mire. I began to eat and sleep again and the fog lifted from my mind. I came round to the idea and fought through the depression by telling myself that I was having to move for positive reasons: I had done so well as a vicar that I was getting my own church early. It was something to rejoice about! Plus I met the new rector, David Kennedy, who turned out to be brand new to the church just like I was and so I wouldn't be alone in having to tackle a new challenge head on. Perhaps things weren't going to be so bad after all.

CHAPTER 16

FINDING MY WAY BACK

On 30th March 2000, my new life kicked into gear. I was to look after the Ormsgill estate which had its fair share of problems, being one of the poorer estates in the area. I relished the challenge, though, and threw myself into my work with gusto.

There were a few teething problems at first. Some of the congregation weren't happy when I invited children from the local school into our services. They didn't like it when I let the kids dress up in the vestments and people thought they were too loud and distracting. It caused some people not to return to services, but I couldn't stop myself from welcoming the children in.

I was still struggling with a crisis of faith and it was a struggle that I kept largely internal, except for the odd discussion with David. He reassured me that things would get better, but our discussions didn't go into any more detail than that because he had his own new-starter teething problems to sort out. For this reason I just kept ploughing on and working hard, hoping that I would feel God's presence again soon enough.

Something else was on my mind too. I was 39 now and Lesley was 40, but after much discussion and prayer we'd decided to start trying for another baby. We did everything in our power to make things happen including fertility tests, but with each disappointment every month came a kind of heartbreak. This did nothing to help with my faith issues and I was just about keeping my depression at bay, though I could feel it trying to knock down the door within my mind. I hid it very well behind my dog collar, but I was slipping.

Eventually the doctors gave us the worst news. The fertility tests showed that we were unlikely to ever conceive again.

'What will we do, Mark?' Lesley sobbed to me that night. 'Maybe we left it too late, but I so wanted another child.'

I held her in my arms and tried my best to reassure her. 'Let's pray,' I said to her, sounding far more confident about God than I actually felt. 'If anything can make this happen for us, He can.'

I admit I felt like a fraud. At this point my faith in God had pretty much disappeared. I was holding things together for Lesley but inside I felt dead. God had left me and I wasn't sure how to find him again. But I didn't want to tell Lesley. Added stress would not help her conceive.

While I felt like I was unable to hear God's voice any more, he must have heard mine and Lesley's. One sunny day in 2001, I was working in my study and was alarmed to hear Lesley crying out.

I ran upstairs to meet her, my eyes searching her body for an injury or ailment. 'What's wrong? What's going on?'

She was crying hysterically and couldn't say anything. But she didn't have to. The positive pregnancy test in her hand said it all. We threw our arms around each other and wept. What a miracle!

We decided not to tell anyone outside of close friends and family for a while that Lesley was pregnant. It was hard not to break the news to people, though, especially as I couldn't stop myself strutting around the place and grinning like the Cheshire Cat. I felt less pressured now, too, and the insecurities I had about possibly being infertile had melted away. No wonder I was enjoying myself!

Despite a few concerns that we were getting on a bit, news of Lesley's pregnancy was met with elation by friends and family alike.

We were given a due date of March 2002 and I just couldn't wait. I supported Lesley through the morning sickness and other side effects, and loved every minute of it. Lesley grew bigger and bigger quite quickly and I often teased her about it, in a nice way. I didn't think anything of it, of course. It was a just a normal part of pregnancy – or so I thought!

But soon it became apparent as to why she was so big. One morning I was heading to the fish and chip shop with a friend of mine and wondering where she'd got to. I knew she was having a scan that morning while I delivered a sermon, but I thought she'd have been back ages ago. I just standing in line at the chippy waiting to be served when she called me up.

'Hello, funny face,' I said into the phone. 'Where are you? You've been gone a while.'

'Mark, I've had the scan,' Lesley said, sounding serious. Immediately my anxiety kicked in full force.

'Are you okay?' I said to her, convinced something horrible had happened. I guess I'd never got out of the habit of catastrophising. I tried to keep things light-hearted though. 'Did you find out the sex of the baby?'

Silence. Panic rose within me.

'I'm expecting twins!'

I didn't speak for a minute.

'Mark, are you there?'

'Yes, I'm here,' I responded. 'That is fantastic news!'

I was shocked but thrilled. I couldn't believe it! Twins!

Lesley's pregnancy progressed well over the next few months. I welcomed that sense of excitement again, the one that came with expecting a new baby. It gave me something to focus on other than my crisis of faith, and quite frankly it kept me going. I still believed in

God as a concept, but I just couldn't feel or hear him any more.

I thought that maybe prayer and more Bible studying would help, but it seemed I was destined to be tested over and over again. This time it was with the death of my father.

When Lesley broke the news to me that he was in hospital in Boston and feared to be dying, I was surprised that the news didn't hit me as hard as I was expecting. I guess it was because he'd never really been present for most of my life. I admit I felt guilty, because all it really felt like was the death of a member of my congregation. I felt sad, but it didn't touch me deeply. And when Shene called to tell me he'd passed away, I felt the same. There was a kind of numbness there, and a deep regret for what could have been.

I wanted to attend the funeral, though, and pay my respects in the same way I would do for anyone else. I wanted to do a gospel reading and say goodbye in the right way. My old best friend Fram still lived in Boston, and so I called him and asked him if we could stay with him.

'Please, come!' Fram said to me down the phone. 'It will be lovely to see you again.'

We took the five-hour drive down to Boston and greeted Fram, his wife Joel, and their beautiful children. I was genuinely thrilled to see my old friend again. It had been about six years since I'd seen him last. He had struggled with leukaemia in recent years but he was in remission, and looked good for it. We hugged tightly and spent a lovely night together with our families, reminiscing about old times back when I was in the children's home. We remembered the humongous meals his mother used to cook for me, and the time I got in serious trouble with Aunty Lindsay for going on the paper round and coming in late. We chuckled all night and it felt so good to remember the past for positive reasons, especially as I knew the next day would be tough.

At some point in the evening I called my sister Jenny, Shene's twin, to make sure that everything was arranged for the next day.

'Oh Mark,' she said to me worriedly down the phone. 'The curate still hasn't been in touch about tomorrow.'

'What? That's not on! How unprofessional,' I responded. 'Let me call him and see what's happening.'

When I finally managed to get through to him, he surprised me by telling me that he believed God wanted me to perform the funeral. In my shock all I could really do was say yes. My sister was horrified, but who was I to argue with the curate if he'd said God had spoken to him? Even if it was a load of rubbish, I didn't feel like there was anything else I could do.

And so it was that the following day I took my father's funeral service. I was honest in my speech. I told people that Dad hadn't been able to look after me and my siblings, but that he'd done the best he could. I told funny stories about some of the happier times with Dad. I tried to drive out the memory of being driven away from him in the car all those years ago. When I thought about this, the pain began to squeeze its grip tighter on my heart. Reliving the past seemed to do something to my emotions where they'd previously been numb.

I held my dad's hand as he laid there in front of me in his coffin. Tears came then, hot and heavy. It was still the regret that hurt me. I could have worked harder at being close to him when I was older. We could have had some kind of relationship, but I'd been far too wrapped up in myself and my own mental health issues to care about anyone else. 'I'm sorry, Dad,' I whispered to him. 'I love you. I forgive you.'

I supported my sisters and brother through the service, all of whom were crying and trying to hold themselves together. Paul was still suffering with depression and anxiety and because I knew all too well what that was like, we all rallied around him. He took it very hard and broke down at the end of the service. My sisters and I had to help him up and out of the crematorium. Lesley comforted me throughout the service, and her love warmed me through. I made a promise to myself then and there that I would be a brilliant father to the twins. I'd made mistakes before, but I hated the idea of failing the way that my dad had. I promised myself that my kids would never feel this deep, sorrowful regret, missing what never was.

Later that night, I found that I couldn't really identify how I was feeling. When I was alone, I spoke to a God I hadn't felt in long time. 'Where are you, Lord?' I whispered. 'This hurts more than I thought it would. Where are you?' Still I sensed no response, no real clue that He was there. The Bible sat on the desk in front of me in my study, and it felt more like a relic than anything else now.

As the months went on, I found myself becoming, quietly, more and more desperate. I continued to carry out my services, but they felt hollow and meaningless. I did my best to stay active and put an effort into engaging with my flock. Throwing myself into tasks was the only thing I could really do. I called out to God every day, but I didn't get anything back.

Lesley continued to grow quickly and became so tired that eventually she had to take to her bed and rest. The twins were due to arrive during the week of Lent, which stressed me out a bit because it meant that me and my colleagues would all be busy. As it turned out, she was two weeks overdue before she went into labour.

I cried with joy when Joshua James and Mark Antony Jr. were brought into the world on 23rd March 2002 – finally, after hours of labour. They were so tiny and perfect. Joshua weighed five pounds and Mark Jr. weighed four pounds. Joshua screamed loudly when he was born, but Mark Jr. stayed eerily silent. After an initial panic, we were told that he had some fluid on his lungs. But the silence didn't last long! We breathed a sigh of relief and went back to revering our beautiful new boys.

That night I returned home for some much-needed rest. I was exhausted, so goodness knows how Lesley was feeling! I flopped onto the bed and was soon in a deep, contented sleep. I managed to get a few hours of shut-eye before the phone rang.

I stared at the clock in the darkness. It was 11.30pm. My blood ran cold. Surely a phone call this late couldn't be good news?

'Hello?' I croaked into the receiver.

'Mark, it's me,' said Lesley. She could barely choke out the words.

'What's wrong, love?'

'It's Mark Junior! They've had to resuscitate him twice, Mark! He stopped breathing and went purple.' Her huge racking sobs tore pieces out of my heart.

'Is he okay now?' I asked her, my heart beating a million times a minute.

'No, he's not! His oesophagus isn't joined to his stomach. He can't eat and he can't breathe properly. He needs to be taken to Liverpool children's hospital for emergency surgery.'

The room spun around me as I listened to her crying down the phone. My baby.

'Mark ...' Lesley said to me, hiccupping. 'Pray. Please pray for him.'

Her words cut me deeply. I would pray; I knew I would pray. But was anybody listening?

Mark Jr. was taken to surgery in the early hours of the next morning. He underwent a six-hour surgical procedure but we were told pretty quickly that it had all gone well. The relief was immense, but as Joshua was so small himself, Lesley was kept in our local hospital with him. I couldn't be with my family all day every day as I was very busy with Holy Week at work, but I visited Lesley and Joshua as often as I could. Lesley found separation from Mark Jr. very difficult, and clearly Joshua did too: he began losing weight after Mark Jr. left. It was a trying, emotional time for all of us but somehow, we saw it through. We had to.

We did manage to visit him once. It was harrowing to see my poor baby hooked up to so many tubes and machines. And despite my crisis of faith, I found myself praying more than ever. I had no idea, and no real conviction, that my prayers were being heard. But all the same, that didn't stop me appealing to God in my biggest hour of need yet. This wasn't about me any more. It was about my family.

And against all the odds, four weeks later our family were back together again. Mark Jr. came forward in leaps and bounds, and soon we were facing the more common, mundane challenges of family life. Lesley and I were now both in our forties and we could really tell the difference between raising babies as 20-year-olds and raising them as older parents. But our house was full of laughter (when I wasn't arguing with Fiona, who'd become a fully fledged teenager with an attitude!) and our community just adored the twins.

Throughout all this I kept my crisis of faith well hidden. To be honest, I was too wrapped up in my beautiful new sons to really pay it much attention. I admit I was relieved – whenever I thought about it too much, I felt a deepening depression creep over me. What was wrong with me that after all these years, after everything I'd been through, I'd managed to lose God along the way? I felt so disappointed in myself that I could feel my mental health slowly but surely deteriorating.

Mark Jr. continued to go in and out of hospital. Every few weeks he would go through a terrifying relapse where he struggled to breathe, vomited, became dehydrated and lost consciousness. It turned out that he also had some kind of congenital problems caused by his emergency surgery when he was born. It was a trying time for all of us.

I also often felt bad about my parenting skills, especially when it came to Jonathan and Fiona. I struggled to understand Jonathan as he entered a Goth phase, and Fiona and I had the most horrific, blazing rows. I'd had no real role model for parenting as a child, and I could feel the effect that my past was having on my home life. No matter what I did I seemed to get things wrong. Lesley was the opposite to me, and I still maintain that it was her calmness and level-headedness that got us through that turbulent time.

Another change came upon us too, one that I'd known was coming for a while. Our house, the vicarage I knew I would have to live in one day, had finally been fully renovated and we were to move into it as soon as we could. It was right opposite St Francis, the church in which I worked.

On top of all this, my work life became harder. David, my rector, had been having issues with a small minority within the troubled community and his mother was seriously ill in another city. I sensed something was happening but it still came as a nasty surprise when he told me that he would be leaving St Matthew's. This meant that both churches would now be under my watch. The pressure was anything but light: I would have to look after two churches and Ormsgill, which was in itself a troubled place.

Perhaps it comes as no surprise, then, that by 2003 I was feeling really rather low and isolated. That connection that I felt with the Lord and with Jesus had gone. No amount of religious ritual or ceremony helped and I was lost.

I decided that it might be a good idea to give volunteering a try, to attempt to reconnect with that part of the gospel that encouraged people to contribute in the wider community outside of their daily duties. I'd been chaplain of the RNLI for a while, and I had applied to join them but been refused. According to them it was because I didn't live close enough to their station, but I suspected it was actually because I was a vicar. The rejection had stung as always, but I'd tried to shake it off. I had had far too much on my plate to worry about it at the time.

Perhaps that was a blessing in disguise, though. One day I was flicking through the local newspaper when an article caught my eye. It was about Duddon Inshore Rescue, and they were looking for volunteers at the lifeboat station. I smiled. Surely this was meant to be?

Before I could get too excited, though, Mark Jr. suffered yet another relapse and I forgot about it for a while. Mark Jr.'s illness felt unrelenting. Every time he went into hospital we feared for his life. Perhaps it was for this reason, then, that quite a few weeks later I still felt the urge to get in contact with Duddon Inshore Rescue.

'Are you still looking for volunteers?' I asked the man on the other end of the phone. 'It's been a few weeks since you last advertised, but I've been rather preoccupied.'

'Yes, absolutely!' came the reply.

'Just one question – I'm actually a vicar. Will this be a problem? Can I still join?'

'That shouldn't be a problem at all,' he said. 'I'll take it to the committee, but I can't see any reason why not.'

Fantastic! I thought.

That weekend I went down to meet the crew and get an idea of what the post would involve. Dave, the station officer, met me and took me on a tour of the boat house and the station, which was situated near the village and past some allotments. He showed me the crew room, mobile response unit, even the uniform that I would get after six months of volunteering!

I was seriously excited! So much so that Lesley had to rein me in a bit and tell me to take things one step at a time. But it was just so nice to have something to feel excited about again. God was still elusive and this gave me a chance to give back in a different capacity. It was one place I knew I could be myself without any worrying or holding back.

After a few nerve-wracking weeks during which I thought I wouldn't be accepted onto the committee (so many people often thought that as a vicar I wanted to spend my time converting people, which is far from the truth) Dave showed up on my doorstep with my pager and information about training schedules. I was on the team! I was delighted.

I was even more delighted when our first call came in and I got to see the mechanics of how it all worked. There was no other feeling like the adrenaline pumping through my body as I drove as fast as I could to the boathouse, got introduced quickly to the rest of the crew, rushed towards Askam pier in a hard hat and floatation suit, and played my part in helping to help someone who had been pulled out of the water. It took my mind off the stresses of arguing with my teenage kids and being convinced they hated me, a sick child, creeping depression and a crisis of faith. I couldn't wait to get really stuck in.

Six months later I'd received my uniform and, through some work I undertook through my own initiative, raised over £3,000 for the team.

The next few years proved both to be a blessing and a challenge for me. While quietly trying to renew my faith through worship and study, I would go out into the community and help the most needy and vulnerable. The area saw a lot of crime and violence, but I even managed to form good relationships with some of the troubled kids who often found themselves in trouble. I did my best to bridge the gap between the two churches I was looking after now that David, the rector, had left, which was a challenge in and of itself, but people appreciated my efforts.

All this was a mask, however, and no one really knew what was going on beyond the collar. No one, that is, except my family, who had now got to a point where they were telling me I had to get help for my anger issues. The depression and deep, ingrained fury, it seemed, were bubbling back up to the surface. It had been quite a few stressful years since I'd last had any counselling and it was beginning to show.

In January 2005, I made a promise to myself – that this would be the 'year of the Lord'. I wasn't even sure what that meant, except that I knew I had to find some way of finding my faith again. Not feeling a connection with God or Jesus while I was going through a lot of upheaval was seriously starting to depress me. I felt let down by God but most of all I felt let down by myself. I thought I'd conquered my mental health issues, and yet here they were creeping back on me, ever closer and ever more sinister. All I could do was keep things going to the best of my ability – with a fair bit of difficulty due to politics within the church and backlash from the community when I got things wrong – but that's all it felt like. Like I was going through the motions with no real joy in what I was doing.

I've done a lot of writing over the years, and I remember at one point writing down the words, 'God is dead and the church sucks!' I honestly, genuinely felt that way. My licence would be up for renewal again in two years and I was terrified, absolutely terrified, that I would be made to move yet again. Maybe when I was mentally stronger I could have handled it, but I could feel myself slipping back into that dark, deep pit of depression and I felt another rejection might just break me.

Jonathan was now a (very hairy!) 20-year-old and Fiona almost 18. They were both ready to fly the nest, to university and elsewhere, and it was hurting. I couldn't quite articulate to them how guilty I felt about how I'd treated them the past few years. I did my best to manipulate the situation so that they could stay at home longer despite our issues, and as you can imagine that went down like a lead balloon. I hated the feeling of losing connection with another important part of my life. I didn't want to alienate my kids but I knew no other way of behaving. Every night I went to bed feeling like a terrible person, and it began to weigh down on my shoulders.

The day came for them to leave and I held it together as best I could. We drove Fiona to her university halls of residence in Preston while Jonathan was moving out to live with his mates (all who looked as yeti-like as Jonathan did!) in Manchester. I hugged them both tightly and told them I loved them when they walked away from me, but I lost my composure when I returned home to two empty bedrooms. I cried and cried a lot that night. Something had been ripped out of me that I could only get back when they visited during holiday times.

Mark Jr. was still very poorly, but that became a normal part of life. Other than that, he and his twin were such happy kids, and that served as a tiny ray of sunshine in my otherwise rather grey outlook on life. I wondered why Lesley wanted to be around me. I felt hollow and depressed and we'd always shared our love of God with one another. Now I didn't even have that to share with her; instead she had to deal with a grumpy, angry, bitter man who had lost his zest for life. I worried about how my older two were getting on and never seemed to be cheerful any more. It must have been so draining for her.

I've said it before in this book and I'll say it again: Lesley is the most wonderful woman in the world. Throughout this horrible depressive phase, she never left my side. She had endless patience and love for me, even though I'd never made her life easy. Having her support and understanding helped me get through the darkest days. She'd even given up drinking alcohol for me so that I was never tempted, as I was well aware of the the role it played in at least one of my suicide attempts in the past.

Something had to be done; I knew it. I knew I was feeling depressed because I didn't like change or stressful situations, but it was more than that. I was depressed because I'd built mine and my family's lives on a foundation of my faith. Without it, I felt like a huge fraud and unable to do my duties as a husband and father properly. Hadn't I failed enough in life?

Despite my depression, therefore, I did feel a motivation to make a change. I sought out help wherever I could find it. And so one night, with this in mind, I said a quick prayer and flicked through the channels on TV, looking for the God channel. When I found it, there was a loud-mouthed Texan shouting and throwing his hands about in the air. He kept yelling something about forgetting all else and putting the word of God first, as the final authority. I immediately felt irritated at his demeanour and how over the top he seemed, labelled him as a fanatic in my mind and switched off the TV.

But something niggled at my brain that night in bed. Despite wanting to dismiss this man as daft and a bit wacky, my mind was telling me that what he'd said had actually made sense. When all was said and done, it was God's word that mattered most to me; I just hadn't felt like I could hear it for so long. It was, after all, the judgement and the pomp and fake piousness of some people within the church community that made me feel so worried and nervous and misunderstood all the time. If I did my best to tune that out, would I be happier? Would I be able find my faith again?

Perhaps if I couldn't hear God directly, what I really needed to do was seek Him out elsewhere, through other people and other mediums. Maybe I could find Him in something other than the overly formal texts and ways of worship that I used in my ministry. Before I fell asleep that night I vowed to myself that I would give this man another go. I just had to find him again first, as I had no idea who he was.

I spent the next few days flicking through the channel, hoping to find the speaker again. It didn't take me long before I chanced upon him again, and found that his name was Kenneth Copeland. Yes, he was quite full-on, but as I watched him speak I knew I'd found something that spoke to me on a level that no one else had done before.

Fair enough, Ken Copeland seemed like a bit of fanatic and over the top, and I found out later on that he was unpopular for a number of reasons, but maybe I just needed God's word communicated to me in a new and different way. Perhaps I needed his level of excitement in order to kick-start my faith again.

Ken Copeland was far from perfect and he had a lot of critics, which I understood. A lot of people around me didn't react that well when I told them about it; many people found Ken Copeland to be money-grabbing and controversial. But I tried to filter out all of the negativity and just focus on what he was saying about God, rather than anything else. It touched me for a reason. Through his preaching he taught me to focus on the Bible and God's message, rather than getting worked up about the bureaucracy of the Church, which had admittedly been causing me so much stress over the years. He taught me to trust that God was the only one I really needed to listen to, that I needed to filter out all of the negativity of my environment when I considered my faith. For this reason, I found Ken Copeland to be absolutely wonderful. He spoke to me on a level that no one else had done for a long time.

I couldn't believe the impact this had on my life. Seemingly overnight my faith returned with full force, and I felt excited about God and Jesus again. I shared my discovery with Lesley, who was worried at first that I'd joined some kind of cult. I understood her reservations as Ken Copeland did come with a reputation for being a bit of a nut, but I explained to her that it was his message and the delivery of his message that had so inspired me again.

Once Lesley realised that I wasn't just developing yet another obsession like I normally did, she confessed that her own faith had been waning recently too. I was shocked – Lesley had always seemed so steadfast in her commitment to God. But then I had to remind myself that she'd been through all the same pain I had too: the stress of arguments, the upheaval of constant relocations, the terrifying realities of having a sick child. Again, my depression had made me become absorbed with my own issues again and I had forgotten to take a good look around me. The good thing is that Lesley fully embraced Ken Copeland as I had, and her faith was strengthened too.

Now it looked like there was some kind of light at the end of the tunnel. I could feel peace spreading itself over my body. I now had a reason to try to drag myself out of this pit I found myself in. I'd realised that despite everything I had around me in my life, I'd lost joy in existence. It hit me just how depressed I'd become and how ashamed I had felt about that. I was supposed to have overcome all this and it hurt me that I hadn't managed to after all.

For this reason I was well aware that I also needed to address my mental health issues in a practical way. I might have found my faith again but I needed to tackle the misery and the anger that my crisis of faith had created within me. And even though being proactive and productive is incredibly hard for someone dealing with mental health issues, I took the momentous decision that my days of curling up in the foetal position on my couch and weeping were over. I wanted to take control of my mind again, now that God had retaken control of my heart and soul. At this stage I was desperate and willing to try anything. I was losing sleep through worry and self-hatred. But something was stirring in me and I finally felt like I might be rediscovering God again. It was also time to rediscover the Mark who was mentally healthy and happy, too.

Counselling wasn't really an option for me as money was tight and my time even tighter. The only way I could really think about tackling my depression, anxiety and unhelpful thinking was through self-help. After all, I was used to using literature to help me find peace in life; there was no reason I couldn't use it to achieve good mental health!

And so it was through my own research that I fell upon the names Dr Caroline Leaf and Joyce Meyer. Yes, they were both Christians and that appealed to me, but more helpfully they both worked in fields that dealt with cognitive neuroscience, emotional wellbeing and mental health. Over the next few months I ordered every book they'd written on mental health and I began to practise mindfulness. I researched these women's scientific methods on retraining your brain and changing your thought patterns in order to change your outlook on life and lift depression and anxiety. Their theories were entirely research and evidence-based, and their insistence that I could take control of my own mind spoke to me on so many levels.

Dr Leaf and Joyce Meyer spoke on TV and online, and discussed the tendency to focus on the problem rather than the solution. They pointed out that many people have the urge to ruminate over the past and I knew they were talking about people like me who'd had turbulent experiences in life. Their books taught me that I wasn't a victim and that I could, with enough effort and time, choose how I react to things. With their help I started to change my way of thinking and, with a lot of hard work and frustration, I was able to start looking at my life in a more productive way. I was in control, and I always had been. I had always been at my most depressed when I felt that this wasn't the case.

I remembered my days of counselling with The King's House and Peter and Jane Haywood. They'd always taught me to tackle my unhelpful thinking patterns and this worked in a very similar way. It wasn't the world around me that needed to change, it was me and how I dealt with my emotions. I just needed guidance to help me achieve it. Through self-help, my mental health began to improve.

Over the months, with Ken Copeland's help and the psychological teachings of Leaf, Meyer and others like them, I found myself looking at things in a much healthier way. It was a bumpy ride and my recovery wasn't instantaneous, but slowly I began to find it easier to get out of bed in a morning. I could feel my spirits and depression lift. My angry outbursts massively reduced in number and my thought patterns became less toxic. I shared my story with friends and family and they were delighted with my progress and my new-found happiness. I had fallen in love with life again, and it showed!

CHAPTER 17

RECEIVING RECOGNITION FOR ALL THE RIGHT REASONS

Volunteering on the lifeboats in Barrow-in-Furness was always rewarding, and I loved it from day one. Of course I was always a bit apprehensive, and actually it turned out I wasn't alone in feeling that way.

The previous captain of the lifeboats and Dave's predecessor, Bernard (nicknamed the Admiral) was a little wary of me when I first joined. I can't say I wasn't used to that at this point in my life, though, and I didn't let it get to me too much. We developed a strong bond eventually, but at first I guess I had to prove myself. And that's okay – everybody does at some point or another. Turns out I hit the ground running anyway, and we hit it off. He was a character and a half! He was always so cheeky and funny and made volunteering a lot of fun.

When I joined the team, the other members saw an opportunity. It turns out that they had been trying to get Bernard an MBE for quite some time. He had done so much for his community and they wanted to show their gratitude and admiration. The trouble was that they just hadn't got very far at all, despite their best efforts. And that's where I came in. As I was a Reverend, they came to me for guidance and advice.

I didn't know anything about the procedure myself, but having seen in a short amount of time how brilliant Bernard was, I was very happy to help. 'What have you done so far, lads?' I asked them, expecting them to talk me through some kind of process.

Instead, they handed me a manila envelope with some paperwork in it. 'This is a photocopy. We've sent all this, but we're not getting anywhere,' one of the lads told me. Intrigued, I had a read through and learnt a lot about Bernard and his contributions to the Barrow-in-Furness community. However, I could tell that this wouldn't really get them anywhere. There didn't seem to be anything very official about how they'd gone about it, although they had managed to put together a lot of great citations and references for him.

I decided to do some research on how to apply for an MBE, and worked out all the official procedures to follow and forms to fill out. I used the information the team had given me and sent it off for them, happy to be of some assistance. The Admiral was a very inspirational man! A jolly-looking fellow with a beaming smile and caring demeanour, he had clearly inspired many others too.

And as it turns out, this was instrumental in helping him to get his MBE. Eventually, and much deservedly, he received it at a ceremony in Buckingham Palace. He had saved many lives in his time; I was absolutely thrilled to help him receive recognition.

Some time passed and my work with the lifeboats continued to go from strength to strength. The more Bernard got to know me, the more he warmed to me and any apprehension on either side melted away. I formed a camaraderie with Bernard and the rest of the team, and I spent some very happy times there.

Sometime in around 2008, on a busy but productive day, Bernard took me aside and said to me, 'I'd like to put you forward for an MBE, Mark. How would you feel about that?'

I was very taken aback. I was thankful but dismissed it a little bit at first. 'To be honest, Bernard, I don't really know that I have done enough to get an MBE.' Self-confidence has never been my strong suit.

'Look,' he said to me, his eyes twinkling and his big broad grin beaming. 'Just give me an outline of all the things you've done in the past.'

'Well, okay,' I replied. I was actually intrigued to see what it would all look like down on paper. And so I went away and put together a list of everything I could remember doing. I went right back to my early days in the city mission, discussed my community work, listed youth projects, and outlined my volunteering posts. I wrote about my work with the homeless, assisting on a difficult estate in Barrow, my role on the lifeboats, fundraising and so forth. When I had finished, it was quite a list! I thought to myself, 'I can't believe I've been involved in all this stuff!' I hadn't realised just how much good work I had pioneered over the years.

Thinking that maybe it was worth a shot after all, I handed the information over to Bernard who, as I found out afterwards, worked alongside his wife to put together the application. He then went, in person, to the local MP's office and said to him, 'I'm not leaving here until you write a citation for Father Mark. Because Mark has contributed to the community in Barrow in a big way.'

Bernard's powers of persuasion were clearly strong as the MP wrote me a citation there and then! Not only that, but Bernard garnered citations from some others, too. He submitted it and I forgot about it for a good long while. In fact, it wasn't until the year after, when I'd moved away from Barrow-in-Furness to Newcastle upon Tyne, that I got a letter informing me that I was to be awarded an MBE.

Her Majesty would be graciously pleased to approve your appointment as a Member of the Order of the British Empire, the letter read. I was stunned!

To be honest with you, even though I knew Bernard had sent off the application, I had still thought, 'Yeah, yeah, it'll never happen. I'll believe it when the fat lady sings!' So when I read that letter I was shaking, speechless! It had always been a dream of mine to prove myself as someone worthy, and now I was going to receive one of the country's highest recognitions. I was so excited.

In many respects, it was also quite unexpected because, as you'll read in the next chapter, the way I left Barrow wasn't great. We didn't leave things on brilliant terms. But this MBE showed me that the people of Barrow really did appreciate what I'd done for them. And considering what a special man Bernard was, it meant a lot to me that he felt that I deserved one too. There really was more to me than my chequered past.

CHAPTER 18

A BATTLE BETWEEN PEACE AND ANXIETY

2008 was bearing down upon us and life was very happy in Barrow-in-Furness. We had been there as a family for almost eight contented years, and I had made it my home. I had made great friends there, and everybody knew me. My family were settled, and I felt like a real member of the community. I could have stayed there for the rest of my life, but it soon became apparent that that's not what God had in store for me. My licence was up for renewal and it didn't look likely that I would be allowed to stay on in Barrow. I felt incredibly nervous about it.

In my mind, Barrow was where I was supposed to stay and I desperately didn't want to move. But there had been some significant changes within the team in the past few years. David, our rector, had left and had eventually, after some time, been replaced with Reverend Stuart Evason who also looked after a church in the next parish. William Dean was to be the new priest at St Matthew's, and Stuart would oversee us both as a team. This meant that I would be priest only for St Francis, but that William and I would share duties as and when schedules called for it. I liked William fine, but our personalities and methods of worship clashed and William most definitely didn't like me.

William was the kind of man that liked to stick rigidly to strict rules of worship. His style was more formal and dignified, closely associated with that of the High Church. He liked to do things methodically and in a very different way to me. When he witnessed me carrying out Mass for the congregation, he was deeply unimpressed.

'Where did you learn how to celebrate Mass?' he asked me after the service.

Taken aback, I said, 'Under my vicar, Ian Davies. We practised together before I went solo. Why do you want to know?'

'No reason,' he said to me. That was the end of it then, but as we continued to work together it was obvious that things were strained between us and that he really didn't approve of my methods. He stopped asking me to cover his services, which was strange as he'd never minded it before. I started to feel disheartened; my services had never been an issue with David Kennedy but it was becoming an obvious bone of contention between us.

Eventually, I had a meeting with the archdeacon about the issues that were occurring between William and me. I was very nervous about it as he was an intimidating man. He listened closely to me as I told him all about how great my life was in Barrow and all the things I'd done to serve the community. I felt that I made my case well, backed up with plenty of evidence of how I'd contributed positively to the area.

'Mark, your licence renewal will happen anyway, and whether or not you can stay in Barrow very much rests on your relationship with William. It depends on how you can function within the team ministry,' he told me seriously.

'It takes time to build up a good relationship, archdeacon,' I said to him, unsure of who I was trying to convince more. 'There's no reason we can't come to a place of understanding. I also think there's space for two kinds of worship and two kinds of personalities.'

But it soon became obvious that the archdeacon and William Dean just didn't agree. We all went out for a lunch together and it wasn't a pleasant experience. William made it obvious from the outset that he had no time for me or my ways.

'You have to learn to keep your personality at the door,' he told me. 'There's no place for personality and eccentricity to taint the sanctity of public worship.'

'I have to disagree,' I replied. 'There are clergymen of all shapes and sizes in every church. There's no reason our two methods can't work in harmony.'

William shook his head. The archdeacon tried to remain impartial but I had a sickening feeling in my gut that told me that this wasn't going to go my way.

The consultation process went on despite my protestations. The church wardens assessed the situation between me and William and then handed me the document which summed up the process and the final decision. As I read through the document, I felt angry and let down. The authorities had seemingly undertaken the review without asking anyone from St Francis to contribute. Instead, the decision was made that my licence was only to be renewed for two years, during which time I would have to find a new parish.

I was absolutely heartbroken, and felt defeated and rejected all over again. Ian Davies tried to cheer me up as best he could, but even he acknowledged that I'd been screwed over royally. I had a bad few days and spiralled into a pit of self-pity. The community were outraged, like they were back at my previous posting, that I was being made to leave against my will. But this time it was up to me, with the help of Lesley, to make sure that I didn't sink any deeper into despair or mental illness. I couldn't do it all over again. I had to try to be strong and brave things out.

It seemed like I had been sent a lifeline, then, when I discovered that a position for priest, in charge of the Bardsea, Lindal and Pennington parish, opened up just down the road from where I lived. What's more, it was associated with youth work! It couldn't have been more perfect! Lesley could stay at work, and the twins would still be near the school and hospital. Okay, so it was a lot of work, being three churches and a youth work posting, but I thought it was great – clearly God's doing!

I applied straight away, feeling happy and fairly confident that I would receive an interview. But I was wrong. The archdeacon got in touch with me to tell me that they were re-advertising the job. I wasn't best pleased. I thought to myself, 'They can't do that! That's not on!' But they did it anyway.

I was disappointed, but it was okay because as it turned out, I was contacted about another post. This one was in Askew-in-Furness, right down the road from the Duddon Estuary! Again, I felt incredibly excited. I was even more chuffed when I was invited for an interview. I was so excited about the prospect of getting the job. I desperately wanted to stay in Barrow, and I was willing to do everything I could to stay here.

I thought the interview went well, if perhaps a bit short. But I guess it didn't go well enough, because one evening I got the call to tell me that I hadn't been successful. My chest heaved with the injustice of it all. I was so, so sick of being rejected. But the more I came to terms with the fact that perhaps this just wasn't God's plan for me at all, the better I felt. The archdeacon wasn't a big fan of me anyway, and I'd had a niggling suspicion that I wouldn't have got along with the rector.

Soon it felt that it had happened for the best, however, because the opportunities just kept on coming. After this let-down, the Bardsea, Lindal, and Pennington job came back around. I gave it a shot and tried again. I figured that they couldn't ignore me if I kept applying! At this time I was so desperate for a job to keep me in Barrow that I couldn't hear God's voice at all. I was squeezing him out; I didn't go to him for advice or guidance as to what I should do. I knew I wanted to stay in Barrow, and so I persisted.

Eventually they contacted me and told me that I would be called in for interview just before Christmas. But again, I didn't hear anything for a good long while. Feeling frustrated, I called the archdeacon, only to be told, 'Oh, it's been moved back to January now, because there's someone else in another parish who won't be able to apply or interview for the job until then.'

I blinked, confused. 'So,' I replied. 'You're saying I'm still the only applicant at the moment, again?'

'Yes,' said the archdeacon, sounding unconcerned. 'But someone will be applying after Christmas.'

'But you've moved the goalposts again! Will I still be getting an interview?'

'Oh, yes, you'll definitely still get an interview,' he replied, his tone of voice making it clear he was trying to mollify me.'

'Well, okay,' I replied, hesitantly. This still all felt wrong. I didn't see why they needed to wait for more applicants, when I was clearly keen and well qualified. They were just wasting their own time! But as there was nothing more I could do about it, I decided to leave it. I didn't hear anything about it after that.

One night I was sitting in my study with my Bible, preparing for one of my upcoming services, when my mind wandered over to the job. I really, really wanted the job. It felt like it had been put in my path as a saving grace. 'I hope I get an interview,' I thought to myself. 'I hope I get a chance.' And then something went off in my spirit. Something said to me, from deep down inside, 'Mark, I want you to withdraw from the process.'

I thought, 'It can't be God. He knows how much I want this job. I want to stay in Barrow.' And so I dismissed it. I carried on with my preparation, but then something went off in my spirit again. I can't describe it any better than that.

I stood up and paced up and down, trying to understand what was going on in my mind and my soul. They seemed to be completely contradicting each other, but I wanted to pay more attention to my mind. My anxiety was incredibly strong, and my deep, ingrained fear of change meant that I couldn't face doing something that I knew would be a challenge. I didn't feel mentally healthy or strong enough to be able to cope with it. And having had a history of struggling mentally after big life changes, I desperately didn't want to go through it all again. I was feeling like that little child all over again – scared, anxious, and completely without any kind of control. I wanted the job so that things could stay the same.

I sat down again, but I couldn't relax or concentrate. And that's when it hit me. I couldn't find any peace because I was trying to dismiss the will of God. This is how it felt for me. But following God was not always easy for me, especially since I struggled so much with my mental health. It wasn't a case of simply deciding to do the right thing.

And so for the next few days this internal battle raged inside me. I wanted to listen to God, but I was too wrapped up in what I wanted. I'd never been good at listening to authority figures, and I was fed up of never getting my own way. I challenged my own thoughts and stopped telling myself that I was under spiritual attack. Finally I made the decision to email the archdeacon and withdrew from the process. And immediately, amazingly, the peace returned. I felt calmer in my soul.

Of course, my anxiety was still strong, as I was a mentally fragile man walking, yet again, into the unknown. But knowing that I was following what was set out for me – however mentally trying it was going to be – helped me realise that this was the right thing to do.

Looking back now, I know I was being stitched up. Hindsight is a wonderful thing, and I wish I'd realised sooner what was going on. Certain people in Barrow did not want me around, and it turned out that the authorities had already decided who they wanted for the clergyman job. Needless to say, it wasn't me. The guy they had lined up for the post was a teacher who had already done youth work. What's more, he didn't have a dark and troubled past like me.

It seemed that stigma was still rife and my past was still managing to catch up with me. But this time, it was okay. I didn't know it then, but life was only about to get better. In early January a post came up in the diocese of Newcastle. It was the position of vicar for two small village churches in Dinnington and Brunswick, with a part-time post of chaplain to Northumbria Police. After a nerve-wracking interview process in both places, I was offered the job.

Perhaps things were going to be okay after all!

CHAPTER 19

STARTING A NEW LIFE IN NEWCASTLE

What felt like a cruel blow at the time actually turned out to be one of the best things that's ever happened to me. In 2008 I became a parish priest and moved to Seaton Burn in Newcastle upon Tyne. Since then I have also been working in the local community as an ambulance first responder and chaplain for the Northumbria police force.

Things haven't been perfect. Mark Jr. has been in and out of hospital a few times, sometimes at risk of losing his life, leaving Lesley and me terrified and vulnerable each time. But somehow the lad has pulled through every time, defying the odds at every turn. Lesley has started working with children with mental illnesses and learning difficulties, and she tells me that her job has helped her to understand me more than she ever had before. It's been a real blessing and has brought us even closer.

Jonathan and Fiona have flown the nest, heading off to university and pastures new, starting relationships and families and forging their own paths in life. It's been very hard to adjust to the change, but I am incredibly proud of both of them. They've turned out better than I ever could have imagined, and I know I have Lesley and God to thank for that. And though I know the anger over the years hasn't helped, I like to think that I've done my bit too.

Meanwhile, I've been doing my best to serve the community and heal people myself. Being part of something makes me feel good and valuable, and I've always had a lot of time for the emergency services. I think they do a great job. They're under a lot of stress and they're under-resourced, so to be able to help them is a dream come true for me. I see what they do when I go out with the ambulance on observations and when I interact with police officers.

When I left the lifeboats, I was sad. I loved being around ordinary people. I loved the camaraderie, the banter, and going out to rescue people. And when I came here to Newcastle, I was too far away from the sea to do any of that. But then I saw a poster for first responders at the police station. I knew a little bit about first responders because my station officer was one.

What did I have to lose? I made the decision to give it a shot and applied, and I was invited to go through two weekends of training. We covered basic life support and another essential skills. It seemed like no time at all before I got the kit and went live. It's one of the best decisions I've ever made.

So when I'm up for it and not undertaking my duties as a vicar, I book in as available on my pager and wait for the calls to come through.

It's part of the gospel to care for the community. Jesus tells us to be in the community and to reach out to the needy and the sick and suffering, and do something worthwhile. As a priest and a Christian. I'm contextualising my faith. It's not all about being in the pulpit and being a preacher. It's about being a real person. People have to see an authenticity in you when you're a priest. They shouldn't just see a vicar or a clergyman; they should see you as a real person with real value. I'm Jesus's ambassador.

The Christian Church always talks about contextualisation, and teaches Christians to take their faith out into the wider community. But many people spend so much time talking about it that they often forget to actually do it. I would like to say to people, 'Hands up those who go to an ordinary club. Hands up those who go to a bowls club.

Hands up if you go to a hobby group ...' Many of them would not put their hands up. So many of them are just part of church groups. They talk about going into society beyond the church, and so few of them actually do it! It's crazy. I'm proof that it can be incredibly rewarding.

This part of my life makes me happy. And as you've read earlier, my faith is now stronger than ever. But perhaps the best area of my life is still my family.

In 2009, Lesley and I celebrated our 25th wedding anniversary. I can't really put into words how momentous an occasion this was for me. I still have to pinch myself now that any such woman would want to spend their whole life with me. Especially one as wonderful as my Lesley. I often say to people that my wife Lesley is the closest I can get to God with skin on. I joke to them, 'Do you know how difficult it is to live with someone so sanctified? Because she makes me look bad!'

She is, and always has been, an amazing woman through and through. Lesley has not abandoned me, despite all my expectations of her doing so. To find a soulmate and a partner in life that fully understands unconditional love is important. Things like that are few and far between. A lot of people in life will say, 'I will love you, if you meet these criteria.' But Lesley always loved me regardless. That's unconditional love. You don't see true unconditional love very often. It's very rare. But it's stood the test of time – 33 years in April 2017.

A lot of people in Lesley's life, around the time of university, tried to talk her out of going out with me. The lovely Pastor Coombs even played the devil's advocate, and he was just trying to be realistic. I had plugged into people emotionally in the past, but I had never had a girlfriend before. I remember the night I rushed around to tell him about our engagement. He spent the next hour or so trying to talk me out of marrying Lesley! And I was thinking, 'What are you doing?'

'Let's look at this objectively, Mark. Lesley is from a middle-class, secure background who's just finishing her degree. You've got no qualifications. You've just come out of a mental health institution.

And these two worlds are going to clash. They're going to collide. Are you sure you've thought through the implications of what this means, if I marry you two? You're going to have to meet her parents eventually. How are they going to view this?'

I genuinely did understand this. I ask a similar question of couples in my parish now! It's very rare nowadays that I get people asking me to marry them who are not already living together anyway, but there have been a couple of young couples who have approached me about it, who are not living together. And I ask them to make sure they've thought through things properly. So I understood where the pastor's reservations were coming from.

I didn't like it, but Lesley was far more mature than me. She'd weighed it up and prayed about whether she should go out with me. She took her time and so she knew what she was letting herself in for.

The night before our wedding, Pastor Coombs said to me, 'Mark I wanted you to be realistic about this relationship. You *are* from the wrong side of the tracks, so to speak. I can see that you've made a genuine commitment. You are on a journey, and I don't know where that journey will take you, but I believe you and Lesley are right for each other.'

And lo and behold, it turns out he was right. It's a good job, and all! No one else would put up with me like Lesley does. I can barely put up with myself sometimes!

She wrote the following letter to me on our anniversary. It still gets me every time I see it.

Mark,

Who would have thought it, when we said 'I do' 25 years ago, that so much would happen? That we would still be together, deeply in love and, yes – a family of six!

We were young and naive on that sunny afternoon. You, in your suit, and me in my white dress. The song Bind Us Together *rang out, and over the years it had its work to do.*

Pastor Coombs told us that a three-way cord could not be broken, and because God was always part of our lives, it rang true. There would be lots of strain on that cord, and it was pulled taut on many occasions over those 25 years.

The first ten years were an adventure. We grew in our love and overcame our differences ... or some of them. You tested my love over and over again. Your past stopped you from trusting in me and my love. You couldn't relax. Only when you'd pushed my love to the limit did you eventually grasp that it was for real!

We had our first children, Jonathan and Fiona, when we were still young. There was much joy to be had, and although we had little in worldly terms, we had everything that we could desire.

You went to college, and then got a job. Responsibilities grew, but you were still a kid in lots of ways. Scared and frightened of the big new world. But you always had that ROCKY *spirit. You would get up and try again. No matter how many times you were knocked to the ground, you got up and tried again.*

Over the years I admired you so much for this. I also admired your passion and love for God and your empathy for people. You had been through so much in your life that you could understand when others were hurting.

In contrast my life had been sheltered ... getting to know your troubled past and your pain was an eye opener for me. It brought me into a whole new world, one I had never seen before. As a Christian I was grateful over the years for this, as it would make us more sensitive to the needs of those around us.

But for you it was a world you desperately wanted to escape from and later in our marriage it would insist on haunting you and leaving its mark. You needed to mature, develop and face the past, over and over again. It was a painful process and you needed all of your ROCKY *spirit. There were many times in our marriage that you care not to remember. There have been difficulties and pain beyond anything I ever experienced before. It was a hard marriage sometimes.*

It wasn't only you who made it like that. I had my faults, as well you know. I wasn't used to showing affection, and you craved that. I had to physically respond to your needs, and I am grateful that you developed that in me over the years. I may not be the most demonstrative person, but you have helped me along that road.

I love you so much for so much that we have shared. For those moments when we have held each other close physically, but also when we have connected emotionally. When we have been there for each other and strengthened each other. You always proclaim me to be the 'heroine'. But you will always be my hero.

Only once did you lose that accolade. That was when things were at their worst. When you had lost your faith and that three-way cord seemed severed. Everything I did was wrong at that time, and I could no longer reach you. I became an enemy and you were driving me away. I held onto God as he was my rock. You were miserable, and felt like giving up. But we had four children at this point.

The burdens were great, but the glass was half full, not half empty. God heard your cry for help and lifted you out of the mire. Ken Copeland became your best friend. God used his ministry to breathe his life back into you.

Hallelujah! I could love you and respect you again. God hadn't let our love for each other, or for him, die. We still face pressures and strains on our marriage, but we are older and wiser. You are a diamond with many facets, and believe me, I have seen all of them. You are a polished diamond now, with so many of the rough edges gone and a real sparkle about you. You are beautiful and people here in Newcastle see you shine. They love you for that and so do I.

I love the way that you can talk to anyone, whether prince or pauper. I delight in watching you at work, and in the love you show to others. I know that it is genuine and deep. I can relax in your love now as we have gone through so much together. I know that your love is real and that it always has been.

If could turn back the clock 25 years, would I choose to walk away? I don't think so. Despite all the pain, it has been (and still is) a privilege to have walked this path together with you, to share our lives together and to face the world as a team.

Thank you for all the years of love and affection. For the fun and the laughter. For being willing to change and go the extra mile. For being a fighter and overcoming the odds. For being passionate about life and about God. For loving your family and being a brilliant husband and dad.

For your energy and strength, and all that is you.

I love you for ever and always.

Lesley

Over the years there have been times where I thought my wife Lesley would leave me. It took me a long time to realise that she wasn't going to do that and that she was the real deal. And looking back on my diary entries and remembering the early years of my life, it's not hard to understand why that happened. That's why so many times I tried to push her away, because I didn't want to wait for her to abandon me. I had become very cynical. I thought trying to chuck her out with her suitcase and telling her to go away was the right thing to do. I was convinced of it, because I was convinced she was going to leave just like everyone else. Thank God I didn't stick to my guns, though, when she was banging on the door and yelling 'But I love you!' at me.

Lesley is amazing. If it was me, I would have left a long time ago. But she had no understanding at the time of mental illness. She has understanding now, because she deals with it in her work, but back when she met me she was naive and from a very privileged and together background. I was a guy from the wrong side of the tracks, if you like. Lesley took the lead at the beginning of our relationship. Then as the years went by and I started to grow and mature and develop, I started to take the lead sometimes. We're a partnership, a collaboration. It's a game of two halves. We're Team Edwards. And that's what family and marriage should be about.

Soulmates and partners can be an important part of the healing process. We need to choose wisely. Although, having said that, would someone have chosen someone like me, from the 'wrong side of the tracks', deliberately, if they had to choose wisely?

The truth is that I honestly don't know. Lesley didn't know *all* of my baggage when we first got together. She said it was a big shock and an eye opener to her when I told her. But it didn't scare her away! I've done so much over the years that hasn't scared her away.

Her parents have been wonderful in that respect, too. I mean, we all make jokes about the in-laws, but I really have to take my hat off to them because if my daughter brought someone home like me, I would have been concerned. But I would have to try to put that to one side. And I do have to check myself sometimes and tell myself, 'Well hold on a minute – you need to remember where you come from.'

When I first started courting Lesley, I was jealous of her because of her parents and because she was brought up in such a stable home. I desperately wanted a stable upbringing like hers. And I think that's why initially, I struggled to really be myself around them. I kept them at a distance for a while, but gradually I let my guard down, because they never showed an ounce of judgement. When Lesley presented me to her mother she said, 'He's been in a mental health hospital. He's got no qualifications. He was brought up in care,' I can imagine their jaws dropped to the floor! They would have been well within their rights to be wary of me, but they never made me feel unwelcome. They've supported us in many different ways, and I will always be grateful to them for their kindness.

A lot of my recovery is down to Lesley's unconditional love. She's borne the brunt of my anger, my rejection, and my pain. And she's been there through thick and thin. Apart from God, she's been the one constant in my life. She's protected me, shielded me, and understood me. She's not once judged me. Never once, even though she's come from such a wildly different background to me. She had no real understanding of it when she first met me, but she had a whole load of love. She took the time to learn from me.

I've often said to her, 'How could you love me so much? I don't understand it. Why do you still love me like you do, despite everything I've put you through?'

Lesley will say she's not perfect. And none of us are. But I think the fact that because I'm a dominant person, and I like my own space, and Lesley gives me all that freedom – well, it means she's pretty perfect to me. And I know that a lot of clergy wives rule the roost! But Lesley has never done that. She trusts me 100%. She never asks where I've been. If I go to bed at three in the morning, she doesn't know because she's always in bed before me, because she gets twitchy leg syndrome! She doesn't wait up for me wondering what I'm up to. She doesn't criticise or hold a grudge.

It's extraordinary really, her love and commitment to me. I wish I could bottle it! Whenever I've been a reactionary, she's been able to step back and look at things objectively. In my marriage, more often than not I'm the problem, not her. I can get bent out of shape very quickly. If I'm out of fellowship with Lesley, I'm automatically out of fellowship with God. God can't have anything to do with me if I'm out of fellowship with anybody. So if we've argued, and I've gone storming into my study, kicking my heels, God will tell me to go back and apologise to her. I play it out like a little conversation in my mind.

I'll say to God, 'You don't know what she's done!'

And in my mind he'll say, 'I don't care what she's done, but I do care about your reaction to it. Go over there and say sorry!' And inevitably I do, because I have to remember that God is a loving father and knows what's best for me. And what's best for me is Lesley and my beautiful family.

For the first part of my life I never had a real family. And it was precisely that that caused me so much psychological damage. I admit that I've said to my own kids at times that I'm jealous of the family they have, because it was what I always wanted and never had! I dreamt about it. I longed for it.

My family have been a huge, huge part of my healing process. Although we've protected the children a lot from my mental health issues, their love and warmth have seen me through some of the darkest times.

They've also been very forgiving of the mistakes I've made. Particularly my two oldest children. I haven't made the same mistakes with the twins, but I did a lot of things wrong with Fiona and Jonathan. And yet, they still turn to me now and tell me that I'm their hero. It means more to me than they could ever know, because I beat myself up a lot for how I handled their teenage years. They bore the brunt of my depression and anger issues just as much as Lesley did.

Because of this, I convinced myself that I wasn't a good father for the longest time. Jonathan was the one that had to face most of my anger, and forgiving myself for that was very hard. Perhaps that's why one of the birthday cards he sent me as an adult touched me so deeply:

Dear Dad,

I hope you have a wonderful birthday. You deserve to. You are a remarkable man who I'm so proud of. You're my mentor and my hero. All that you do is an inspiration to me. Continue to do all of your good work. I am forever in awe of your compassion and your grace. It's because of you that I am who I am.

This card almost broke my heart, because at the time I really didn't feel that I deserved that accolade. I wasn't there for them for a long time because I was so absorbed in my own issues, and Lord knows I've been accused of that many times throughout my life. I wasn't a great father to them because I was so turned in on myself and my pain.

When the twins came along, I felt like I'd been given a second chance to do things differently and get things right. And I've not made the same mistakes at all; I learnt from experience. I changed my outlook. I used to tell myself, 'Oh, they're going to grow up to hate me too.' But if I'd have continued saying that it would have become a self-fulfilling prophecy. Words are very powerful.

Instead, I've been far more relaxed in bringing the twins up. They've been set the same boundaries as Fiona and Jonathan, but I've been more relaxed, and I haven't made the same mistakes.

I'm also a grandparent now. And that is a surreal feeling. I don't feel old enough to be a grandparent! But it's amazing. She's at crawling age now, and I can't wait until she says 'Granddad' for the first time. Here again is a whole new opportunity to do things better and improve upon the past. I'm so lucky I have a forgiving, Christian family that will let me do that.

There are, of course, times when I need a bit of alone time too. I always say let there be space in the togetherness. I need that space sometimes and my family acknowledge that. A lot of people wouldn't. But they understand that sometimes the way I am means I need solitude in order to process things and not get overwhelmed with what life throws at me. Understanding like that goes a long way towards helping a recovering mental illness sufferer.

I have gone from having nothing to having everything. I'm not talking about having a bank balance bulging with money. I'm talking about being prosperous in my relationships, prosperous in my profession and my volunteering, just prosperous in life. Prosperity is not just about wealth. It's borne out of my faith, which is supported by my family. For so long I had to live a fantasy life around Aunty Lindsay, but now I have absolutely no reason to.

I pay tribute to my family. They're wonderful. They've enriched my life beyond anything that I could possibly imagine. Family alone can't get you through depression, but they can help you tackle it.

And of course, standing up and receiving my MBE from Prince Charles in 2010 felt completely unreal. I was like a child in a sweet shop! I have a DVD of it and you can see me on the footage, staring up in awe at my surroundings as I walk through the palace. I was also completely starstruck around the Prince and was humbled by his kind words. After all, if a member of royalty was not put off by my past, then that was definitely saying something!

Receiving my MBE was important to me in terms of validating all of my achievements. But for me it also represented something else: the fact that nobody, no matter how bad things have been, is ever a lost cause.

It all felt completely unreal. I never believed it was possible for someone like me to be standing there for such a momentous lifetime achievement. Me, Mark Edwards, who in the past had been written off by society. The same Mark Edwards who was rejected by social services, condemned by the education system, abused by authority figures, ostracised from the workplace, and misunderstood by general society. To actually be standing there in Buckingham Palace receiving an MBE was beyond my wildest dreams.

And yet at the same time I thought, *Well, this could be for anybody. I'm living proof that your past does not have to be a barrier to your future.* I'm not 100% where I'm meant to be, because I'm on a journey, but I'm glad I'm not where I was.

Mark showing off his MBE.

Police chaplain to Northumbria Police.

CHAPTER 20

RECOVERY DOES NOT MAKE ME PERFECT

Writing this book has been fresh and emotive, and it's made me realise that there's still some issues there, lying under the surface, that I'd convinced myself were gone. But when I think about my story and reflect upon it, it does become emotional and complex.

I do believe that I am stronger today, but I have to work at it every day. The old Mark is still there, and he can come back up to the surface. I don't like him. He's vindictive, he's deviant, and he loves to be a victim. He's a child and I can often recognise when the child is dominant within me. But as an adult who is constantly trying to practise self-awareness, I have got used to asking myself, 'Is this the child speaking, or the adult?'

Having had a history of having zero control in my life, I now really don't like being told what to do and I hate it when something happens that I have no control over. When this happens, I often withdraw into myself and go back into that dark place, and it's very hard for my family to reach me when I do this.

Perhaps it's a good idea to give you some examples of when young Mark springs to the surface. Perhaps this will help readers who are suffering or recovering to see that it's completely normal to relapse from time to time.

My twin boys are getting to an age where you can really tell they're growing up. They're 15-years-old at the time of me writing. They still share a bedroom and I like that. A part of me, as a parent, is struggling with the fact that they're growing up. I don't want to keep them as children, but I need to do things and make changes at a pace I can cope with, so that's why it's nice that they're still sharing some space. The boys like it too, so that's great.

The first two beds we had for them in their room were fairly small, so they fit into the room quite well. When the time came for us to replace them, we thought we were replacing them with beds of the same size – three-foot-long ones. But when they were put up and put in the room together, they were actually four-foot-long and almost touching.

When Lesley sent me a photo of them I started to panic. I kept thinking, 'I've got to go back. I've got to get rid of these beds. I can't deal with it.' It was bad enough for my anxious brain that we'd just got rid of something that was connected to the boys' childhood, but now that they'd been replaced it all looked far too different and just wrong. It became too much for me to handle.

I got home and as soon as I saw them, Lesley saw my face go pale. She has told me that whenever I'm faced with a situation that I'm unhappy with or that threatens me, she can see the blood drain away from my face. I just go white.

Still to this day I don't know why I reacted so strongly. But I hated the beds. I hated them. I couldn't think properly. I felt physically sick. No one could talk to me. I was angry. I was anxious. It was all I could think about. I told Lesley we needed to send the beds back.

'I don't care how much it costs,' I yelled at her. 'We've got to send those beds back!' But she couldn't understand it. She was trying to be sympathetic, but I couldn't explain how I was feeling and so she was very taken aback. I just went into a very dark place. It was almost like I'd regressed to a previous form of myself.

I thought to myself, 'I'm a man of faith here, and I'm losing the plot.' I grabbed a spanner, and I started taking down the beds. And it wasn't until they were completely dismantled, and the room was back to how it was before, that I could breathe again. I remember thinking to myself, 'Where did that come from?' I've been taught to analyse things and unpack things and look at things logically, but I was still trying to make sense of that bed situation for weeks after.

If only Lesley hadn't sent me the picture when I was out. If only I'd have just discovered it when I got home. I wouldn't have had the kind of meltdown I had. I could have dismantled them straight away and dealt with my emotions immediately! But instead it all blew out of proportion. I got angry with Lesley. I shut her out and closed down completely. I just could not think about anything else until the beds were taken apart.

But now I know that it came from somewhere in the past. I can reflect back, and when I do that I know where it's coming from. It comes from that feeling of not being in control.

As I child, I spent time in four, five, six – I've actually lost count – foster homes. The fact is, when you're moved from home to home, you're just taken. You're just snatched and whisked away to the next home. You have no control. You internalise all your pain, your frustration, your sense of rejection, your anger. You internalise all that as a child. People say that children are very resilient, but they're not, not always. So, I think some of my issues right now are because, when even the smallest things happen that make me feel like they're out of my control, subconsciously it reminds me of my childhood. I was just snatched from somewhere that was meant to be my home so many times and I had no control over it.

When these beds went up, and they weren't what I had envisaged; when it turned out they weren't what I had in mind and I wasn't at home to sort out the problem, I just regressed back to that teenager who hated everything that was going on around him. I was struggling with idea of changing the beds anyway. I wanted to hold onto the idea of the twins being young children just that little bit longer.

I remember another such incident from when we moved from Barrow-in-Furness to Newcastle. It's obvious what was happening then. I was being forced to move from a home and a job that made me happy, to a completely different city and community. I felt rejected, and I had no control over what was happening. I didn't want to move – I felt secure and safe, and it was the longest I'd ever lived in any one place. It was like being wrenched from the foster home again. Barrow was my home – I was established there. People knew me. I had a ministry, and I was in the lifeboat volunteering group. I didn't want to give it all up.

But inevitably I had to go despite my wishes. And sooner or later we had to start packing. So one morning Lesley, thinking she was being helpful while I was in my study, started taking down all the pictures. I came out, saw all the pictures taken off the wall, and I had a complete and utter meltdown to the point where I started getting aggressive and angry. I started yelling 'PUT THE PICTURES BACK!' at my poor wife. I couldn't cope. Lesley had to unpack the boxes and put the pictures back on the wall. And then I was fine! Several weeks down the line, I packed them myself. Because at that point I had processed the change that was happening. I needed time to process things.

She did a similar thing with the kitchen one time. Lesley had a big clean up one day. I came home, walked into the kitchen, opened the cupboard, and she'd moved everything. It was too much of a shock for my messed-up mind to cope with! And there I was, freaking out again. 'PUT THEM BACK!' I yelled. I was crying and bawling. She literally had to put every single object back to where it was before. And they had to stay there, because I couldn't cope with the sudden change.

I'm still like this now; I don't think I'll ever change. For instance, I have a neurosis about walking into banks or building societies. If Lesley knows we have to visit one, she comes to me and tries to sweet-talk me.

'Mark ...' she whispers quietly and delicately. 'I need you to come to the bank.'

This is always met with quite a strong reaction. 'Oh, JEEZ! Noooo. I don't want to!' springs to mind as a common response!

I don't know why I developed an anxiety about banks. I have no clue! It seems crazy. For those readers old enough to remember this, I like to compare myself to Luther in Coach! I adopted Hayden Fox's character for a long time, but sometimes there's a bit of Luther in me too. If you talk about change to him, he freaks out! And that's just like me.

I also had anxiety attacks when the twins joined the cadets. Josh really took to it and enjoyed it straight away. But Mark Jr. told me he didn't like it. And so straight away I started to panic. Lesley told me later on that the colour had drained away from my face again. Instead of trying to be encouraging, I had a major meltdown over it.

I was trying to be a good parent and to be encouraging. I told him, 'I've never run away from anything in my life. I've wanted to! So many times I wanted to escape and not face the hardship. But I'm only doing what I'm doing today because I've faced my fears. I don't want you to give it up. You *are* going to do this.'

It all sounds reasonable like that. I knew it was good for his overall development and I thought he would get a lot of good out of it, but my reaction was still severe. I endured three weeks of hell and constant fretting and worrying. I didn't sleep properly. My mind was in torment. In the fourth week, Mark Jr. came to me and said, 'I enjoyed it tonight, Dad.' And it was an immediate relief. Suddenly I didn't feel so horrendous any more.

Each time these meltdowns happen I think to myself, 'I make myself seem crazy to other people.' But being aware of this doesn't make it any easier. I have to process things at a speed that I'm comfortable with. If I'm too overwhelmed by something, then I'm back in that dark, scary, place as a child where I don't have any control. It is scary.

When I go into those meltdowns, I'm not just one person any more. I'm an adult *and* a child. The family man, the man of faith, the ambulance first responder in me gets pushed aside and the child becomes dominant in my personality. I know that.

People who haven't actually been there, or struggled with mental health issues, often they dismiss it so quickly and easily. My daughter is lovely, and she's a person of faith too, but even she said to me, 'Well, it's only beds.' But it clearly wasn't as simple as that for me. I know it's only beds. I'm well aware. But I suppose that if people have never had mental health issues, they're never going to truly understand. And I can't hold that against anyone.

When I do relapse, I feel disappointed in myself. It feels like I've taken one step forward and five steps back. I beat myself up about it afterwards and condemn myself. Lesley often tells me, 'Don't beat yourself up, it's forgotten.' But no matter how hard I've been towards her, she always forgives me. She's always been very together and I'm so grateful for that.

I know I mustn't allow condemnation and guilt in, because that's not part of how I live my life spiritually. Christianity isn't about that. Religion is! Religion will make you heap guilt and condemnation upon yourself! It's terrible for that. But that's why I say I'm not a religious person. I'm just a man of faith. I don't want to spend my life feeling guilty. And I do try my hardest not to, even though that can be very hard.

I want to continue to grow as a person, and do the best I can. I want to help people along the way as well, and serve the community as a medic, a priest, a good father, a husband, and now a mental health advocate. I will always try to do my best, and accept it as a normal part of life if I can't always achieve it.

In many respects, I'm in the perfect role because for the most part, I'm my own boss. The only higher authority I ever need to answer to, at least on a daily basis, is God.

Part of me didn't want to admit, while writing this book, that I was 'in recovery' rather than fully recovered. I wanted to pretend that I am now 100% fine, because that would seem more impressive somehow. So, to admit that I'm actually always going to be in a process of recovery is a big thing to me. I'm a recovering depressive. I'm in recovery from mental health issues. Panic attacks, rejection, low self-esteem, abandonment complex, fear – I'm in recovery from all of those things. I didn't want to admit that because I'm a professional.

People only really see me behave in a 'childlike' way in the home. Because I'm a professional person, people don't see me in crisis when I'm working with the public, when I'm wearing this dog collar or my ambulance uniform. While I'm happy to be open and honest about my past and my struggles, the only people who really witness it first-hand are my family.

When you're a vicar and an ambulance first responder, people look to you for leadership and support. And rightly so, because that's what we're called to do. And I often say to people when I'm teaching, 'Look, what I'm doing here may look effortless, but behind this exterior is a spiritual discipline, a self-discipline, and a self-motivation. And behind this exterior is a daily battle to stay well.'

It comes back, again, to this collar, and the expectations of someone who wears this collar. A police officer or a paramedic enters a situation, and everyone expects that person to have it together and take charge, because they're wearing a uniform.

One day I was speaking to new recruits in my role as police chaplain. One of them told me about this part of his exam. He was told to imagine that he is in the following situation: a bad road accident has occurred, and he's on his own. Back-up is 20 minutes away. Just then he's told that a burglary has happened in one of the houses down the street. Nearby, a woman's going into labour and is about to give birth. Across the street, a house is on fire and there's people screaming for help … When asked what he would do, he replied flippantly, 'I would take off my uniform and merge into the crowd.' And I laughed because I knew just what he meant. Sometimes, I want to take off my uniform and merge into the crowd. I love the Lord, and God and Jesus, but don't you think sometimes I want to hide away?

Keeping myself together for my ministry and my patients takes a lot of discipline. Athletes don't just arrive at the podium with a gold medal, with people clapping and cheering for them. A whole lot of work goes into it beforehand. You don't see them getting up at six o'clock in the morning to train. You don't see them going to bed at eight o'clock in the evening. You don't see them running in all weathers. You don't see the sacrifices that that person has made to get where they are, to get that medal. You just see them up on the podium after a successful run.

People see my strength and faith and say to me, 'I wish I had your faith. I wish I had your discipline.' But I don't just wake up in the morning feeling mentally well. I have to keep working on it, just like the athlete does. Or a piano player. Or anyone! Sometimes people call me lucky because I have so much now whereas before I was in a terrible place physically, emotionally and mentally. But would you call an athlete lucky? Can you imagine the athlete saying, 'Yes! The more I practise the luckier I get!'?

My point here is that I have to keep practising my faith and my mindfulness and my mental health, in order to keep myself on the right track. If I stop practising, I become like an athlete who hasn't trained. I become a flabby Christian!

CHAPTER 21

THE LESSONS I'VE LEARNT

Throughout my journey, I've come to a number of realisations that have helped me recover and become the man I am today. Some people might disagree with some of my thoughts or methods, but some might find them very helpful. I'm also aware that a lot of what I say won't apply to many people. But for people who have been in a similar situation to mine, the following advice and insight might help you. Again, I don't ever wish to preach or to prescribe, but instead I want to take the chance to pass on some wisdom I very much wish someone had given me over the years!

1) Try to filter out any unnecessary negativity and increase the positive things in your life.

When I'm having a particularly anxious time, or feel like things are getting on top of me emotionally or mentally, I decide to filter out the things that trigger me or bring me down. For this reason, I decided at the beginning of the year to do a 'detox of the soul'. I decided to spend more time studying the scriptures. I also scaled back how much of the news I was reading and watching – not to such a degree that I became ignorant to important things, but enough that I didn't feel I was being dragged down emotionally. I also avoided soap operas – *EastEnders* was particularly depressing to me! (I mean, who would want to live there, seriously? You'd move straight away!)

Perhaps you want to watch less violence on TV, or cut down on your social media use. Personally, I cut down on soap operas, because the constant misery in them really got to me. If you're not a person of faith, an option to offset that could be to do more of your hobbies or something that relaxes you. Just start to feed your mind with good things and make more of an effort to cast out the bad. It's not always so easy, but even small decisions can help you feel less anxious generally.

2) Find something you're passionate about. Even better if it's something selfless or giving in nature.

Those who are, or have been, depressed become very introspective. And I understand that completely; I should know! In my darkest times I always used to try to bring the conversation around to myself. I wanted to wallow in my own misery. When getting through each moment is so difficult, you don't give a monkeys about what's going on around you! Or perhaps I should say, you don't notice. But staying introspective can feed your depression and so I think it's worthwhile to try to distract yourself, in a positive way, to help you through the hard times while you're recovering.

This helps you get outside of your own head and focus on the world around you. Helping people is a brilliant way of doing that. By volunteering for the lifeboats and then the ambulance response service, I truly found something that filled the void. Every day, I feel passionate, excited, and fulfilled when I help others in times of crisis. It helps me to think about things beyond myself, and that's quite helpful if you have struggled with depression in the past. Suddenly you can look at yourself in the context of the wider world, and it's a very rewarding and healing thing to do. It also helps distract your mind if you feel depression pulling you back under.

3) Always surround yourself with friends and family who are positive.

Avoid, wherever you can, anyone who routinely brings negativity into your life. It's toxic to people with mental health issues. External negativity can contaminate you so easily. Of course we must always be compassionate, and loving and caring. But we also need the wisdom to know when someone is toxic and is sucking the very life out of us, because there are others who genuinely do want to bring positivity into your life, and support you. Don't feel guilty about doing this. Self-care is very important.

I have strict boundaries, even as a clergyman. It's not always open-door access. I need to be wise, otherwise some people could sap the life out of me very quickly. That won't help me. To the best of your ability, you have to surround yourself with positive people.

4) Learn to forgive.

Not everyone will feel able to do this depending on how bad their circumstances are, but it has worked well for me. And you don't need to be a Christian to do it.

I hated everybody when I left the care home. I hated all of those who, I felt, had caused me so much pain. I was planning my revenge on lots of people! But if those bad thoughts had continued, who knows where I might be now? Think about it, anyone who goes mad with a gun has thought about it, at length, first. They've stewed over some kind of injustice or resentment. But if you keep dwelling on anger and resentment, it will keep feeding back into your psyche and affect the way you live the rest of your life. Whatever you think about the most is the direction that your mind is going to take you in.

I'm thankful I didn't continue to be resentful, but I did think and feel that way for a while. Hating people made me feel unhappy, and so I've had to let a lot of things go and do a lot of forgiving. It doesn't mean I have to like everybody in life! Not everybody has to be my best friend. But if I want to grow and develop, and if I want peace of mind, then I have to forgive.

It wasn't actually until many years later, as an adult, that I learnt that we'd been taken away from the Taits because the educational psychologist believed that we weren't developing quickly enough, educationally and mentally. But I didn't know about that for a long, long time, and so in the meantime I had to find it in myself, over the years, to forgive something that was traumatic and made no sense to me. If I hadn't learnt to let it go, it would still be eating me up inside to this day.

As they say, 'Unforgiveness is like taking poison yourself and hoping the other person dies.' Often other people don't give a monkeys whether you forgive them or not. All that happens is that you carry that person around with you for the rest of your life. It's like handcuffs that you can't shake off. Forgiveness releases you, not them.

5) Try to live in the present, not the past.

As you now know, I've had terrible periods in my life where I have obsessed over the past, particularly the mental institution.

Even now, I sometimes wish I could go back in time to the children's home with Aunty Lindsay and make sure it had a different outcome. But all this serves to do is torment you.

I've been badly mistreated in the past. I understand the pain people go through. But I'm in my fifties now and it's just detrimental to wellbeing to keep obsessing over it. I know it's easier said than done. I have plenty of relapses where my mind goes back to a dark place. I've been abused by the system, put in care, and written off by superiors. But I find no value in keeping that going around and around in my head, in ruminating. Of course people should be held to account where necessary, but now I can only go forward, you see.

You've got to be able to sympathise and empathise with victims of abuse and neglect. You've got to be able to get down on your knees and cry with them. But eventually you both have to get up off that floor, and face the world and fight back. If you have a scab, that scab is never going to heal if you keep picking at it. If you have a mental scar, it's never going to heal if you keep agitating it. Joy and happiness belong in the present.

6) Remember that maintaining good mental health takes effort, even for those who have it together the most.

I'm not passive in my own recovery. I have to put the work in too. A lot of people of faith think they can just sit around and God will sort things out for them. In the same way, a small minority of mentally ill people just sit around and wait for their medication to kick in. But it's a discipline of the mind that's just as important in the recovery process. Becoming well is hard work, but it won't happen if you don't at least try. I know that for some, whose illnesses are debilitating, effort alone isn't enough. But for people in similar predicaments to me, I think it holds true.

And if you're forever looking for other people to prop you up or wave a magic wand over it all for you, you'll never gain that mental strength you need. I want to speak as someone with integrity, as someone who's been there, done that, bought the T-shirt. I know it sounds harsh, but in all of this recovery there has to be tough love with yourself. Recognise that recovery takes effort: whether that's with CBT, therapy, faith or other means. Don't give up just because it's hard, or because it takes time. Nothing worth having comes easy, as they say.

7) Re-evaluate yourself and try to see yourself as someone other than 'the victim'.

I played the victim for a long time. I knew how to play the victim, and I played it well! I could have got an Oscar! And that's because it invoked people's sympathy, to a degree. And then eventually, after a long time of being sympathetic, people would clear off because they'd get sick of me. But then I just moved on to the next person.

But there came a point in my journey where, by my faith, my family, and by people like Ian and John, I was told 'Mark, you've been through a hell of a lot. You've been hurt, but you're not going to move on until you stop thinking of yourself as a victim. Tell yourself you are more than that. It will help you to heal.'

Sometimes I wonder if there's some people who don't want to get well, because for a while I'm not sure that I did. I just wanted to be the victim instead, because I wanted the sympathy. I thrived on it. It was satisfying in a strange kind of way, because it absolved me of any blame and stopped me taking control or ownership of my life. And this in itself is probably an illness.

At the end of the day, I want my story to be a blessing, and to give other sufferers hope. I don't discount the pain that anyone is going through, at all. I will get down on that floor and cry with you if that's what you need me to do. But eventually I will pull you back up and encourage you to stop letting the past hold you back. Because I think I'm living proof that you don't have to do that. You can turn things around if you really want it enough. You don't have to be a victim of your bad start in life.

When you redefine who you are in your own head, you can recognise that you are capable of moving on and moving past what has happened to you. You can decide that you want to get well and recognise that recovery is possible. And that's how change begins to happen.

8) Get the right kind of counselling.

Talking therapy has its place, but sometimes it's static. A lot of people find they don't really make any progress because all they're actually doing is regurgitating their story and their past, week after week. They continue to dredge up their sorrows without processing them properly or solving their underlying issues. There's no real resolution.

Counsellors are a fine body of people, and they do their utmost. But I think for people who have suffered abuse and suicidal tendencies, counselling needs to be *constructive* and *productive* rather than just reflective. If you just sit and moan every time, unfortunately that doesn't cut the mustard. I think this is why I needed quite a lot of counselling from different people over the years. Sometimes I just did it to jump through hoops and to pass my psychiatric assessment for my vicar studies. I wasn't going at it from the right place half of the time.

If you feel that counselling is right for you, I would suggest asking your doctor to refer you to someone who will give you productive, evidence-based therapy (one such example is cognitive behavioural therapy, but there are others). Talking counselling is nice in principle, but if you're anything like me, you need something more dynamic and effective. I will always be very thankful for the counsellors in my life who helped me reprogram my thinking.

9) For those supporting loved ones through depression or anxiety: look after yourself.

Supporting a loved one through such a difficult time is hard. Heaven knows Lesley has been through some rough stuff with me! I've tried to throw her out on a number of occasions, and shut myself off emotionally from her. During those times, she was of course worried about me but she knew she had to protect and take care of herself.

Always try to be discerning and wise and help in any way you can, but remember that if you don't always manage that, it's okay. If you feel you've made a mistake or you've got something wrong, don't beat yourself up about it. You are only human, like the rest of us. It's not your job to be perfect. Remember: even if we're not always in a position to show it, we appreciate your help more than you will ever know!

CONCLUSION

Perhaps the most important reason I chose to publish my diaries now, 35 years after my time sectioned on a mental health ward, is because of the many issues surrounding mental health today, particularly with young people. The need for action to promote and safeguard children and young people's mental health has never been more acute. You'd have to be very out of touch with media and with society in general not to have ever noticed this. It's *always* on the news, and I notice it still even when I'm detoxifying. I can't help it; my ears always prick up when it comes up on the TV or radio. But I suppose that it's a good thing that we're at least talking about it and trying to find a solution now, when previously the whole subject was so wrapped up in stigma that it was pretty much untouchable.

People who have suffered with mental health problems say that the social stigma attached to mental health, and the discrimination experienced as a result, can make their difficulties worse and make it harder to recover. That was certainly my experience. After I was discharged from hospital it became impossible for me to find work. The very mention of the fact that I had been in psychiatric care stigmatised me, preventing me from finding employment, which added to my sense of alienation, fear and lack of self-worth, plunging me for a time back into depression. Even within the church I found that there were times when I felt stigmatised and alienated, and discriminated against by the Christian community.

This simply has to stop. There's no two ways about it. And that's why it's so positive that more and more celebrities and people of influence are coming forward to tell the world that they have or they are suffering from mental health issues. It gets people interested in the cause. It makes people feel less isolated. That's why I'm a big fan of movements like *Heads Together* and *Time to Change*, which is England's largest programme to challenge mental health stigma and discrimination. It is run by the leading mental health charities and supported by celebrities such as Stephen Fry, Ruby Wax, Patsy Palmer, Frank Bruno, Fiona Philips, Trisha Goddard and many others. They are all committed to ending the stigma surrounding mental health issues. While you'd never be able to call me a celebrity, I hope, nonetheless, that my story might help others in a similar situation to have hope. At the same time, I hope it challenges people to be more sympathetic towards those who have suffered any form of depression or mental illness.

Even though my experience of a mental institution was far from good, I can't deny that mental health hospitals today do a lot of good work. From my admittedly limited knowledge, it seems that things have improved massively in this area. It helps that my old mental institution in Chester has been torn down now and replaced with a new building – so there's no more dark, depressing dormitories and eerie, Victorian corridors.

And I try my best not to get political in life, but when Margaret Thatcher introduced Care in the Community in the 1980s, it looked good on paper (despite huge funding gaps), but I think it made some people discount the value of mental hospitals. It also undermined the severity of some people's illnesses. You had people who were previously institutionalised suddenly thrust back out into the community. Their issues and difficulties were managed in hospital because they were in a safe environment where they could be cared for. But if a person was institutionalised for a long period of time with no support network, is there any wonder there were problems?

I'm a simple person, but didn't anyone think that through? And it's certainly a lot of empty rhetoric when there's no funding to back up the ideas. This is a problem that has definitely not gone away. In fact, it's even more dire than ever today.

As much as we'd like to think that in an ideal world we'd get rid of all the institutions, in reality institutions are for people who can't cope with life outside. It's a safe place for them, and often it can be a safe place for society if certain illnesses cause a person to be violent through no fault of their own. I have great respect for the work they do, despite the issues I personally had in mine.

I'm happy to be telling my story to you now for these reasons, but I also want to tell it from a positive point of view. I don't want to invoke sympathy. I want to tell it because, while I'll never be 100% recovered, I *am* in recovery and there's every reason that you can reach a place of recovery too. I might not be completely where I'm meant to be yet, but I'm glad I'm no longer where I've been.

As a teenager, deep in the depths of despair and depression, I never would have dreamt that I'd be doing what I'm doing now. Even when I was ordained, and sometimes even now, I have to pinch myself. Getting that MBE was surreal – and it's a long way from the steps of a Lincolnshire children's home to the steps of Buckingham Palace.

Someone once described me as a 'walking miracle'. It sounds quite extreme, and they don't mean it in a biblical sense. But I understand what they meant. If you look at case studies or items on the news about people in my situation, it's amazing I am where I am. Many would have expected me to end up in prison, or homeless, or an addict. Or, as that occupational therapist said to me, '… in and out of institutions all your life, if you don't do us all a favour and kill yourself first.'

And so the fact that I've managed to turn my life around, from a lost cause to an MBE, is a personal miracle. And there are lots of walking miracles out there. There are plenty of people who can show us that we can overcome mental illness and hardship. We *don't* have to become that stereotype.

I hope that authenticity is what defines me. I don't pretend to be something I'm not. When I stand in front of my congregation, I don't pretend to have it all together. I want people to know that just because I wear this collar of confidence, it doesn't mean I don't face the same challenges that everyone else faces. I have been in some very dark, scary places. I have experienced the dark night of the soul. And sometimes I haven't felt worthy of being a priest.

It's so easy to look at everyone else around you and think they're perfect. But in reality, they're all just protecting themselves by hiding behind masks. Few people today seem to feel confident and secure enough in themselves to come out and say, 'This is the real me. This is what I've done and where I've been in the past.' Because they feel like they're going to be judged. And we all do sometimes. Every single one of us wears a mask in society. And some of us dare not let it slip, in case the world labels you for life. People are still wary of me now, a vicar who has been in a mental institution. But even though there will always be nasty people out there, it is always worth opening up. People can help you, and it can only help to raise awareness and tackle stigma.

One of the messages that I'd like to get across in this book is that no matter what you're suffering with, you shouldn't ever feel ashamed. I've been guilty of feeling ashamed in the past, and a lot of that has been down to other people putting me down. But now I am not ashamed of writing this story and you shouldn't feel ashamed of yours.

When they think of mental illness nowadays a lot of people think of the criminally insane. But mental health now covers such a wide spectrum of conditions. It's a wide label. We're not talking about people locked up in Broadmoor. We're talking about people like Hope Virgo, who suffered from anorexia. We're talking about people like me who have suffered from abandonment complex and anxiety and rejection. And this is the kind of stigma we need to fight against.

I absolutely see myself as a new person now. And I have a lot of people to thank for that. At one point in my life, all the 'trustworthy' professionals had written me off – my employees, social services, the medical profession, psychologists, the care system, the mental institution all gave up on me. But when the people who matter in life – family, friends, and in my case, God – stick by you, it's still possible to get better even when it feels like the odds are against you.

I wanted to give up the fight many times. There's been times I've been laid on the sofa, in the foetal position, not wanting to move. There's a reason we want to stay like that. It's warm, it's comfortable, it feels safe. It reminds us of the womb.

But every knockback can be an opportunity. I didn't stay down there in that pit. I could still be where I was 20, 30 years ago, sucking my thumb, cuddling my blanket, thinking 'Woe is me.' Oh, I've *wanted* to, many times! It's comforting! But eventually I stopped feeling sorry for myself and helped myself, with God and my family's help, to climb out of that place.

Because when I'm at my lowest ebb and all the lights go out, there's something within me – something quite apart from my family, faith, friends, anything else – that just kicks in when I need it to. There's something I always liken it to, and I'm going to use a TARDIS analogy here, because I'm a *Doctor Who* fan. Even when the TARDIS almost died completely, there was just the tiniest flicker of power that saved it. It was barely there, but that was all that was needed to bring that TARDIS back to life.

I tell my congregation, and now my readers, that I'm on a journey with them. And there's certain things that I have to do on this journey to maintain a healthy lifestyle and a healthy mind. If I don't do those things, I could degenerate.

I'm genuinely in the business of giving people hope in the Church, and now I want to give people hope in the mental health community too. It is about hope. If I'd have read a book such as this way back when, I wouldn't have felt alone. When I was taken from the general hospital to the psychiatric hospital with a bandage around my wrist, I could see no future beyond the bars on the windows. I was desolate and had never been shown an example of anyone getting through this. I was in the very place I was terrified of, and believed I was resigned to the 'nut house'. But I wasn't; I just needed some help and some kind of indication that I wasn't a freak or a lost cause.

The best part is that your journey is not yet over. The best is yet to come. For me, *and* for you. Things may have started badly, but they can finish well.

ACKNOWLEDGEMENTS

Thanks to my sister, Shene, and her husband, Graham, who gave me a home after I left local authority care. Your endless support and love, even when I pushed you away, was invaluable.

To Lesley, your unconditional love has brought healing and wholeness to my life.

A final thank you must go to my lovely editor Stephanie Cox for helping me share my story.

the *Shaw* mind
FOUNDATION

Supporting children, adults and families
for better mental health. **#lets**do**stuff**

Sign up to our charity, The Shaw Mind Foundation
www.shawmindfoundation.org
and keep in touch with us; we would love to hear from you.

*We aim to bring to an end the suffering and despair caused
by mental health issues. Our goal is to make help and support
available for every single person in society, from all walks of life.
We will never stop offering hope. These are our promises.*